THE LAW RELATING TO FINANCIAL CRIME IN THE UNITED KINGDOM

The Law Relating to Financial Crime in the United Kingdom

KAREN HARRISON
University of Hull, UK

NICHOLAS RYDER
University of the West of England, UK

ASHGATE

Published by
Ashgate Publishing Limited
Wey Court East
Union Road
Farnham
Surrey, GU9 7PT
England

Ashgate Publishing Company
110 Cherry Street
Suite 3-1
Burlington, VT 05401-3818
USA

www.ashgate.com

British Library Cataloguing in Publication Data
Harrison, Karen, 1974-
  The law relating to financial crime in the United Kingdom.
  1. Commercial crimes--Great Britain. 2. Terrorism--
  Finance--Law and legislation--Great Britain--Criminal
  provisions.
  I. Title II. Ryder, Nicholas.
  346.4'107-dc23

Library of Congress Cataloging-in-Publication Data
Harrison, Karen, 1974-
  The law relating to financial crime / by Karen Harrison and Nicholas Ryder.
    p. cm.
  Includes bibliographical references and index.
  ISBN 978-1-4094-2388-1 (hardback) -- ISBN 978-1-4094-2389-8 (pbk) --
ISBN 978-1-4094-2390-4 (ebook) 1. Commercial crimes--Great Britain. 2. Terrorism--
Finance--Law and legislation--Great Britain--Criminal provisions. I. Ryder, Nicholas. II.
Title.
  KD7990.H37 2012
  346.4107--dc23

                                                                    2012022537

ISBN 9781409423881 (hbk)
ISBN 9781409423898 (pbk)
ISBN 9781409423904 (ebk – PDF)
ISBN 9781409472438 (ebk – ePUB)

Printed and bound in Great Britain by the
MPG Books Group, UK.

Contents

List of Abbreviations

AML	Anti-Money Laundering
CJA	Criminal Justice Act 1993
CPS	Crown Prosecution Service
CRO	Civil Recovery Order
CTF	Counter-Terrorist Financing
DTI	Department of Trade and Industry
ECA	Economic Crime Agency
ECHR	European Convention on Human Rights
EU	European Union
FATF	Financial Action Task Force
FIU	Financial Intelligence Unit
FSA	Financial Services Authority
FSMA	Financial Services and Markets Act 2000
GDP	Gross Domestic Product
HMRC	HM Revenue and Customs
IMF	International Monetary Fund
IRA	Irish Republican Army
JMLSG	Joint Money Laundering Steering Group
MAD	Market Abuse Directive
MAR	Market Abuse Regime
MIB	Markets and Investment Board
MLRO	Money Laundering Reporting Officer
NCA	National Crime Authority
NCIS	National Criminal Intelligence Service
NFA	National Fraud Authority
NFIB	National Fraud Intelligence Bureau
OECD	Organisation for Economic Co-operation and Development
OFT	Office of Fair Trading
POCA	Proceeds of Crime Act 2002
SAR	Suspicious Activity Report
SCPO	Serious Crime Prevention Order
SFO	Serious Fraud Office
SIB	Securities and Investment Board
SOCA	Serious Organised Crime Agency
SYSC	Senior Management Arrangements, Systems and Controls

UK	United Kingdom
UN	United Nations
USA	United States of America

Chapter 1

Introduction

What is Financial Crime?

The term financial crime, is often used in common parlance and thus is one of which we assume we know its meaning, despite the fact that there is 'no internationally accepted definition'[1] of it. As outlined throughout this book, definitions are abundant for fraud, money laundering, terrorist financing and market abuse, but are less precise for the collective expressions of both financial crime and financial abuse. For a book which purports to be about financial crime however, it is probably fairly important that some attempt is made at defining these latter terms.

In England and Wales, financial crime can be said to include 'any offence involving fraud or dishonesty; misconduct in, or misuse of information relating to, a financial market; or handling the proceeds of crime.'[2] This can therefore include the activities of money laundering and terrorist funding. The Financial Services Authority (FSA) offers a similar definition, stating that it is 'any offence involving money laundering, fraud or dishonesty, or market abuse.'[3] The European Commission does not appear to provide an actual definition of the term; but on looking at the legislation and Directives which have been issued to cover financial crime, it would appear that these only cover the areas of money laundering and terrorist financing.[4] The Federal Bureau of Investigation, in the United States of America (USA) however, has a much more far-ranging definition, which includes the criminal activities of corporate fraud, commodities and securities fraud, mortgage fraud, healthcare fraud, financial institution fraud, insurance fraud, mass marketing fraud and money laundering.[5] The International Monetary Fund (IMF) goes further by stating that it 'can refer to *any* non-violent crime that generally

---

1   International Monetary Fund, *Financial System Abuse, Financial Crime and Money Laundering – Background Paper* (International Monetary Fund, 12 February 2001, 5).

2   Financial Services and Markets Act 2000, s 6(3).

3   Financial Services Authority, 'Fighting Financial Crime' <http://www.fsa.gov.uk/about/what/financial_crime> accessed 21 March 2012.

4   European Commission, 'Financial Crime' <http://ec.europa.eu/internal_market/company/financial-crime/index_en.htm> accessed 21 March 2012.

5   The Federal Bureau of Investigation, 'Financial Crimes Report to the Public' <http://www.fbi.gov/stats-services/publications/financial-crimes-report-2010-2011/financial-crimes-report-2010-2011#Financial> accessed 21 March 2012.

results in a financial loss' (emphasis added).[6] This can therefore include tax evasion, money laundering and financial fraud, but essentially allows for anything which causes a financial loss. It further states that where the loss involves a financial institution, then the term 'financial sector crime'[7] can also be used.

Definitions of the term, financial crime, have also been presented by academics. For example, Gottschalk states that it is 'a crime against property, involving the unlawful conversion of property belonging to another to one's own personal use and benefit', stating that it is often 'profit driven ... to gain access to and control over property that belonged to someone else.'[8] Pickett and Pickett define financial crime as 'the use of deception for illegal gain, normally involving a breach of trust, and some concealment of the true nature of the activities.'[9] This can include fraud, insider trading, embezzlements, tax evasion, kickbacks, identity theft, cyber attacks, social engineering and money laundering.

Financial abuse is another term which is sometimes used synonymously with financial crime and is defined in the United Kingdom (UK) as:

> Financial or material abuse, including theft, fraud, exploitation, pressure in connection with wills, property or inheritance or financial transactions, or the misuse or misappropriation of property, possessions or benefits.[10]

Under section 44 of the Mental Capacity Act 2005, this therefore includes the offences of: theft, forgery, fraud by abuse of position, fraud by false representation, fraud by failing to disclose information, and blackmail.[11] The IMF also defines what is meant by financial abuse, but does this in rather broad terms. This is due to the fact that it argues its meaning can vary between different occasions and different jurisdictions; precisely in the same way that the term financial crime can vary. For example, the government of the UK has previously included money laundering, drug trafficking, illegal capital flight, tax evasion and fraud under the term financial abuse; while the USA Department of State refer to it as including

---

6   International Monetary Fund, *Financial System Abuse, Financial Crime and Money Laundering – Background Paper* (International Monetary Fund, 12 February 2001, 3).

7   International Monetary Fund, *Financial System Abuse, Financial Crime and Money Laundering – Background Paper* (International Monetary Fund, 12 February 2001, 5).

8   P. Gottschalk, 'Categories of Financial Crime' (2010) *Journal of Financial Crime*, 17(4), 441–458.

9   Pickett, K.H.S. and Pickett, J.M. (2002), Financial Crime Investigation and Control, Wiley, New York, NY. As cited in P. Gottschalk, 'Categories of Financial Crime' (2010) *Journal of Financial Crime*, 17(4), 441–442.

10   City of London Police, *Assessment: Financial Crime Against Vulnerable Adults* (Social Care Institute for Excellence, November 2011, 2).

11   City of London Police, *Assessment: Financial Crime Against Vulnerable Adults* (Social Care Institute for Excellence, November 2011, 3).

money laundering, tax evasion and terrorism.[12] Different jurisdictions around the world thus define the component offences (such as fraud and money laundering) differently and while some make certain actions criminal, while others do not.. An example of the latter situation is tax evasion where some countries have very low or lax tax laws while others have the practical opposite. To recognize this disparity, the IMF states that financial abuse includes 'financial activities, many of which have the potential to harm financial systems, and legal activities that exploit undesirable features of tax and regulatory systems.'[13] Another term which has been used as well as or instead of financial crime includes illicit finance which has been used by the USA's Department of Treasury and the UK's HM Treasury.[14]

A person who has committed such offences must therefore be able to be described as a financial criminal. Other perhaps more common terms of vernacular include that of the white collar criminal and the offender who has committed corporate crime although, as acknowledged by Croall, there are also problems with how these terms are defined.[15] For example, while we might often regard the white collar criminal as someone who has high social status, is respectable, powerful and at management level, this is not always true, with many corporate crimes involving employees acting in the course of trade and business and with their offences relating to matters of hygiene and other health and safety issues.[16] While it may therefore be true, as suggested by Croall, that the vast majority of white collar crime is not committed by the high status offender, this is not the type of offence or offender which this book focuses upon. Therefore, for the purpose of this book, a financial criminal will be defined as someone who has committed a financial crime and who has a certain level of standing (i.e. that of management) within a business or corporation.

The Extent of Financial Crime

Despite concerted efforts by national and international agencies such as the United Nations, the Financial Action Task Force (FATF) and the IMF it is impossible to accurately quantify the true extent of financial crime/financial abuse which is taking place on a daily basis around the globe. This is partly due to the fact that significant amounts of all criminal behaviour will often go undiscovered and thus

---

12   International Monetary Fund, *Financial System Abuse, Financial Crime and Money Laundering – Background Paper* (International Monetary Fund, 12 February 2001, 4).

13   International Monetary Fund, *Financial System Abuse, Financial Crime and Money Laundering – Background Paper* (International Monetary Fund, 12 February 2001, 4).

14   N. Ryder, *Financial Crime in the 21st Century* (Edward Elgar 2011).

15   H. Croall, 'Who is the White-Collar Criminal?' (1989) *British Journal of Criminology*, 29(2), 157.

16   Ibid.

unreported, but it is also due to the many methodological difficulties which are often encountered when trying to pull statistics of this kind together.[17] The only estimations which can thus be provided are those for individual financial crimes.[18]

In the UK, for example, for the period of 2011/2012, the National Fraud Authority estimated that the cost of fraud to the UK's economy was in the region of £73 billion. This can be broken down into losses of £20.3 billion for the public sector (predominantly through tax, benefits and tax credits and governmental frauds), £45.5 billion for the private sector (including financial services, professional services, construction and engineering, natural resources, retail, wholesale and distribution and manufacturing), £1.1 billion for the non-profit sector and £6.1 billion for UK individuals (mass marketing, rental and online tickets).[19] In the European Union, according to a study prepared for the European Commission, fraud is estimated to range between 0.2 and 2 per cent of Gross Domestic Product (GDP), with the notorious examples of Barings, Drexel and Sumitomo and Daiwa, each involving losses in excess of US$1 billion. Fraud by banks, for example that seen by BCCI and Meridien, has contributed to considerable losses to depositors in a few countries, and seriously damaged the banking systems of some of the smaller African nations.[20]

In terms of money laundering, the FATF, on the basis of information about final sales of some illegal drugs (approximately US$120 billion a year in Europe and the USA in the late 1980s) and estimating worldwide and generalizing to include all drugs, have extrapolated that on the basis of assuming that 50–70 per cent of that amount would be laundered, the approximate amount of the laundered profits could be in the region of 2 per cent of the global GDP. In one FATF member country alone, 1,233 cases of money laundering were prosecuted in one year, with a total value of US$1.6 billion. Furthermore, an Australian study, from 1995, estimated money laundering there to amount to nearly US$3 billion or about 0.75 per cent of GDP. As with all estimations of financial crime though, given that these two latter examples were based on recorded crime, the true extent of money laundering there has been significantly underestimated.[21]

Further costs associated with other elements of financial crime often include the damage caused by the financial abuse of poor regulatory frameworks, which may subsequently contribute to financial crises or undermine confidence in a

---

17   N. Ryder, *Financial Crime in the 21st Century* (Edward Elgar 2011).

18   While some examples of these are included below, a fuller assessment of the extent of each individual crime is provided throughout this book.

19   National Fraud Authority, *Annual Fraud Indicator* (National Fraud Authority 2012, 3).

20   International Monetary Fund, *Financial System Abuse, Financial Crime and Money Laundering – Background Paper* (International Monetary Fund, 12 February 2001, 11).

21   International Monetary Fund, *Financial System Abuse, Financial Crime and Money Laundering – Background Paper* (International Monetary Fund, 12 February 2001, 11).

country's financial system. Such losses relate to the total costs of the crises and in essence are impossible to quantify. There are also similar difficulties in attempting to estimate the effects of tax evasion, harmful tax competition and corruption.[22]

The Importance of Financial Crime Regulation

Even though financial crime is often thought to be victimless; this is far from true. As explained by the FATF, 'criminal proceeds have the power to corrupt and ultimately destabilize communities or [even] whole national economies.'[23] The integrity of a nation's financial institutions can be eroded by those organized criminals who seek to maximize their illegal profits so that they are able to enjoy, the so called champagne lifestyle,[24] and as further explained by Vaithilingam and Nair it can weaken the financial systems which are the main players in many global financial transactions.[25] Moreover, as Ryder argues, the effects of financial crime can ultimately threaten national security on the basis that terrorists need money and resources so that they can carry out their illegal activities.[26] The IMF additionally argues that financial system abuse,

> ... could compromise bank soundness with potentially large fiscal liabilities, lessen the ability to attract foreign investment, and increase the volatility of international capital flows and exchange rates ... financial system abuse, financial crime, and money laundering may also distort the allocation of resources and the distribution of wealth.[27]

Financial crime will almost certainly also have an adverse impact on the economies of countries. Scanlan, for example, notes how the bomb attacks in London on the 7 and 21 July 2005 and the subsequent disruption to the transport system in London, cost the UK government in excess of £3 billion.[28] In addition to this,

---

22   International Monetary Fund, *Financial System Abuse, Financial Crime and Money Laundering – Background Paper* (International Monetary Fund, 12 February 2001, 11).

23   Financial Action Task Force, *Report on Money Laundering and Terrorist Financing Typologies 2003–2004* (Financial Action Task Force 2004).

24   N. Ryder, *Financial Crime in the 21st Century* (Edward Elgar 2011).

25   S. Vaithilingam and M. Nair, 'Factors affecting money laundering: lesson for developing countries' (2008) *Journal of Money Laundering Control*, 10(3), 352–366.

26   N. Ryder, *Financial Crime in the 21st Century* (Edward Elgar 2011).

27   International Monetary Fund, *Financial System Abuse, Financial Crime and Money Laundering – Background Paper* (International Monetary Fund, 12 February 2001, 9).

28   G. Scanlan, 'The Enterprise of Crime and Terror – The Implications for Good Business. Looking to the Future – Old and New Threats' (2006) *Journal of Financial Crime*, 13(2), 164–176.

further economic damage for a country may arise through the loss of reputation which may prevent businesses conducting future or further financial transactions in that country.

The impact of financial crime can also be seen on an individual level. Although losses to individuals may be small, especially when compared to public sector and private sector losses, they can still have a significant impact on that given individual. This may include a reduced flow of wealth between generations in families and a subsequent loss of tax revenue for the government through inheritance tax. This may also have real consequences for the public purse. For example, victims of financial crime who need care in their old age may no longer have the means to pay for it themselves and so become dependent on state funding. Also, where crime is perpetrated by a professional, such as a solicitor or financial professional, there may be harm to the reputation of individuals and organizations, leading not only to a decrease in confidence and trust,[29] but as emphasized by the IMF, can consequently result in a weakening of the entire financial system.[30]

The impact of financial crime should therefore not be underestimated and can be every bit as significant as physical abuse. Deem, for example, suggests that victims of financial crime can suffer as much as those who have been victims of a violent crime.[31] Spalek notes that outrage and anger, as well as fear, stress, anxiety, and depression, were experienced by victims of the Maxwell pension fraud[32] and how many victims of this fraud thought that their husbands' deaths had been accelerated as a result of said events.[33]

Bearing in mind the vast figures involved in financial crime, especially when it is likely that these estimations may only be the tip of the iceberg, and with such far-ranging impacts, it is essential that the UK has regulatory systems and legislation in place which effectively work to prevent and reduce the commission of such activities. The rationale of this book is therefore to look at the regulatory processes, systems and pieces of legislation which exist in the UK and offer both an assessment of these in terms of their effectiveness and a discussion on their potential reform. We hope to achieve this by not only providing a commentary

---

29 City of London Police, *Assessment: Financial Crime Against Vulnerable Adults* (Social Care Institute for Excellence, November 2011).

30 International Monetary Fund, *Financial System Abuse, Financial Crime and Money Laundering – Background Paper* (International Monetary Fund, 12 February 2001, 9).

31 D. Deem, 'Notes from the Field: Observations in Working with the Forgotten Victims of Personal Financial Crimes' (2000) *Journal of Elder Abuse & Neglect*, 12(2), 33–48.

32 B. Spalek, *Knowledgeable Consumers? Corporate Fraud and its Devastating Impacts, Briefing 4* (Centre for Crime and Justice Studies 2007).

33 B. Spalek, 'Exploring the Impact of Financial Crime: A Study Looking into the Effects of the Maxwell Scandal Upon the Maxwell Pensioners' (1999) *International Review of Victimology*, 6, 213–220.

on the law relating to financial crime in the UK but also presenting this in an innovative holistic style.

Contents Overview

The contents of this book are thus divided into seven further chapters. Chapters 2 to 6 deal with the individual financial crimes of money laundering, terrorist financing, fraud, insider dealing, market abuse and finally bribery and corruption. Each of these chapters has a similar structure. After a general introduction to the individual offence, the chapter outlines what the offence is, including relevant actus reus, mens rea and defence elements. Next follows a consideration of the extent of the financial crime in question. As noted above, this is often difficult to quantify, although through using a collection of international and national documents, an attempt at this has been made. Following on from this, each chapter then turns to the question of policy background. Initially this looks at where the offence originated from but then moves on to a detailed assessment of the financial institutions and regulatory bodies which exist to control and prevent the commission of such abuse. Whether such institutions and bodies are actually achieving their listed aims is additionally analysed. Finally, each chapter looks at the sentencing options and policy applicable to each financial crime. This includes sentencing examples and provides details on how the UK can achieve the recovery of criminal proceeds. Again the effectiveness of such options is discussed. The final chapter in the book, chapter eight, draws together the themes of the book and makes a number of future recommendations. Our fundamental aim here is to provoke further thought and discussion, but also to offer a way forward for the regulation and prevention of financial crime in the twenty-first century.

Chapter 2
Money Laundering

Introduction

Money laundering can be defined as the process utilized by criminals to disguise or convert the proceeds of crime (dirty money) into clean money. In this sense, the term criminal can include drug dealers, burglars, fraudsters, people traffickers, smugglers, terrorists, extortionists, tax evaders and illegal arms dealers, but can also include lawyers, accountants and other financial experts. The laundering of money is usually achieved by placing it into the financial system where it can be transferred between different financial products and bank accounts.[1] Due to the extent and threat of the problem, the United Kingdom (UK) has adopted an aggressive policy towards the offence and is an integral member of the global battle against money laundering. The primary focus of this chapter will therefore be to cover three of the UK's anti-money laundering initiatives including also an attempt at quantifying the extent of the problem. The chapter will then consider background to the policy of criminalizing and regulating money laundering, plus an evaluation of the financial institutions and regulatory bodies involved. Finally we look at how dirty money is recovered, including a brief analysis of sentencing options and practices.

The Money Laundering Process

Due to the fact that the goal of many criminal acts is to generate a profit for the individual or group involved, the ability to change dirty money into clean untraceable money is paramount for many criminals. Money laundering is thus the process by which organized criminals and drug cartels disguise their proceeds of crime. It is of critical importance to them, as it enables them to enjoy the profits without jeopardizing their source. Money laundering is therefore a criminal activity, which involves the practice of concealing assets to avoid any discovery of the unlawful activity that fashioned them. In order to achieve this, the practice involves three recognizable stages: placement, layering and integration. In the first stage, the money launderer places the illegal profits of crime into for

---

1   Financial Services Authority, 'Frequently Asked Questions' (Financial Services Authority 2011) <http://www.fsa.gov.uk/pages/About/What/financial_crime/money_laundering/faqs/index.shtml> accessed 6 June 2011.

example, the financial system.[2] This is sometimes achieved by separating larger sums of money into smaller amounts which are then deposited into several bank accounts in order to avoid money laundering reporting requirements. This process is commonly referred to as smurfing where criminals will deposit money in a financial institution in amounts that are lower than the level at which the financial institution must complete a suspicious activity report (SAR).[3] At the second step, layering, the launderer enters into numerous transactions to distance the illegal money from its original source. The final stage is referred to as integration, and it is at this phase of the money laundering cycle that the monies re-enter the economy. Although there are too many money laundering mechanisms to mention them all, the most common examples in the UK include cash couriers, money transmission systems, cash intensive businesses, shell corporations, high value assets and property transactions.[4] The National Criminal Intelligence Service (NCIS) has stated that the most common means of laundering money includes the purchasing of property, investment in front companies, high levels of conspicuous consumption and moving large amounts of cash to foreign jurisdictions.[5] Other mechanisms include money service bureaus, smuggling, the depositing of bogus salaries and via financial institutions.

What is the Offence of Money Laundering?

The offence of money laundering is currently contained within Part 7 of the Proceeds of Crime Act (POCA) 2002. This received Royal Assent on 24 July 2002 and applies to money laundering activities on or after 23 February 2003.[6] The Act contains three principal offences: i) concealing, disguising converting, transferring or removing criminal property from the jurisdiction;[7] ii) entering into or becoming concerned in an arrangement, knowing or suspecting it to facilitate the acquisition,

---

2   For an excellent commentary on how organized criminals will seek to hide their proceeds of crime at the placement stage of the layering process see J. Simser, 'Money Laundering and Asset Cloaking Techniques' (2008) *Journal of Money Laundering Control*, 11(1), 15–24.

3   For a more detailed and fascinating discussion about smurfing and money laundering see S. Welling, 'Smurfs, Money Laundering, and the Federal Criminal Law: The Crime of Structuring Transactions' (1989) *Florida Law Review*, 41, 287–339.

4   Financial Action Task Force, *Third Mutual Evaluation Report Anti-Money Laundering and Combating the Financing of Terrorism – United Kingdom* (Financial Action Task Force 2007, 15).

5   National Criminal Intelligence Service, *UK Threat Assessment* (National Criminal Intelligence Service 2007, 53).

6   R. Forston, 'Money Laundering Offences under POCA 2002' in W. Blair and R. Brent (eds) *Banks and Financial Crime – The International Law of Tainted Money* (Oxford University Press 2010, 157).

7   Proceeds of Crime Act 2002, s 327.

retention, use or control of criminal property on behalf of another person;[8] and iii) acquiring, using or possessing criminal property.[9] It is also an offence to be part of a conspiracy, to attempt to commit, or to counsel, aid, abet or procure any of the above. All three offences can be committed by any person, irrespective of the fact that they work within the regulated sector (including banks, insurers, accountants, credit institutions, financial institutions, lawyers etc.) or undertake a relevant business (including casino operators, estate agents and insolvency practitioners). Other offences, mainly focused on disclosure, including failing to disclose suspicions or knowledge of money laundering,[10] failing to pass on these aforementioned disclosures to an authorized person,[11] disclosing that a person or persons are subject to an investigation due to allegations of money laundering (tipping off),[12] and finally making disclosures which are likely to prejudice an investigation.[13] On the basis that the first three offences are the primary ones, it is these which will be considered in more detail.

Concealing, disguising converting, transferring or removing criminal property from the jurisdiction – section 327 POCA 2002

Section 327 of POCA 2002 generates the first of the three primary money laundering offences, with a person committing an offence if he conceals, disguises, converts, transfers or removes criminal property from England and Wales, Scotland or Northern Ireland. This also includes concealing or disguising the nature, source, location, movement, ownership or disposal of the property.[14] For the purposes of the Act, property includes money; real, personal, heritable or moveable property; things in action and other incorporeal or intangible property.[15] Property is considered to be criminal property if '(a) it constitutes a person's benefit from criminal conduct or it represents such a benefit (in whole or part and whether directly or indirectly); and (b) the alleged offender knows or suspects that it constitutes or represents such a benefit.'[16] This interpretation of criminal property is somewhat contentious, mainly because its scope allows the inclusion of property from anywhere in the world.[17] Furthermore, Forston states that element (b) provides 'a somewhat artificial meaning because the knowledge

8   Proceeds of Crime Act 2002, s 328.
9   Proceeds of Crime Act 2002, s 329.
10   Proceeds of Crime Act 2002, s 330.
11   Proceeds of Crime Act 2002, s 331 and s 332.
12   Proceeds of Crime Act 2002, s 333A.
13   Proceeds of Crime Act 2002, s 342.
14   Proceeds of Crime Act 2002, s 327(3).
15   Proceeds of Crime Act 2002, s 340(9).
16   Proceeds of Crime Act 2002, s 340(3). For a critical discussion of the interpretation of this phrase see D. Bentley and R. Fisher 'Criminal Property Under PCOA 2002 – Time to Clean up the Law?' (2009) *Archbold News*, 2, 7–9.
17   Proceeds of Crime Act 2002, s 340(9).

of the person dealing with the property only becomes relevant at this point.'[18] Hudson, therefore, argues that the section has two specific requirements. First, that the criminal property constitutes a benefit and second, that the defendant had suspicion or knowledge of this fact.[19]

The phrase benefit is broadly defined and is applied universally by the Act.[20] Under section 340(5), 'a person benefits from conduct if he obtains property as a result of or in connection with the conduct.'[21] The phrase includes 'not only the property that the offender directly obtained as a result of or in connection with the offence, but also any pecuniary advantage that he or she obtained from it.'[22] A benefit therefore includes three key concepts. The first is that any gain is directly related to criminal behaviour. The scope of section 340 is extremely wide and it is possible for *any* person to have made a gain, not just the person who committed the offence. Indeed, the Act goes as far as stating that in assessing whether or not an offence has been committed, it is immaterial 'who carried out the conduct' or 'who benefited from it' or whether the conduct occurred before or even after the passing of the Act.[23] Secondly the gain must flow from the criminal activity involved. This doesn't necessarily mean just financial gain and could include improvements to someone's standard of living or profits derived from the illegal activity.[24] It can also include anything which represents a benefit,[25] with a person committing an offence if they know or suspect that what has been given to them constitutes or represents such a benefit.[26] This suggests that it could include gain which has been made in lieu of property as defined above. This would again make the provision extremely far reaching.

Finally, it must be proven that the property or benefit derives from criminal conduct. This is defined as all conduct which constitutes a criminal offence under UK law. Offences which are committed abroad can still be brought within the jurisdiction of the UK if the laundering acts are committed within the UK. It is also

---

18   R. Forston, 'Money Laundering Offences under POCA 2002' in W. Blair and R. Brent (eds) *Banks and Financial Crime – The International Law of Tainted Money* (Oxford University Press 2010, 165).

19   A. Hudson, *The Law of Finance* (Sweet and Maxwell 2009, 345).

20   R. Forston, 'Money Laundering Offences under POCA 2002' in W. Blair and R. Brent (eds) *Banks and Financial Crime – The International Law of Tainted Money* (Oxford University Press 2010, 163–164).

21   For a more detailed interpretation of this phrase see for example *R v Rowbotton* [2006] EWCA Crim 747, *R v Gabriel* [2006] EWCA Crim 229 and *R v IK* [2007] EWCA Crim 491.

22   R. Forston, 'Money Laundering Offences under POCA 2002' in W. Blair and R. Brent (eds) *Banks and Financial Crime – The International Law of Tainted Money* (Oxford University Press 2010, 163).

23   Proceeds of Crime Act 2002, s 340(3)(a).

24   A. Hudson, *The Law of Finance* (Sweet and Maxwell 2009, 345).

25   A. Hudson, *The Law of Finance* (Sweet and Maxwell 2009, 344).

26   Proceeds of Crime Act 2002, s 340(3)(b).

worth noting that it is immaterial whether the criminal conduct took place prior to the POCA 2002 coming into force, as long as the laundering act took place after its commencement.[27]

Entering into or becoming concerned in an arrangement knowing or suspecting it to facilitate the acquisition, retention, use and control of criminal property on behalf of another person – section 328 POCA 2002

Section 328 of POCA 2002 provides that 'A person commits an offence if he enters into or becomes concerned in an arrangement which he know or suspects facilitates (by whatever means) the acquisition, retention, use or control of criminal property by or on behalf of another person.'[28] To establish a conviction, the prosecution must prove not only that a person became concerned in an arrangement which they knew or suspected would make it simpler for another person to acquire, retain, use or control criminal property, but furthermore, that the person concerned also knew or suspected that the property constituted or represented benefit from criminal conduct.[29] The offence can be committed in a number of ways and covers the situation where a third party is handling money which is derived from the proceeds of crime. Forston therefore takes the view that 'this offence is of considerable concern to those who handle or advise third parties in connection with money and other types of property.'[30] In order for a person to be guilty of the offence the definition of criminal property is again of central importance as, too, are the concepts of knowledge and suspicion. While knowledge is a fairly straightforward idea, the meaning of suspicion has caused uncertainty and anxiety, particularly in relation to what will amount to suspicion for the purposes of the offence. Harvey, for example, notes that 'suspicious itself is a wide-reaching term of which there is no objective definition: suspicious is personal and subjective and falls far short of proof based on firm evidence.'[31] Perhaps due to this subjectiveness and in an attempt to clarify meaning, the courts have defined suspicion as,

---

27   Crown Prosecution Service 'Proceeds of Crime Act 2002 Part 7 – Money Laundering Offences' <http://www.cps.gov.uk/legal/p_to_r/proceeds_of_crime_money_la undering/> accessed 6 July 2011.

28   Proceeds of Crime Act 2002, s 328(1).

29   This section amends and updates section 50 of the Drug Trafficking Act 1994 and section 93A of the Criminal Justice Act 1988, section 38 of the Criminal Law (Consolidation) (Scotland) Act 1995 and Article 46 of the Proceeds of Crime (Northern Ireland) Order 1996.

30   R. Forston, 'Money Laundering Offences under POCA 2002' in W. Blair and R. Brent (eds) *Banks and Financial Crime – The International Law of Tainted Money* (Oxford University Press 2010, 181).

31   J. Harvey, 'Compliance and Reporting Issues Arising for Financial Institutions from Money Laundering Regulations: A Preliminary Cost Benefit Study' (2004) *Journal of Money Laundering Control*, 7(4), 333–346, 335.

... being beyond mere speculation and based on some foundation, for example: a degree of satisfaction and not necessarily amounting to belief but at least extending beyond speculation as to whether an event has occurred or not; and, although the creation of suspicion requires a lesser factual basis than the creation of belief, it must nonetheless be built upon some foundation.[32]

In *R* v *DA Silva*, Longmore L.J. took the view that,

... the essential element of the word "suspect" and its affiliates, in this context, is that the defendant must think that there is a possibility, which is more than fanciful, that the relevant facts exist. A vague feeling of unease would not suffice. But the statute does not require the suspicion to be "clear" or "firmly grounded and targeted on specific facts", or based upon "reasonable grounds".[33]

Furthermore, Lord Hope in *R v Sail (Abdulrahman)* stated,

... the assumption is that the person has a suspicion, otherwise he would not be thinking of doing what the statute contemplates. The objective test is introduced in the interest of fairness, to ensure that the suspicion has a reasonable basis for it. The subjective test – actual suspicion – is not enough. The objective test – that there were reasonable grounds for it – must be satisfied too.[34]

Moreover, according to the Court of Appeal in *K v National Westminster Bank and HM Revenue and Customs and Serious Organised Crime Agency*,[35] the interpretation of suspicion is the same in civil law as it is in criminal law. Applying case law, we therefore have what is often referred to as the 'more than fanciful possibility test.'[36] Therefore, Hudson takes the view that 'the defendant must have

---

32   The Financial Services Commission, *Guidance Notes – Systems of Control to Prevent the Financial System from Being Used for Money Laundering or Terrorist Financing Activities* (Financial Services Commission 2011, 8.1).

33   *R v Da Silva* [2006] EWCA Crim 1654. This case related to the interpretation of the phrase under the Criminal Justice Act 1988. For a more detailed discussion about the decision in this case see G. Brown and T. Evans 'The Impact: The Breadth and Depth of the Anti-Money Laundering Provisions Requiring Reporting of Suspicious Activities' (2008) *Journal of International Banking Law and Regulation*, 23(5), 274–277. The decision in this case was recently confirmed in *Shah v. HSBC Private Bank Ltd* [2012] EWHC 1283 (QB) at para. 112.

34   *R v Sail (Abdulrahman)* [2006] UKHL 18, para. 52.

35   [2006] EWCA Civ 1039.

36   The Financial Services Commission, *Guidance Notes – Systems of Control to Prevent the Financial System From Being Used for Money Laundering or Terrorist Financing Activities* (Financial Services Commission 2011, 8.1).

actual suspicion and also [that] there must have been a reasonable basis for having that suspicion, as well as the property being used for criminal purposes.'[37]

Section 328 has also caused problems with respect to what an arrangement is, particularly with regard to those working within the legal profession. For example in *P v P*[38] Dame Butler-Sloss, in the Family Division of the High Court, held that a legal professional, if acting for a client in divorce proceedings, is required to investigate the financial affairs of both parties in some detail, and any irregularity such as an over-claimed benefit payment or undeclared VAT transaction requires the solicitor to stop proceedings while he makes his disclosure to the relevant body and awaits guidance. This caused Collins and Kennedy to note that 'many professionals will soon be committing criminal offences if they fail to report suspicions about money laundering activity.'[39] Further clarity was however provided the following year in *Bowman v Fels*,[40] a Court of Appeal judgment, which disapproved of *P v P*. In this case, the judgment concerned two important points. The first, at the very centre of the appeal, related to 'whether s. 328 applies to the ordinary conduct of legal proceedings or any aspect of such conduct – including, in particular, any step taken to pursue proceedings and the obtaining of a judgement.'[41] In its decision, the Court of Appeal made it clear that the proper interpretation of section 328 did not cover or affect legal proceedings. The Court arguably came to this decision through its interpretation of 'being concerned in an arrangement', with Brooke L.J. stating that there was a 'strong argument for a restricted understanding of the concept',[42] and that 'as a matter of ordinary language, our impression on reading s. 328 was and remains that, whatever Parliament may have had in mind by the phrase "entering into or becomes concerned in an arrangement which ... facilitates" it is most unlikely that it was thinking of legal proceedings.'[43] Ordinary legal activities such as securing injunctive relief, steps needed to be taken in litigation, dividing assets in accordance with judgment, alternative dispute resolutions and securing freezing orders therefore fall outside what is considered under section 328 to be an arrangement.

Acquiring, using or possessing criminal property – section 329 POCA 2002

The third principal money laundering offence is found in section 329(1) of POCA 2002.[44] This section provides that a person commits an offence if they acquire,

37   A. Hudson, *The Law of Finance* (Sweet and Maxwell 2009, 350).
38   [2004] Fam 1.
39   J. Collins and A. Kennedy, 'The Cheat, His Wife and Her Lawyer' (2003) *Taxation*, November 136.
40   [2005] EWCA Civ 226.
41   [2005] EWCA Civ 226 para 52.
42   [2005] EWCA Civ 226 para 63.
43   [2005] EWCA Civ 226 para 64.
44   This unifies and replaces Drug Trafficking Act 1994, s 51 and Criminal Justice Act 1988, s 93B.

use or have in their possession criminal property. For the purposes of the offence, possession means physical custody. In order for a person to be convicted of an offence, it has to be proven that the property handled is criminal property and that it comprises a benefit. Furthermore, the prosecution has to prove that the defendant knows or suspects that the property is obtained from criminal conduct.

Defences

A person does not commit an offence under section 327 POCA 2002 if, 'he makes an authorised disclosure under section 338 and (if the disclosure is made before he does the act mentioned in subsection (1)) he has the appropriate consent.'[45] This is known as the consent defence[46] and relates to consent given to the defendant that he can proceed on the basis of the authorized disclosure. An authorized disclosure is 'a disclosure to a constable, a customs officer or a nominated officer by the alleged offender that property is criminal property',[47] with the defence also applying to situations whether the defendant intended to make a disclosure but had a reasonable excuse for not doing so: the reasonable excuse defence. Furthermore, a person does not commit an offence if,

    a. he knows or believes on reasonable grounds, that the relevant criminal conduct occurred in a particular country or territory outside the United Kingdom, and

    b. the relevant criminal conduct –

        i. was not, at the time it occurred, unlawful under the criminal law then applying in that country or territory, and

        ii. is not of a description prescribed by an order made by the Secretary of State.[48]

Finally and applying only to deposit-taking institutions, a body does not commit an offence if 'a) it does the act in operating an account maintained with it; and b) the value of the criminal property concerned is less than the threshold amount determined under s. 339A for the act.'[49] This is currently set at £250. Similar defences also exist for section 328 and section 329 offences.

In addition to those defences outlined above and only in relation to a section 329 offence, section 329(2)(c) provides the adequate consideration defence. This covers those people who have accepted dirty money for ordinary consumable goods and/or services. In such cases, the person receiving the money is not

---

45   Proceeds of Crime Act 2002, s 327(2).
46   See *Hosni Tayeb v HSBC Bank plc* [2004] EWHC 1529.
47   Proceeds of Crime Act 2002, s 338(1).
48   Proceeds of Crime Act 2002, s 327(2A).
49   Proceeds of Crime Act 2002, s 327(2C).

obliged to question the source of it.[50] It can also be relied upon by professional advisors who have received money for or on account of costs (unless it is a gross overpayment of the services given), but will not apply if the defendant knows or suspects that the payment will help another to carry out criminal conduct. If this is the case the person is treated as not having paid proper consideration.[51] Employees working within the regulated sector may also have a defence if they can prove that they have received inadequate training from their employers on matters of money laundering and/or their requirements to disclose.

The Extent of Money Laundering

Due to the secretive nature of money laundering, it is extremely difficult to measure the true extent of the problem, with many previous attempts proving largely unsuccessful. This is further hampered by the fact there are so many different ways that organized criminals launder money, as discussed above. Despite these difficulties there have been claims that money laundering is one of the world's largest industries, with an International Monetary Fund (IMF) assessment in 1998 suggesting that it was equal to 2–5 per cent of global gross domestic product (GDP).[52] Furthermore, Spalek claims that the amount is approximately $500 billion per year;[53] Maylam argues that it could be as much as $1.5 trillion[54] while Walker estimates that in fact it could be nearer $2.85 trillion.[55] The latest figures provided by the United Nations (UN) Office on Drugs and Crime in 2009 agree with the IMF 2–5 per cent of global GDP, estimating that this equates to an annual amount of between $800 billion and $2 trillion.[56] In the UK, it was once thought that the amount of money laundered on an annual basis ranged from £19 billion to £48 billion.[57] These figures based on a 1999 HM Customs and Excise assessment

---

50   Annotation notes to Proceeds of Crime Act 2002, s 327.

51   Crown Prosecution Service 'Proceeds of Crime Act 2002 Part 7 – Money Laundering Offences' <http://www.cps.gov.uk/legal/p_to_r/proceeds_of_crime_money_la undering/> accessed 6 July 2011.

52   Financial Services Authority, 'Frequently Asked Questions' (Financial Services Authority 2011) <http://www.fsa.gov.uk/pages/About/What/financial_crime/money_laund ering/faqs/index.shtml> accessed 6 June 2011.

53   R. Spalek, 'Regulation, White–Collar Crime and the Bank of Credit and Commerce International' (2001) *Howard Journal of Criminal Justice*, 40, 166–179, 167.

54   S. Maylam, 'Prosecution for Money Laundering in the UK' (2002) *Journal of Financial Crime*, 10, 157–158, 158.

55   J. Walker, 'Modelling Global Money Laundering Flows – Some Findings' <http:// www.johnwalkercrimetrendsanalysis.com.au/ML%20method.htm> accessed 6 June 2011.

56   UN Office on Drugs and Crime, 'Money-Laundering and Globalization' <http:// www.unodc.org/unodc/en/money-laundering/globalization.html> accessed 6 July 2011.

57   J. Harvey, 'An Evaluation of Money Laundering Policies' (2005) *Journal of Money Laundering Control*, 8(4), 339–345, 340.

would now produce estimates of between £23 billion and £57 billion.[58] Although, if we take the IMF estimation of between 2 and 5 per cent GDP and base it on the GDP figures for the UK in 2010 (£1473 billion[59]) we are looking at between £29.46 billion and £73.65 billion. The amount of money involved is therefore of epic proportions and requires an effective monitoring and prevention strategy.

Policy Background – From Where did the Offence Originate?

The origins of the UK's money laundering policy are to be found not in the European Union (EU), but in the declaration of the 'War on Drugs' by President Richard Nixon in the 1970s. Money laundering is inherently linked with the sale, production and manufacture of illegal narcotic substances which, in the 1980s, resulted in its prevention being pushed to the top of the international community's criminal justice agenda. This community, largely led by the UN and the EU, introduced a wide range of legislative measures that aimed to tackle money laundering and the problems it presents. These measures included, for example, the UN Convention against Illicit Traffic in Narcotic Drugs and Psychotropic Substances, which is more commonly referred to as the Vienna Convention.[60] The Vienna Convention provides that signatories must: criminalize the laundering of drug proceeds; implement instruments to allow for the determination of jurisdiction over the offence of money laundering; permit the confiscation of the proceeds of the sale of illegal drugs and/or materials used in their manufacturing; introduce mechanisms to facilitate extradition matters and provide measures to improve mutual legal assistance. The UK signed the Vienna Convention in December 1988 and ratified it in June 1991.[61] The impact of the Vienna Convention is illustrated by the Criminal Justice (International Co-operation) Act 1990,[62] part two of which is entitled the Vienna Convention. It is also important to note that the Convention only applies to drug trafficking offences. The scope of the UN's legislative measures

---

58   Financial Services Authority, 'Frequently Asked Questions' (Financial Services Authority 2011) <http://www.fsa.gov.uk/pages/About/What/financial_crime/money_laund ering/faqs/index.shtml> accessed 6 June 2011.

59   UK Public Spending 'UK Gross Domestic Product' <http://www.ukpublicspend ing.co.uk/downchart_ukgs.php?title=UK%20Gross%20Domestic%20Product&year =1950_2010&chart=> accessed 6 June 2011.

60   United Nations Convention against Illicit Traffic in Narcotic Drugs and Psychotropic Substances (1988).

61   Financial Action Task Force, *Third Mutual Evaluation Report Anti-Money Laundering and Combating the Financing of Terrorism – United Kingdom* (Financial Action Task Force 2007, 250).

62   Booth et al. noted that this Act was 'enacted partly to enable the United Kingdom to implement the Vienna Convention'. See R. Booth, S. Farrell, G. Bastable and N. Yeo, *Money Laundering Law and Regulation: A Practical Guide* (Oxford University Press 2011, 15).

was thus extended by the UN Convention against Transnational Organised Crime, or the Palermo Convention,[63] to include the 'proceeds of serious crime'.[64] The UK signed the Palermo Convention in December 2000, and ratified it in February 2006.[65] Evidence of its influence, is illustrated by the fact that it is referred to in the Serious Organised Crime and Police Act 2005.[66]

In addition to the UN Anti-Money Laundering (AML) measures, the EU has also introduced a series of money laundering initiatives that have influenced the UK's policy. For example, in 1990 the EU implemented the Council of Europe Convention on Laundering, Search, Seizure and Confiscation of the Proceeds from Crime and on the Financing of Terrorism.[67] The UK signed the Convention in November 1990, and ratified it in September 1992.[68] The scope of the 1990 Convention was further broadened by the subsequent Council of Europe Convention on Laundering, Search, Seizure and Confiscation of the Proceeds from Crime and on the Financing of Terrorism in 2005, which was adopted in Warsaw in 2005 and entered into force in 2008. It is important to note, however, that at the time of writing the UK has not yet incorporated this. Through the 1990 Convention, the EU requires its Member States to implement three Money Laundering Directives. The First Directive was introduced in 1991 and concentrates on what are referred to as preventive measures including client identification, the examination and reporting of suspicious transactions, indemnities to be given for good faith reporting of suspicions transactions, identification records to be kept for five years after the client relationship has ended, co-operation with the authorities and the provision of adequate internal procedures and training programmes. These are based upon the 40 recommendations of the Financial Action Task Force (FATF),[69]

---

63   United Nations Convention against Transnational Organized Crime, G.A. Res. 55/25, U.N. GAOR, 55th Sess., Supp. No. 49, Vol. I at 43, U.N. Doc. A/55/49.

64   UN Convention against Transnational Organised Crime, article 12. A serious crime is defined in article 2 of the Convention as including 'conduct constituting an offence punishable by a maximum deprivation of liberty of at least four years or a more serious penalty'.

65   Financial Action Task Force, *Third Mutual Evaluation Report Anti-Money Laundering and Combating the Financing of Terrorism – United Kingdom* (Financial Action Task Force 2007, 250).

66   Serious Organised Crime and Police Act 2005, s 95.

67   This is more commonly referred to as the Strasbourg Treaty.

68   Financial Action Task Force, *Third Mutual Evaluation Report Anti-Money Laundering and Combating the Financing of Terrorism – United Kingdom* (Financial Action Task Force 2007, 250).

69   See V. Mitsilegas and B. Gilmore, 'The EU Legislative Framework Against Money Laundering and Terrorist Finance: A Critical Analysis in Light of Evolving Global Standards' (2007) *International and Comparative Law Quarterly*, 56(1), 119–140, 120. It is important to note that the FATF merged its money laundering recommendations with the terrorist financing recommendations in February 2012. See Financial Action Task Force 'FATF steps up the fight against money laundering and

as discussed below, and were implemented by the UK in 1993.[70] The Second Money Laundering Directive increases the scope of the suspicious transaction reporting requirements and the scope of the reporting obligations to a wider range of professions, thus extending the scope of the UK's AML obligations. This has been achieved through the Money Laundering Regulations 2003.[71] Finally, the Third Money Laundering Directive was implemented by Member States in 2007. This broadens the scope of predicate offences and provides more guidance in improving customer identification procedures. It currently applies to all proceeds of serious crime,[72] and in the UK has been implemented through the Money Laundering Regulations 2007.[73]

In addition to these measures, the UK's money laundering policy has also been influenced by a series of international best practices and industry guidelines. This includes, for example, the aforementioned 40 Recommendations of the FATF. This inter-governmental body was created in 1989 as a result of the UNs bold pledge to stop money laundering.[74] Its purpose is to establish a set of international acceptable standards of AML recommendations that can be implemented by nation states. The FATF published its original 40 Recommendations in 1990 although these have been subsequently amended, both in 1996 and in 2003. Such amendments were largely in response to new money laundering practices adopted by organized criminals and drug cartels. The scope of the Recommendations was also further extended following the terrorist attacks of 9/11 to include the financing of terrorism.[75] This has resulted in the significant step of creating nine Special Recommendations, the last of which was added in October 2004. Under the Recommendations, countries must: criminalize the financing of terrorism; freeze and confiscate terrorist assets; require financial institutions to report suspicious activities that relate to terrorism; promote international co-operation; and, provide measures to deal with alternative remittance systems, wire transfers, non-profit entities and cash couriers.

In addition, countries should ratify and implement the UN counter-terrorist financing (CTF) measures. In February 2012, the FATF published its revised set of International Standards on Combating Money Laundering and the Financing of Terrorism and Proliferation. The standards have amended the 40 Recommendations and the nine Special Recommendations and have attempted

---

terrorist financing', 16 February 2012 <http://www.fatf-gafi.org/document/17/0,3746,en_3225 0379_32236920_49656209_1_1_1_1,00.html> accessed 14 March 2012.

70 European Council, *Directive on the Prevention of the Use of the Financial System to Launder Money* 91/308, 1993 O.J. (L 166). This Directive was implemented by Money Laundering Regulations 1993, S.I. 1993/1933.

71 S.I. 2003/3075.

72 J. Fisher, 'Recent Development in the Fight Against Money Laundering' (2002) *Journal of International Banking Law*, 17(3), 67–72, 67.

73 S.I. 2007/2157.

74 J. Johnson, 'Is the Global Financial System AML/CTF Prepared?' (2008) *Journal of Financial Crime*, 15(1), 7–21, 8.

75 For a more detailed discussion of this see Chapter 3.

to provide governments with stronger mechanisms to tackle financial crime. Importantly, the revised standards have been extended to include corruption and tax crimes.[76] The UK is an active member of the FATF and as such acted as chair of the organization in 2007. The influence of the FATF over the UK's AML policy and legislative framework is illustrated through the money laundering and terrorist finance strategy of 2007.[77] In the accompanying press release HM Treasury stated 'the FATF is central to the UK's international objectives within the strategy.'[78] Furthermore, in its 2007 Mutual Evaluation Report the FATF concluded that the UK was fully compliant on 19 out of the 40 Recommendations, largely compliant on nine, partially compliant on nine and non-compliant on only three.[79] The report concluded that the UK has a far reaching AML legislative framework that fully complies with both the Vienna and Palermo Conventions.[80]

In addition to the 40 Recommendations, another important industry guideline is the Basel Committee on Banking Regulation and Supervisory Principles. The Committee has published a Statement of Principles, which is consistent with the 40 Recommendations, and also a number of best practice papers that highlight ways to prevent the financial system becoming an instrument for financial crime clients.[81] The UK is also a member of the Basel Committee on Banking Supervision and a founding member of the Egmont Group of Financial Intelligence Units (FIU). The objective of the Egmont group is to 'increase and improve the communication between FIUs worldwide to help fight what is recognized as a universal problem.'[82] The UK's AML policy has therefore been influenced by the legislative and preventative measures of the international community and by international best practices and industry guidelines. The UK's money laundering

---

76   Financial Action Task Force, *International Standards on Combating Money Laundering and the Financing of Terrorism & Proliferation* (Financial Action Task Force 2012).

77   HM Treasury, *The Financial Challenge of Terrorism and Crime* (HM Treasury 2007).

78   HM Treasury, 'Appointment of the UK President of the Financial Action Task Force' <http://www.gov-news.org/gov/uk/news/appointment_uk_president_financial_act ion/36083.html> accessed 3 July 2011.

79   Financial Action Task Force, *Third Mutual Evaluation Report Anti-Money Laundering and Combating the Financing of Terrorism – United Kingdom* (Financial Action Task Force 2007, 10–15).

80   Financial Action Task Force, *Third Mutual Evaluation Report Anti-Money Laundering and Combating the Financing of Terrorism – United Kingdom* (Financial Action Task Force 2007, 10–15).

81   M. Simpson, 'International Initiatives' in M. Simpson, N. Smith and A. Srivastava (eds) *International Guide to Money Laundering Law and Practice* (Bloomsbury Professional 2010, 202).

82   M. Simpson, 'International Initiatives' in M. Simpson, N. Smith and A. Srivastava (eds) *International Guide to Money Laundering Law and Practice* (Bloomsbury Professional 2010, 202).

policy is managed and implemented by several government departments, financial regulatory and law enforcement agencies, many of which are considered below.

Financial Institutions and Regulatory Bodies

HM Treasury and the Home Office

HM Treasury is the leading AML authority in the UK and is responsible for the implementation of Money Laundering Directives and the execution of the UN's financial sanctions regime. It is the UK's representative at the FATF and sanctions the industry guidelines on compliance with money laundering controls.[83] The importance of the role of HM Treasury is illustrated by the publication of its first money laundering strategy in 2004,[84] where the objective is to create an effective AML framework that seeks to achieve an appropriate balance between tackling money laundering while preventing the imposition of burdensome compliance regulations. In relation to this, HM Treasury has taken the view that 'the existing [AML] regime consists of measures ranging from provisions in the criminal law to punish money launderers and to deprive them of their proceeds, to the obligation on the financial services industry and certain other sectors and professions to identify their customers and to report suspicious activities when necessary.'[85] The objective of HM Treasury is thus to safeguard 'the integrity of the financial system from exploitation by criminals and terrorists. It does this by deploying financial tools to deter, detect and disrupt crime and security threats. The approach taken is effective and proportionate to the risks posed as well as engaging with business, law makers and law enforcers.'[86] This is clearly illustrated by the publication of its second strategy document in 2007 which outlined how the government intended to tackle the problems associated with money laundering and the financing of terrorism.[87]

    HM Treasury also chairs the Money Laundering Advisory Committee which is a 'forum for all relevant stakeholders [including] financial institutions, trade and consumer organizations, government and law enforcement representatives.'[88]

---

83   Financial Action Task Force, *Third Mutual Evaluation Report Anti-Money Laundering and Combating the Financing of Terrorism – United Kingdom* (Financial Action Task Force 2007, 24).

84   HM Treasury, *Anti-Money Laundering Strategy* (HM Treasury 2004).

85   HM Treasury, *The Financial Challenge of Terrorism and Crime* (HM Treasury 2007, 11).

86   HM Treasury, *The Financial Challenge of Terrorism and Crime* (HM Treasury 2007).

87   HM Treasury, *The Financial Challenge of Terrorism and Crime* (HM Treasury 2007).

88   Oxford Analytica Ltd, 'Country Report: Anti-Money Laundering Rules in the United Kingdom' in M. Pieith and G. Aiolfi (eds) *A Comparative Guide to Anti-Money*

In this role, HM Treasury is further supported by the Home Office, which is responsible for managing police forces in England and Wales, and the Serious Organised Crime Agency (SOCA), which tackles organized crime, counter terrorism, crime and immigration. In relation to money laundering, the Home Office manages the asset recovery scheme and the mutual legal assistance regime. However, as discussed below, the Home Office announced in June 2011 that it intends to establish a National Crime Agency (NCA), which will have a significant impact on the role of SOCA and several other financial crime agencies.

The Financial Services Authority

Another important body is the Financial Services Authority (FSA) which acts as a key policymaker in the UK. The Authority was established following a number of high profile financial scandals between the 1970s and 1990s which were arguably caused by poor banking regulation by the Bank of England. The FSA were therefore given extensive rule making and enforcement powers under the Financial Services and Markets Act (FSMA) 2000. Under this Act the FSA has a duty to reduce financial crime by ensuring that financial institutions have systems and practices in place which protect themselves against being used as vehicles to launder money by financial criminals. Financial crime is broadly defined within the FSMA 2000 as incorporating any offence including fraud or dishonesty,[89] misconduct in, or misuse of, information relating to a financial market;[90] or handling the proceeds of crime.[91] The principal objective of the FSA has therefore been to focus on the AML systems and controls that the regulated sector has in place.[92] Under the FSMA 2000, the FSA makes rules in relation to the prevention and detection of money laundering.[93] The rule-making powers of the FSA were originally contained in the Money Laundering Sourcebook,[94] but these were detailed, burdensome and very similar to those in the Money Laundering Regulations 1993. The Money Laundering Sourcebook has therefore been replaced by a principles-based approach in the Senior Management Arrangements, Systems and Controls (SYSC) part of

Laundering: A Critical Analysis of Systems in Singapore, Switzerland, the UK and the USA (Edward Elgar 2004, 271).

89   Financial Services and Markets Act 2000, s 6 (3)(a).

90   Financial Services and Markets Act 2000, s 6 (3)(b).

91   Financial Services and Markets Act 2000, s 6 (3)(c).

92   A. Proctor, 'Supporting a Risk-Based Anti-Money Laundering Approach Through Enforcement Action' (2004) *Journal of Financial Regulation and Compliance*, 13(1), 10–14, 11. Members of the regulated sector are defined in the Financial Services and Markets Act 2000 (Regulated Activities) Order 2001 S.I. 2001/544.

93   Financial Services and Markets Act 2000, s 146.

94   Financial Services Authority, *Money Laundering Handbook* (Financial Services Authority 2006). The FSA adopted the Money Laundering Regulation 1993 via the Financial Services and Markets Act 2000 Regulations (Relating to Money Laundering Regulations) 2001, S.I. 2001/1819.

the FSA's Handbook.[95] The new version provides that firms must have in place systems and controls which are appropriate for the firm to conduct its business.[96] This includes: a requirement to carry out regular assessments of the adequacy of AML systems so as to protect themselves from being used to further financial crime;[97] allocation of a director or senior manager with overall responsibility for establishing and maintaining an AML system; and, the appointment of a Money Laundering Reporting Officer (MLRO).[98] The SYSC regime seeks to provide the regulated sector with an even higher degree of flexibility, which allows them to identify the risks and determine how they can best allocate their resources in areas which are most vulnerable. This approach seeks to encourage and enable the regulated sector to target their resources most appropriately on activities at risk from money laundering, thus reducing AML compliance costs.

The most important tools that the FSA has in the fight against money laundering are its extensive investigative and enforcement powers.[99] The FSA has the ability to require information from firms,[100] to appoint investigators,[101] to obtain the assistance of overseas financial regulators[102] and provide appointed investigators with additional powers.[103] Furthermore, the FSA has become a prosecuting authority in respect of certain money laundering offences.[104] These powers apply whether or not the entity to be prosecuted is actually regulated by the FSA.[105] The FSA also has the power to impose a financial penalty where it establishes that there has been a contravention by an authorized person of any requirement imposed under the FSMA 2000.[106] For example, the FSA has fined firms, MLROs and imposed a series of fines on firms who have breached its AML rules even where there was no evidence of money being laundered.[107]

---

95   The FSA Handbook contains the FSA's legal rules and guidance on a wide range of measures and can be accessed from <http://www.fsa.gov.uk/Pages/handbook/index.shtml>.

96   Financial Services Authority, *FSA Handbook* (Financial Services Authority 2006, SYSC 3.1.1).

97   Financial Services Authority, *FSA Handbook* (Financial Services Authority 2006, SYSC 3.2.6 C).

98   Financial Services Authority, *FSA Handbook* (Financial Services Authority 2006, SYSC 3.2.6 H and I).

99   J. Bagge, 'The Future for Enforcement Under the New Financial Services Authority' (1998) *Company Lawyer*, 19(7), 194–197, 195.

100   Financial Services and Markets Act 2000, ss 165–166.

101   Financial Services and Markets Act 2000, ss 167–168.

102   Financial Services and Markets Act 2000, s 169.

103   Financial Services and Markets Act 2000, s 172.

104   The prosecutorial powers of the FSA were confirmed by the Supreme Court in *R v Rollins* [2010] UK SC 39.

105   Financial Services and Markets Act 2000, s 402 (1)(a).

106   Financial Services and Markets Act 2000, s 206 (1).

107   See Financial Services Authority, Press Release 'FSA Fines Alpari and its Former Money Laundering Reporting Officer, Sudipto Chattopadhyay for Anti-money

At the time of writing, the FSA remains the UK's financial regulatory agency. A position that is likely to change following the expected publication of the Financial Services Bill (2012) and the creation of the Financial Conduct Authority and Prudential Regulation Authority. These reforms will have a fundamental impact on financial regulation in the UK and the statutory objective of the FSA to reduce financial crime.

The Serious Organised Crime Agency

SOCA is the UK's FIU and as such administers the assets recovering provisions under the POCA 2002.[108] It took over this role from the NCIS in 2005. SOCA was created by the Serious Organised Crime and Police Act 2005 and at that time was a major part of the then government's organized crime strategy. SOCA has three objectives: i) to tackle serious organized crime, ii) to gather information relating to crime and iii) other general considerations. In relation to organized crime, the Act states that SOCA has the function of preventing and detecting serious organized crime, in addition to contributing to the reduction of such crime and the mitigation of its consequences.[109] Furthermore, section 3 provides that in relation to information on serious crime, the function of SOCA is the 'gathering, storing, analysing and disseminating [of] information relevant to (a) the prevention, detection, investigation or prosecution of offences, or (b) the reduction of crime in other ways or the mitigation of its consequences.'[110]

The National Crime Agency

In May 2010, the Coalition government (Conservatives and Liberal Democrats) published its Coalition Agreement, which contained a commitment to tackle economic crime. The Agreement proposed that the roles of the Serious Fraud Office (SFO), the FSA and the Office of Fair Trading (OFT) would be merged into the Economic Crime Agency (ECA). The Chancellor of the Exchequer stated 'we take white collar crime as seriously as other crime and we are determined to simplify the confusing and overlapping responsibilities in this area in order to improve detection and enforcement.'[111] It was made clear that the government's ambition was to get serious about white collar crime, including fraud, insider

---

Laundering Failings' (5 May 2010) <http://www.fsa.gov.uk/pages/Library/Communication/PR/2010/077.shtml> accessed 6 July 2011.

108   However, it is important to note that it is likely this role will transfer to the National Crime Agency during the next parliamentary year.

109   Serious Organised Crime and Police Act 2005, s 2(1)(a)(b).

110   Serious Organised Crime and Police Act 2005, s 3(1)(a)(b).

111   HM Treasury, 'George Osborne, Chancellor of the Exchequer. Speech at The Lord Mayor's Dinner for Bankers and Merchants of the City of London, at Mansion House 16 June 2010', <www.hm-treasury.gov.uk/press_12_10.htm> accessed 26 June 2010.

dealing, bribery, corruption and, relevant for this chapter, money laundering. The government has therefore arguably recognized that the existing multiplicity of disparate agencies has led to conflicting priorities and ineffective outcomes. The proposal to create a one stop shop has been advocated for many years but has been given fresh impetus by the Policy Exchange research note on Fighting Fraud and Financial Crime.[112] This paper argued that the interests of fraud detection, investigation and prosecution would be better served by a unified approach mandated to tackle economic crime. The Coalition Government has proposed that the ECA would be led by the Home Office, which historically has adopted a piecemeal approach towards tackling financial crime.[113] To further this endeavour, the Home Office began a consultation process with key stakeholders and expected the 'initial elements of the ECA' to be in place by 2011.[114]

However, before this could take place, in June 2010, the Home Secretary announced the creation of the NCA which has been set up to tackle organized crime, fraud, cyber crime, maintain border protection and protect children and young people. The NCA is to be divided into four distinct divisions: i) Organised Crime Command; ii) Border Policing Command; iii) Economic Crime Command; and iv) the Child Exploitation and Online Protection Centre.[115] The Home Office envisages the role of the Economic Crime Command to 'ensure a coherent approach to the use of resources focused on economic crime across the full range of agencies deploying them.'[116] Furthermore, it is hoped that it will 'maintain an overview' of a wide range of economic crime agencies including the City of London Police and the SFO.[117] The legislative provisions to create the NCA, which are an integral part of the Coalition organised crime policy,[118] were published Crime and Courts Bill 2012,[119] although it is not expected to receive Royal Assent until 2013. The Bill transfers SOCA's role under the Proceeds of Crime Act 2002 to the NCA.[120] SOCA

---

112   J. Fisher and T. Sumpster, *Fighting Fraud and Financial Crime* (Policy Exchange 2010, 12).

113   Home Office, 'Economic Crime Press Release, 17 January 2011' <//www.homeoffice.gov.uk/media-centre/news/economic-crime> accessed 22 January 2011.

114   Home Office, 'Economic Crime Press Release, 17 January 2011' <//www.homeoffice.gov.uk/media-centre/news/economic-crime> accessed 22 January 2011.

115   The Home Office, *The National Crime Agency – A Plan for the Creation of a National Crime-Fighting Capability* (Home Office 2011).

116   The Home Office, *The National Crime Agency – A Plan for the Creation of a National Crime-Fighting Capability* (Home Office 2011, 20).

117   The Home Office, *The National Crime Agency – A Plan for the Creation of a National Crime Fighting Capability* (Home Office 2011, 20).

118   Home Office *Local to Global: Reducing the Risk from Organised Crime* (Home Office: London, 2011).

119   A full copy of the Bill can be accessed from <http://www.publications.parliament.uk/pa/bills/lbill/2012-2013/0004/lbill_2012-20130004_en_2.htm#pt1-pb1-l1g3> accessed 18 July.

120   Crime and Courts Bill 2012, clause 3(1)(b).

will cease to exist when these reforms are implemented and the management of the UK's confiscation regime will transfer to the NCA. No mention, however, has been made regarding SOCA's role as the UK's FIU.

HM Revenue and Customs

HM Revenue and Customs (HMRC) plays an important role in the prevention of money laundering on the basis that it is a designated supervisory authority under the Money Laundering Regulations 2007. It is responsible for high value dealers, money services businesses, auditors, bill payment service providers and telecommunications firms.

Crown Prosecution Service

The Crown Prosecution Service was established by the Prosecution of Offences Act 1985 and is one of the prosecuting authorities in the UK in relation to the offences of money laundering. In conjunction with the FSA, it initiates criminal proceedings on receiving financial intelligence from SOCA.

The Office of Fair Trading

The role of the OFT is chiefly concerned with the protection of consumers, through the regulation of competition across businesses.[121] In this role it has three regulatory objectives: the investigation of whether markets are working well for consumers; the enforcement of competition laws; and the enforcement of consumer protection laws. Additionally, some businesses need to register with the OFT to comply with the Money Laundering Regulations 2007.[122]

British Bankers Association and Building Societies Association

The British Bankers Association, created in 1919, is the leading trade association for banks operating in the UK. It has approximately 300 members with its principle purposes being to combat money laundering. In this role it has produced AML guidelines for banks, which are published by the Joint Money Laundering Steering Group (JMLSG). The Building Societies Association performs a very similar role to the British Bankers Association in that it seeks to tackle money laundering

---

121   P. Kiernan, 'The Regulatory Bodies Fraud: Its Enforcement in the Twenty-First Century' (2003) *Company Lawyer*, 24(10), 293–299, 295.

122   For a more detailed discussion of this role see Office of Fair Trading, *Anti-Money Laundering Future Supervisory Approach Consultation* (Office of Fair Trading 2010).

by providing AML guidance notes, information and the latest money laundering trends. This is similarly disseminated via the JMLSG.[123]

Joint Money Laundering Steering Group

The JMLSG consists of 17 of the leading UK trade associations in the financial services industry.[124] Its objectives are to disseminate good practice amongst the financial services sector; to counter the threat posed by money laundering; and, to provide workable and practical assistance in interpreting the 2007 Money Laundering Regulations. This is achieved by issuing detailed Guidance Notes, which are regularly amended to coincide with the publication and implementation of new Money Laundering Regulations.[125] Leong notes that its aim is 'to provide an indication of good generic industry practice and a base from which management can develop tailored policies and procedures that are appropriate to their businesses.'[126] Hopton furthermore, argues that 'they are also a good source of industry practice and provide management with advice and assistance.'[127] Importantly, the FSA has recommended that firms should 'read the JMLSG guidance notes in conjunction with the FSA's rules.'[128]

Finance and Leasing Association

The Finance and Leasing Association is the trade association for asset, consumer and the motor finance industries in the UK. Members come from the banking sector, subsidiaries of banks and building societies, the finance divisions of retail companies and a number of independent firms. The Finance and Leasing Association represents its members on a wide range of AML initiatives including: the City of London Police's Economic Crime Unit; SOCA's work in non-fiscal and identification related crime; the National Fraud Authority's (NFA) work, which includes coordinating the fight against financial crime and fraud between

---

123   Building Societies Association 'Financial Crime Prevention' <//www.bsa.org.uk/policy/policyissues/fcpandphysec/financialcrime.htm> accessed 1 July 2011.

124   Joint Money Laundering Steering Group 'Who are the Members of the JMLSG?' <http://www.jmlsg.org.uk/bba/jsp/polopoly.jsp?d=777&a=9907> accessed 18 June 2010.

125   D. Hopton, *Money Laundering: A Concise Guide for all Businesses* (Gower 2009, 43).

126   A. Leong, 'Chasing Dirty Money: Domestic and International Measures Against Money Laundering' (2007) *Journal of Money Laundering Control*, 10(2), 140–156, 144–145.

127   D. Hopton, *Money Laundering: A Concise Guide for all Businesses* (Gower 2009, 43).

128   Oxford Analytica Ltd, 'Country Report: Anti-Money Laundering Rules in the United Kingdom' in M. Pieith and G. Aiolfi (eds) *A Comparative Guide to Anti-Money Laundering: A Critical Analysis of Systems in Singapore, Switzerland, the UK and the USA* (Edward Elgar 2004, 276).

the National Fraud Reporting Centre and the National Fraud Intelligence Bureau; and, the work of JMLSG.

Association of British Insurers

The Association of British Insurers is the trade association for the UK's insurance industry. It has over 400 members, who are authorized by the FSA and are bound by its AML rules.

Royal Institute of Chartered Surveyors

The Royal Institute of Chartered Surveyors is an industry representative for estate agents and other specialized firms involved in land, construction and environmental issues. It publishes AML guidance notes and liaises with the National Association of Estate Agents.[129] Its members are bound by the Money Laundering Regulations 2007 and rely on guidance notes provided by SOCA, the OFT, HMRC and HM Treasury.

The Law Society England and Wales

The Law Society represents solicitors in England and Wales and as such is committed to assisting solicitors in meeting their AML obligations.[130] Solicitors are bound by the Money Laundering Regulations 2007 with guidance on this issued by the Law Society via an AML practice note published in 2009.[131]

Financial Intelligence

With the existence of so many authorities and bodies involved in AML measures, one of the most important and traditional money laundering counter measures is the use of financial intelligence. The UK introduced its first money laundering reporting requirements by virtue of the Drug Trafficking Offences Act 1986 which has since been amended by the POCA 2002 and the Money Laundering Regulations 2007. A wide range of financial institutions in the regulated sector are thus required to report any allegations of money laundering to SOCA. The 2007 Regulations, as described above, were introduced to implement the Third Money Laundering Directive,[132] with its purpose being to 'impose standards of behaviour

---

129   Royal Institute of Chartered Surveyors, *Money Laundering Guidance* (Royal Institute of Chartered Surveyors 2010).

130   The Law Society, 'Anti-money Laundering' <http://www.lawsociety.org.uk/prod uctsandservices/antimoneylaundering.page> accessed 1 July 2011.

131   The Law Society, *Anti-Money Laundering Practice Note* (The Law Society 2009).

132   Council Directive (EC) 2005/60 of 26 October 2005, [2005] OJ L309/15.

governing "know your client" regulations in relation to customers.'[133] The 2007 Regulations apply to a wide range of financial services institutions including credit institutions,[134] financial institutions,[135] auditors,[136] insolvency practitioners,[137] external accountants,[138] tax advisers,[139] independent legal professionals,[140] trust or company service providers,[141] estate agents,[142] high value dealers[143] and casinos.[144] For institutions in the financial services sector, Regulation 7 additionally requires them to apply customer due diligence measures where they suspect the transaction concerns money laundering or terrorist financing, or where they distrust a customer's identification. Customer due diligence measures are defined in Regulation 5 as,

    a. Identifying the customer and verifying the customer's identity on the basis of documents, data or information obtained from a reliable and independent source;

    b. Identifying, where there is a beneficial owner who is not the customer, the beneficial owner and taking adequate measures, on a risk-sensitive basis,

---

133   A. Hudson, *The Law of Finance* (Sweet and Maxwell 2009, 360).

134   As defined in Article 4(1)(a) of the Banking Consolidation Directive 2000/12/EC of the European Parliament and of the Council of 20 March 2000 relating to the taking up and pursuit of the business of credit institutions.

135   This is defined as an undertaking, including a money service business, when it carries out one or more of the activities listed in points 2 to 12 and 14 of Annex 1 to the Banking Consolidation Directive.

136   An auditor is defined as 'any firm or individual who is a statutory auditor within the meaning of the Companies Act 2006'.

137   Any person who acts as an insolvency practitioner within the meaning of the Insolvency Act 1986, s 388 as amended by the Insolvency Act 2000, s 3.

138   This is a firm or sole practitioner who by way of business provides accountancy services to other persons, when providing such services. Money Laundering Regulations 2007, regulation 3(7).

139   This is defined as a firm or sole practitioner who by way of business provides advice about the tax affairs of other persons, when providing such services. Money Laundering Regulations 2007, regulation 3(8).

140   An Independent legal professional is a firm or sole practitioner who provides services of a legal nature concerning the sale and acquisition of real property, the administration of client money and other related activities. Money Laundering Regulations 2007, regulation 3(9).

141   A trust or company service provider is defined as a firm or sole practitioner who provides business services relating to the formation of legal entities or acting as an agent for another party to operate as a director or other relevant position within a company. Money Laundering Regulations 2007, regulation 3(10).

142   As defined by the Estate Agents Act 1979, s 1.

143   A high value dealer is a business or sole trader that deals in goods where the payment is at least 15,000 Euros in total. Money Laundering Regulations 2007, regulation 3(12).

144   A casino holds an operating licence by virtue of the Gambling Act 2005, s 65(2).

to verify his identity, so that the relevant person is satisfied that he knows who the beneficial owner is, including, in the case of a legal person, trust, or similar legal arrangement, measures to understand the ownership and control structure of the person, trust or arrangement; and

c. Obtaining information on the purpose and intended nature of the business relationship.

This means that the firm is required to authenticate the identity of the customer and monitor their business relationships (Regulation 8). Moreover, casinos are under an individual obligation to determine the identity of customers by virtue of Regulation 10. The 2007 Regulation also imposes obligations relating to record keeping (Regulation 19), policies and procedures (Regulation 20) and staff training (Regulation 21) and contains provisions and obligations relating to supervision and registration (Regulations 23-36), creating enforcement powers for supervisors (Regulations 34-47), provisions for the recovery of penalties and charges (Regulation 48) and imposes an obligation on some public authorities to report suspicions of money laundering or terrorist financing (Regulation 49).

If a firm suspects that it is being used for the purposes of money laundering, it is required to notify its MLRO who will complete a Suspicious Activity Report (SAR) and file it with SOCA, who determines if further action is to be taken. The overall effectiveness of the SAR regime has been questioned. For example, its deficiencies include an ineffective SARs database, weak monitoring of enforcement outcomes, inadequate training and a lack of governmental support for the scheme.[145] It has also been suggested that SARs are under-used by law enforcement agencies, and law enforcement bodies continue to have poor management information on how SARs are utilized.[146] Despite these criticisms, the existence of these reporting requirements has created a fear factor amongst the regulated sector and has thus resulted in a significant increase in the number of SARs submitted to SOCA.[147] The accountancy firm KPMG noted that the number of SARs submitted between 1995 and 2002 increased from 5,000 to 60,000.[148] In 2008, SOCA reported that it had received 210,524 SARs;[149] which increased to 240,582 in 2010[150] and to 247,601 in 2011.[151]

---

145   KPMG, *Money Laundering: Review of the Reporting System* (KPMG 2003, 14).

146   KPMG, *Money Laundering: Review of the Reporting System* (KPMG 2003, 14).

147   R. Sarker, 'Anti-Money Laundering Requirements: Too Much Pain for Too Little Gain' (2006) *Company Lawyer*, 27(8), 250–251, 251.

148   KPMG, *Money Laundering: Review of the Reporting System* (KPMG 2003, 14).

149   Serious Organised Crime Agency, *The Suspicious Activity Reports Regime Annual Report 2008* (Serious Organised Crime Agency 2008, 15).

150   Serious Organised Crime Agency, *The Suspicious Activity Reports Regime Annual Report 2010* (Serious Organised Crime Agency 2010, 4).

151   Serious Organised Crime Agency, *The Suspicious Activity Reports Regime Annual Report 2011* (Serious Organised Crime Agency 2011, 10).

This increase is directly attributable to the threat of sanctions by such organizations as the FSA, which in the regulated sector, has adopted a tactic that has been referred to as defensive or preventative reporting.[152] Reporting entities have also complained about the significant increase in compliance costs,[153] which has resulted in suggestions that the AML reporting requirements should be abandoned and that the resources should be redirected elsewhere. Estimates of the compliance costs vary. For example, the British Bankers Association claims that their members spend £250 million each year in complying with the regulations,[154] while KPMG estimate that annual costs are nearer £90 million.[155] Research has suggested that the AML costs in the UK are higher than in other European countries including Germany, France and Italy.[156] In its 2004 AML strategy paper, HM Treasury asserted that one of the fundamental aims of its policy was to ensure that the compliance costs imposed were proportionate. We would argue however, that this is simply not the case.

Sentencing and Recovery

Due to the importance of and devastating effect caused by money laundering, it is perhaps unsurprising that the maximum penalty for the offences contained within sections 327–329 POCA 2002 is 14 years,[157] although in the United States of America (USA) this maximum is set at 20 years.[158] In all cases, a fine can be imposed instead of or as well as imprisonment. While in the UK there is no maximum fine, the maximum financial penalty in the USA for money laundering is set at $500,000 or twice the value of the property involved in the crime.[159] It is also worth noting that in addition to the courts and under the Money Laundering Regulations 2001 15(1) the Commissioners may impose a penalty of such amount as they consider appropriate, not exceeding £5,000, on a person to whom

---

152   A. Leong, 'Chasing Dirty Money: Domestic and International Measures Against Money Laundering' (2007) *Journal of Money Laundering Control*, 10(2), 140–156, 142.

153   Home Office, *Report on the Operation in 2004 of the Terrorism Act 2000* (Home Office 2004, 19–20).

154   Home Office, *Report on the Operation in 2004 of the Terrorism Act 2000* (Home Office 2004, 19–20).

155   KPMG, *Money Laundering: Review of the Reporting System* (KPMG 2003, 46–47).

156   M. Yeandle, M. Mainelli, A. Berendt and B. Healy, *Anti-Money Laundering Requirements: Costs, Benefits and Perceptions* (Corporation of London 2005).

157   Proceeds of Crime Act 2002, s 334(1).

158   Australian Government and Australian Institute of Criminology, *Charges and Offences of Money Laundering* Transnational Crime Brief No. 4 (Australian Institute of Criminology 2008).

159   C. van Cleef, H. Silets and P. Motz, 'Does the Punishment Fit the Crime' (2004) *Journal of Financial Crime*, 12(1), 57.

Regulation 5 (requirement to be registered) applies or where that person fails to comply with any requirements in Regulation 5, 6 (supplementary information), 9 (fees) or 10 (entry, inspection etc). Between 1999 and 2007, there were 7,569 money laundering prosecutions[160] in the UK, resulting in 3,796 convictions. This amounts to a 50.15 per cent conviction rate.[161] Detailed below in Table 2.1, the number of money laundering prosecutions and convictions in the UK between 1999 and 2007 have been steadily increasing each year, although in 2008 convictions decreased slightly to 1,286.[162] Arguably, however, the conviction rate of over 50 per cent suggests that the mechanisms as described above are working fairly well within the UK.

Table 2.1   Money laundering prosecutions and convictions in the UK from 1999 to 2007[163]

	1999	2000	2001	2002	2003	2004	2005	2006	2007
Prosecutions	126	129	182	256	300	552	1,327	2,379	2,318
Convictions	39	50	75	86	123	207	595	1,273	1,348
Convictions (%)	30.95	38.76	41.21	33.59	41	37.5	44.84	53.51	58.15

When deciding on the length of sentence to impose, the court must take into account the seriousness of the offence, balancing it with other issues such as mitigating factors and the existence of a guilty plea.[164] It will also consider precedent and the existence of guideline judgments. For example, *R v Basra*[165] provides general advice concerning the sentencing of money laundering offences

---

160   Following the cases of *R v Rollins, R v McInerney* [2009] EWCA Crim [1941], the Financial Services Authority has the power to prosecute money laundering offences as well as the Crown Prosecution Service.

161   A.O. Alkaabi, G. Mohay, A. Mccullagh and N.A. Chantler, 'Comparative Analysis of the Extent of Money Laundering in Australia, UAE, UK and the USA' (20 January, 2010) *Finance and Corporate Governance Conference 2010 Paper* <http://ssrn.com/abstract=1539843> accessed 6 July 2011.

162   HC Deb, 26 July 2010, c689W.

163   A.O. Alkaabi, G. Mohay, A. Mccullagh and N.A. Chantler, 'Comparative Analysis of the Extent of Money Laundering in Australia, UAE, UK and the USA' (20 January, 2010) *Finance and Corporate Governance Conference 2010 Paper* <http://ssrn.com/abstract=1539843> accessed 6 July 2011.

164   For more on this complicated process see K. Harrison, 'Sentencing Financial Crime in England and Wales' in N. Ryder (ed.) *Financial Crime in the 21st Century – Law and Policy* (Edward Elgar 2011).

165   [2002] 2 Cr. App. R. (S) 100.

and *R v El-Delbi*[166] concentrates on the proceeds of drug trafficking. In the latter circumstances the Court of Appeal advised that,

> those who launder large sums that are the proceeds of drug trafficking play an essential role in enabling the drugs conspiracy to succeed and, as such, can expect severe sentences comparable to those given to others playing a significant role in the supply of drugs.

> However, it has to be borne in mind that Parliament has provided different upper limits to a judge's sentencing process for dealing in Class A drugs (life imprisonment) and money laundering (14 years).

> There will be no direct arithmetical relationship between the sums recovered by Customs or shown to be involved; nonetheless sentences very close to the maximum have to be reserved for cases where the evidence establishes laundering on a very large scale.[167]

Perhaps different to other financial crimes (see Chapter 4), the court does appear to be using its maxima when it comes to sentencing those convicted of money laundering offences. For example, Ussama El-Kurd,[168] in 1999, was sentenced to the maximum penalty of 14 years' imprisonment and fined £1 million for being involved in a £70 million money laundering operation. The operation was described as the largest in Europe, with El-Kurd being the first person in England and Wales to be convicted on sole money laundering charges, i.e. not additionally connected to other drug or terrorist offences.[169] Likewise, Tarsemwal Lal Sabharwal[170] received 12 years' imprisonment for the laundering of over £53 million of drug trafficking proceeds. While the Court of Appeal acknowledged that this was at the top end of sentencing; it stated that the offence was also at the top end in terms of seriousness[171] and that it thus felt that the model of just deserts had been properly applied. Similarly, David Simpson[172] received 11 years' imprisonment for the laundering of money worth £2.5 million. The Court of Appeal acknowledged that he was not the most seriously involved in the scam, but his role was still said to be 'crucial and pivotal.'[173]

---

166   [2003] EWCA Crim 1767.
167   Sentencing Guidelines Council 'Guideline Judgments Case Compendium' <http://sentencingcouncil.judiciary.gov.uk/docs/web_case_compendium.pdf> accessed 6 June 2011.
168   *R v Ussama-el-Kurd* [2001] Crim. L.R. 234 (CA).
169   BBC News, 'UK Maximum Sentence for Money Launder' (*BBC Online Network*, 25 February 1999) <http://news.bbc.co.uk/1/hi/uk/285759.stm> accessed 6 June 2011.
170   *R v Tarsemwal Lal Sabharwal* [2001] 2 Cr. App. R. (S.) 81.
171   *R v Tarsemwal Lal Sabharwal* [2001] 2 Cr. App. R. (S.) 375.
172   *R v Simpson* [1998] 2 Cr. App. R. (S.) 111.
173   *R v Simpson* [1998] 2 Cr. App. R. (S.) 114.

At the other end of the spectrum is the case of Philip Griffiths,[174] a solicitor, who received a term of six months' imprisonment for failing to disclose a financial transaction where he had reasonable grounds for knowing or suspecting that it involved money laundering. While the judge acknowledged that Griffiths had lost his practice; had not made any money out of the transaction (apart from his usual conveyancing fee); and the dramatic impact it had had on his health and life; it was still felt that a custodial sentence was proportionate and justified. Leveson J. argued, 'Organising the cover-up or laundering the proceeds of crime is always particularly serious, especially if organized or set up as an operation. Custodial sentences are absolutely inevitable in almost every case, if not every case.'[175] This was also shown in *R v Duff*[176] where the Court of Appeal upheld a six month custodial sentence against a solicitor who had failed to report the fact that he had received £70,000 to invest in a joint business, from a client who was later charged with drugs offences.[177] Even though he took advice from another solicitor as to his duty to notify and consulted the Law Society's guidance notes, the Court still held that the sentence was not 'in any way excessive'.[178] What is interesting here, therefore, is the penalizing of someone who fails to act; rather than punishing someone for committing a positive act. In English and Welsh Criminal Law, there are very few situations where a failure to act will initiate criminal proceedings; although being under a duty to act is obviously one such exception. The fact that the government has created such a duty and that a failure in this duty has been criminalized and severely punished, shows how serious the government is in tackling this particular crime.[179]

In addition to terms of imprisonment and/or financial penalties, the courts will also endeavour to recover the proceeds of criminal conduct and/or monitor the offender's financial and business practices after his conviction and/or release from custody. This is achieved through ancillary orders. Such orders can be described as ancillary in that they are often given in addition to the other more general sentencing penalties; rather than instead of. Many of these orders will be assessed through this book, with this chapter concentrating on the recovery of the proceeds of crime. This is largely achieved through the implementation of a confiscation order[180] which can be made against any convicted offender who is thought to have a criminal lifestyle. The interpretation of the term 'criminal lifestyle' is extremely contentious, with the provisions contained within section 10 of the POCA often

---

174 *R v Griffiths (Philip)* [2006] EWCA Crim 2155.
175 *R v Griffiths (Philip)* [2006] EWCA Crim 2155, para 11.
176 [2003] 1 Cr. App. R. (S) 88.
177 *R v Duff* [2003] 1 Cr. App. R. (S) 471.
178 *R v Duff* [2003] 1 Cr. App. R. (S) 471.
179 For the relevant provisions see Proceeds of Crime Act 2002, ss 327–330.
180 Proceeds of Crime Act 2002, ss 6–13.

described as draconian.[181] In deciding whether the offender had such a lifestyle, the sentencing court will use the assumptions as set out in section 10. These are as follows:

> The first assumption is that any property transferred to the defendant at any time after the relevant day, was obtained by him –
>
> a. as a result of his general criminal conduct, and
> b. at the earliest time he appears to have held it.
>
> The second assumption is that any property held by the defendant at any time after the date of conviction, was obtained by him –
>
> a. as a result of his general criminal conduct, and
> b. at the earliest time he appears to have held it.
>
> The third assumption is that any expenditure incurred by the defendant at any time after the relevant day was met from property obtained by him as a result of his general criminal conduct.
>
> The fourth assumption is that, for the purpose of valuing any property obtained (or assumed to have been obtained) by the defendant, he obtained it free of any other interests in it.

If such a lifestyle is found and in addition the offender financially benefited from it, the court can decide what recoverable amount it believes is appropriate in the circumstances and then make an order to ensure that such a payment is made. The amount payable is that which the offender has criminally obtained, an amount which is available to be confiscated, or a nominal amount if all financial assets have been spent.[182] Priority of available funds is given first to court sanctioned financial penalties,[183] with confiscation expected to be achieved within six months.[184] This can be extended to 12 months if the Crown Court believes that exceptional circumstances warrant such an extension. Upon the making of a confiscation order the court should also order a period of imprisonment which will be served if the payment is not made, with the maximum default periods being outlined in section 139(4) of the Powers of the Criminal Courts (Sentencing) Act 2000. As mentioned

---

181   For more on this see R. Alexander, 'Corruption as a Financial Crime' (2009) *Company Lawyer*, 30(4) 98 and J.L. Masters, 'Fraud and Money Laundering: The Evolving Criminalization of Corporate Non-Compliance' (2008) *Journal of Money Laundering Control*, 11(2) 103.

182   Proceeds of Crime Act 2002, s 7.

183   Proceeds of Crime Act 2002, s 9.

184   Proceeds of Crime Act 2002, s 11.

above, the order is ancillary to imprisonment with the effect of a confiscation order having no bearing on the custodial term.[185] The existence of such an order is especially important when HM Treasury currently estimates that serious crime involves approximately £5 billion of assets which are in a seizable form.[186]

In order to try and ensure that available assets exist at the time of sentencing, as soon as a defendant begins to be investigated for a financial crime, the court can issue a restraint order,[187] if there is 'reasonable cause to believe that the defendant has benefitted from his criminal conduct.'[188] The main purpose of a restraint order is to prevent the disposal of criminal assets and can be made even before the defendant has been charged with a criminal offence, provided that this is the expected course of action. If such an order is made, it can instruct a defendant to not only disclose the nature and whereabouts of his assets but also to relocate assets back within the jurisdiction of England and Wales. The order will apply to all realizable property held by the defendant and can additionally include any property which is transferred to him after the order has been made. When deciding which property to seize, the court must take into account the cost of reasonable living and legal expenses and if appropriate allow the defendant to continue in the course of his trade, business, profession or occupation.[189]

Future Recommendations

The UK's money laundering policy is generally compliant with the international measures outlined at the start of this chapter. Its policy is well managed by HM Treasury and assisted by the FSA. However, it is recommended that the newly established NCA is formally recognized as the UK's FIU given the importance of financial intelligence in the fight against money laundering. It is also essential that the Financial Services Bill (2012) retains the statutory objective of the FSA to reduce financial crime.

Further Reading

Alexander, R. *Insider Dealing and Money Laundering in the EU: Law and Regulation* (Ashgate 2007).
Alldridge, P. *Money Laundering Law* (Hart 2003).

---

185 *R v Rogers* [2001] EWCA Crim 1680.
186 HM Treasury, *The Financial Challenge of Terrorism and Crime* (HM Treasury 2007).
187 Proceeds of Crime Act 2002, s 41.
188 Proceeds of Crime Act 2002, s 40.
189 Proceeds of Crime Act 2002, s 41.

Blair, W. and R. Brent, *Banks and Financial Crime: The International Law of Tainted Money* (Oxford University Press 2008).

Booth, R., S. Farrell, G. Bastable and N. Yeo, *Money Laundering Law and Regulation a Practical Guide* (Oxford University Press 2011).

Demetis, D. *Technology and Anti-Money Laundering: A Systems Theory and Risk-based Approach* (Edward Elgar 2010).

Fisher, J. *Money Laundering and Practice* (Oxford University Press 2009).

Gallant, M. *Money Laundering and the Proceeds of Crime – Economic Crime and Civil Remedies* (Edward Elgar 2005).

Gilmore, W. *Dirty Money – The Evolution of International Measures to Counter Money Laundering and the Financing of Terrorism* (Council of Europe 2003).

Hopton, D. *Money Laundering: A Concise Guide for all Business* (Gower 2009).

Ryder, N. *Money Laundering – An Endless Cycle? A Comparative Analysis of the Anti-money Laundering Policies in the United States of America, the United Kingdom, Australia and Canada* (Routledge 2012).

Stessens, G. *Money Laundering – A New International Law Enforcement Model* (Cambridge University Press 2000).

Unger, B. *The Scale and Impacts of Money Laundering* (Edward Elgar 2007).

Chapter 3
Terrorist Financing

Introduction

Prior to the terrorist attacks in the United States of America (USA) on 11 September 2001, the international community's attitude towards financial crime focused on the prevention of money laundering, the illegal drugs trade and fraud. These terrorist attacks, however, resulted in a fundamental change in attitudes towards implementing counter-terrorist financing (CTF) laws. Terrorist financing has been defined as the 'raising, moving, storing and using of financial resources for the purposes of terrorism.'[1] In this context, terrorism is defined as the use or threat of action which involves serious violence against a person; serious damage to property; endangers a person's life; creates a serious risk to the health or safety of the public; or is designed to seriously interfere or disrupt an electronic system.[2] Such attacks caused the international community, largely led by the USA, to instigate the so-called financial war on terrorism. The United Kingdom (UK), largely influenced by the international legislative measures introduced by the United Nations (UN), the European Union (EU) and the then Special Recommendations of the Financial Action Task Force (FATF),[3] has consequentially implemented several pieces of controversial legislation aimed at combating terrorist financing. Such measures include the Terrorism Act 2000, the Anti-terrorism Crime and Security Act 2001, the Prevention of Terrorism Act 2005 and the Counter-Terrorism Act 2008. The primary aim of this chapter will therefore be to cover these important pieces of legislation, including also an attempt at quantifying the extent and level of terrorist financing. The chapter will then consider background to the policy of criminalizing and regulating the problem, plus an evaluation of the financial institutions and regulatory bodies involved. Finally we look at how terrorist assets are recovered.

---

1 Charity Commission, 'Compliance Toolkit: Protecting Charities from Harm' (2009 Module 7, page 1) <http://www.charity-commission.gov.uk/Library/tkch1mod7.pdf> accessed 17 June 2011.

2 Terrorism Act 2000, s 1.

3 It is important to note that the FATF merged its money laundering recommendations with the terrorist financing recommendations in February 2012. See Financial Action Task Force 'FATF steps up the fight against money laundering and terrorist financing', 16 February 2012, available from <http://www.fatf-gafi.org/document/17/0,3746,en_32250379_32236920_49656209_1_1_1_1,00.html>, accessed 14 March 2012.

What is the Offence of Terrorist Financing?

The principal criminal offences relating to terrorist financing can be found in sections 15–18 of the Terrorism Act 2000, which received Royal Assent on 20 July 2000. These include: raising, receiving or providing funds for the purpose of terrorism;[4] using or possessing funds for the purpose of terrorism;[5] becoming involved in an arrangement which makes funds available for the purposes of terrorism;[6] and, facilitating the laundering of terrorist property and money.[7] Additional offences include failing to disclose information about the occurrence of terrorist financing[8] and, for those working in the regulated financial sector, the offence of tipping off.[9] Interestingly, and in accordance with section 63 of the Terrorism Act 2000, if a person does anything outside of the UK which would have been an offence under sections 15–18 of the Act within the UK, he will also be guilty of an offence. Only the four principal offences will be discussed further.

Fundraising – section 15 Terrorism Act 2000

The offence of fundraising is committed if a person facilitates the raising of money for the purposes of terrorism. This can be done through inviting another to provide money or property, receiving such money or other property or through providing money or other property. In all three circumstances the person must either intend that the money (or property) is to be used to fund terrorist activity or have reasonable cause to suspect that it may be used for this purpose. Consideration is not a requisite factor, with the Act defining the provision of money or property to include where it is 'given, lent or otherwise made available'.[10]

Use and possession – section 16 Terrorism Act 2000

The second terrorist financing offence covers the situation where a person uses money or other property for terrorist purposes, or has in his/her possession money or property which he/she intends to be used in this way or has reasonable cause to suspect this to be the case.

---

4   Terrorism Act 2000, s 15.
5   Terrorism Act 2000, s 16.
6   Terrorism Act 2000, s 17.
7   Terrorism Act 2000, s 18.
8   Terrorism Act 2000, s 19 and s 21A.
9   Terrorism Act 2000, s 21D.
10   Terrorism Act 2000, s 15(4).

Funding arrangements – section 17 Terrorism Act 2000

The next offence is found in section 17 of the Terrorism Act 2000 which deals with funding arrangements. Under this section, an offence is committed if a person enters into or becomes concerned in an arrangement and as a result of this arrangement money or other property is made available for the funding of terrorism. As with the other offences, the person needs to either know that the money or property is to be used in this way, or have reasonable cause to suspect that it is to be used for this purpose.

Money laundering – section 18 Terrorism Act 2000

The final principal offence is concerned with money laundering. This is committed if a person deals with terrorist property in a way which conceals it, removes it from the UK, or transfers it to another person. For the purposes of this section, terrorist property is defined to include: '(a) Money or other property which is likely to be used for the purposes of terrorism (including any resources of a proscribed organization); (b) Proceeds of the commission of acts of terrorism; and (c) Proceeds of acts carried out for the purposes of terrorism.'[11] Different from the other offences there is no need to show intention, knowledge or reasonable suspicion. In fact, section 18(2) creates a defence whereby a person is not guilty of the offence if he can prove either that he did not know that the arrangement related to terrorist property, or he had no reasonable cause to suspect this to be so.

Defences

In relation to these four principal offences, the defence of express consent exists.[12] This relates to the situation where an individual is working in cooperation with the police and has express permission to continue with his terrorist financing activities. Originally this defence only applied where a person made a disclosure *after* becoming involved in an arrangement or transaction; through his own initiative and as soon as was deemed to be reasonably practicable.[13] This has now been extended to widen and include the defences of prior consent, consent and reasonable excuse. These were introduced by The Terrorism Act 2000 and Proceeds of Crime Act 2002 (Amendment) Regulations 2007 (which came into force on 26 December 2007) and are found in sections 21ZA, 21ZB and 21ZC of the Terrorism Act 2000. The prior consent defence can be relied upon where a person makes a disclosure to an authorized person *before* becoming involved in a transaction or an arrangement, and the person then becomes involved in such

---

11 Terrorism Act 2000, s 14.
12 Terrorism Act 2000, s 21.
13 Terrorism Act 2000, s 21(3).

an arrangement with the consent of this authorized officer.[14] For the purposes of the defence, an authorized officer is defined as 'a member of the staff of the Serious Organised Crime Agency authorized for the purposes of this section by the Director General of that Agency.'[15]

Similarly, the consent defence is valid where a person is already involved in a transaction or arrangement and makes a disclosure during this stage and the person then acts with the consent of an authorized officer.[16] This is only valid if the person involved can prove that there was a reasonable excuse for his failure in making an advance disclosure, the disclosure was made as soon as reasonably practicable and was of his own volition.[17] A person cannot rely on the defences of either prior consent or consent, if the authorized officer forbids the continued involvement of the person in the arrangement or transaction. Finally, the reasonable excuse defence may be used if a person intended to make a disclosure of the kind mentioned above, and even though he did not, there was a reasonable excuse for not doing so.[18] Other defences relate to those working within the regulated sector, who have failed to make disclosures of activity which they know, suspect or have reasonable grounds for knowing or suspecting relate to terrorist financing. These can be found in sections 21A, 21B, 21E, 21F and 21G of the Terrorism Act 2000. As these offences have not been discussed above, neither will their relevant defences. Without doubt, the aim of all of these defences is the discovery of offending behaviour.

The Extent of Terrorist Financing

The extent of terrorist financing can be contrasted with the other types of financial crime discussed in this book because the objective of a terrorist is not to hide the proceeds of their illegal activity but to use the finances to promote a distorted ideology via a terrorist attack. This is a concept called reverse money laundering and was deemed by President George Bush to be more of a threat to USA national security than money laundering. Gurung, Wijaya and Rao described reverse money laundering as stemming from 'legitimate sources i.e. the fund is obtained to do illegal activity in comparison to money laundering where money is generated from criminal procedures and made legitimate.'[19] Similarly, Hardouin stated that

---

14   Terrorism Act 2000, s 21ZA(1).
15   Terrorism Act 2000, s 21ZA(5).
16   Terrorism Act 2000, s 21ZB(1).
17   Terrorism Act 2000, s 21ZB(2).
18   Terrorism Act 2000, s 21ZC.
19   J. Gurung, M. Wijaya and A. Rao, 'AMLCTF Compliance and SMEs in Australia: A Case Study of the Prepaid Card Industry' (2010) *Journal of Money Laundering Control*, 13(3), 184–201, 199.

'Terrorists practice "reverse" money laundering since they transform clean money into dirty money whereas in the case of organized crime things are happening just the other way round.'[20] Therefore, this chapter adopts the opposite stance to the other chapters in this book and briefly highlights the estimated costs of terrorist attacks and the plethora of sources used to finance these attacks. For example, it is thought that the attacks in Washington and New York on 11 September 2001 cost approximately $500,000 and those in London on 7 July 2005 cost £8,000.[21] Conversely, some commentators have argued that the attacks in London cost between £100 and £200.[22] Furthermore, while the Bishopsgate bomb in London in 1993 caused over £1 billion of property damage, it was estimated to have only cost the terrorists £3,000.[23] This terrorist attack, like the al-Qaeda bombing of the USS Cole (estimated to have cost between $5,000 and $10,000), the train bombings in Madrid ($10,000), the Bali night club attack ($74,000) and 9/11 are all examples of what has become known as cheap terrorism.

The prevention of terrorist financing is very difficult due to not only the low financial costs involved, but also due to the extensive array of financial tools used to fund such attacks.[24] Traditionally, terrorists have relied on two main sources of funding: state and private sponsors.[25] State-sponsorship of terrorism is where national governments provide logistical and financial support to terrorist organizations.[26] The true extent of state sponsored terrorism is impossible to determine, yet it has been suggested that state-sponsors do provide substantial support to terrorists.[27] However, there is evidence to suggest that the extent of state-sponsored terrorism has declined and it is now more likely that terrorists will

---

20   P. Hardouin, 'Banks Governance and Public-Private Partnership in Preventing and Confronting Organized Crime, Corruption and Terrorism Financing' (2009) *Journal of Financial Crime*, 16(3), 199–209, 206.

21   M. Levi, 'Combating the Financing of Terrorism. A History and Assessment of the Control of Threat Finance' (2010) *British Journal of Criminology*, 50, 650–669.

22   See M. Evans, 'Shortage of Money Led to 7/7 Security Failures' *The Times* (London 11 May 2006); M. Townsend, 'Leak Reveals Official Story of London Bombings' *The Observer* (London 9 April 2006).

23   HM Treasury, *Combating the Financing of Terrorism. A Report on UK Action* (HM Treasury 2002, 11).

24   See M. Levitt, 'Stemming the Follow of Terrorist Financing: Practical and Conceptual Challenges' (2003) *The Fletcher Forum of World Affairs*, 27(1) 63, 64.

25   I. Bantekas, 'The International Law of Terrorist Financing' (2003) *American Journal of International Law* 315.

26   A. Chase, 'Legal Mechanisms of the International Community and the United States Concerning the State Sponsorship of Terrorism' (2004) *Virginia Journal of International Law*, 45, 41.

27   A. Chase, 'Legal Mechanisms of the International Community and the United States Concerning the State Sponsorship of Terrorism' (2004) *Virginia Journal of International Law*, 45, 41.

receive funding from private sponsors or donors.[28] This perceived decline in state-sponsored terrorism has forced terrorist organizations to diversify their funding activities and, in effect, become self-funding. Lee has stated that the al-Qaeda 'network increasingly is shifting to non-bank methods of moving and storing value and is relying on a decentralized structure of largely self-financing cells.'[29] The self sufficiency of terrorist cells was also recognized by the official report on the terrorist attacks on London on 7 July 2005.[30] Terrorists have therefore been forced to deploy several mechanisms to raise additional funds, including the collection of membership dues and/or subscriptions; the sale of publications; speaking tours; cultural and social events; door to door solicitation within the community; appeals to wealthy members of the community; and, donations of a portion of personal earnings.[31] Alldridge takes the view that other sources of funding include 'kidnapping for ransom, armed robbery, extortion and drug trading',[32] while Lowe argues that terrorists fund some activities via counterfeiting.[33] Furthermore, it has been reported that another source of funding for terrorist groups is conflict diamonds, and that this source of funding has been used by al-Qaeda and Hamas.[34] Conflict or blood diamonds are those mined in war zones and sold to finance illegal activity. This all means that terrorists are able to 'manipulate an expanding array of tools to shield their wealth, without regard to international borders.'[35] Terrorists are also utilizing new electronic technologies to transfer money over the internet to conceal their true origin.[36] In addition to the above, it has also been mooted that al-Qaeda has obtained monies from both charitable contributions and from legitimate companies.[37] Terrorists have also acquired funding through traditional

28   See for example M. Basile, 'Going to the Source: Why al-Qaeda's Financial Network is Likely to Withstand the Current War on Terrorist Financing' (2004) *Studies in Conflict & Terrorism*, 27, 183.

29   R. Lee, *Terrorist Financing: The US and International Response Report for Congress* (Congressional Research Service 2002, 19).

30   House of Commons, *Report of the Official Account of the Bombings in London on 7th July 2005* (House of Commons 2005, 23).

31   I. Bantekas, 'The International Law of Terrorist Financing' (2003) *American Journal of International Law* 315.

32   P. Alldridge, *Money Laundering Law* (Hart 2003, 215).

33   P. Lowe, 'Counterfeiting: Links to Organised Crime and Terrorist Funding' (2006) *Journal of Financial Crime* 13(2) 255.

34   Global Witness, *Broken Vows – Exposing the "Loupe" Holes in the Diamond Industry's Efforts to Prevent the Trade in Conflict Diamonds* (Global Witness Publishing Inc 2003, 2).

35   K. Alexander, 'The International Anti-Money Laundering Regime: The Role of the Financial Action Task Force' (2001) *Journal of Money Laundering Control*, 4(3), 231–248, 231.

36   R. Lee, *Terrorist Financing: The US and International Response Report for Congress* (Congressional Research Service 2002, 22).

37   N. Ryder, 'Danger Money' (2007) *New Law Journal*, 157, 7300; Supp (Charities Appeals Supplement), 6, 8.

criminal activities, including benefit and credit card fraud, identity theft, the sale of counterfeit goods and drug trafficking.[38]

Policy Background – From Where did the Offence Originate?

The UK's CTF policy has been influenced by the legislative measures introduced by both the UN and the EU. Indeed, the term Terrorist Finance was adopted by the UN in its seminal Declaration to Eliminate International Terrorism in 1994.[39] This was soon followed by a General Assembly Resolution A/RES/51/210 which provided that Member States were to 'take steps to prevent and counteract, through appropriate domestic measures, the financing of terrorists and terrorist organizations.'[40] The scope of this Resolution, however, was limited to terrorist bombings and nuclear terrorism. The al-Qaeda bombings in Kenya and Tanzania in 1998 therefore resulted in a re-think and the subsequent passing of Resolutions A/RES/52/165 in 1997 and A/RES/53/108 in 1998. These highlighted the need to counter terrorist financing as well as a suggestion to form a Convention against the financing of terrorism.[41] Consequently, the International Convention for the Suppression of the Financing of Terrorism 1999 defines funds for terrorism to include 'assets of every kind, whether tangible or intangible, movable or immovable, however acquired, and legal documents or instruments in any form.'[42] The 1999 Convention therefore criminalized the collection or distribution of funds which were to be used in an act of terrorism,[43] and also outlined measures for the freezing and forfeiture of funds used for terrorist acts.[44] Despite the importance of preventing terrorist financing, only 41 Member States signed the Treaty, and only six ratified it.[45]

The terrorist attacks of 9/11, however, led to a monumental shift in attitudes towards the detection and prevention of terrorist financing. The Convention

---

38   C. Linn, 'How Terrorists Exploit Gaps in US Anti-Money Laundering Laws to Secrete Plunder' (2005) *Journal of Money Laundering Control*, 8(3), 200–214, 200.

39   Annex to Resolution 49/60, Measures to eliminate international terrorism, 9 December 1994, 49/60.

40   A/RES/51/210, 88th Plenary Meeting of General Assembly, 17 December; also see A/RES/45/121 of 14 December 1990.

41   A/RES/52/165 15 December 1997, paragraph 3 on pledge to prevent terrorist financing, A/RES/53/108, 8 December 1998, paragraph 11 on a draft International Convention against terrorist financing.

42   Article 1. para. 1 of the Convention, The United Nations (1999).

43   Article 2(1)(a) and (b), also request under Article 4 for domestic states to criminalize terrorist financing, 1999 United Nations Convention for the Suppression of Terrorist Financing, adopted by UN in Resolution 54/109, 9 December 1999.

44   See in general Article 8, 1999 Convention.

45   A. Leong, 'Chasing Dirty Money: Domestic and International Measures Against Money Laundering' (2007) *Journal of Money Laundering Control*, 10(2), 140–156, 45.

therefore served as a precedent for UN Security Council Resolution 1373.[46] This imposes four obligations on members of the UN:[47] i) it specifically requires states to thwart and control the financing of terrorism;[48] ii) it criminalizes the collection of terrorist funds in states territory;[49] iii) it freezes funds, financial assets and economic resources of people who commit or try to commit acts of terrorism;[50] and iv) it prevents any nationals from within their territories providing funds, financial assets and economic resources to people who seek to commit acts of terrorism.[51] Resolution 1373 is therefore the most important international legislative measure that seeks to prevent terrorist financing, with the obligation on Member States to freeze assets described as absolute in compelling collective application.[52] In contrast to the 1999 Convention, all 191 Member States have submitted reports to the UN Security Council Counter-Terrorism Committee on the actions they have taken to suppress international terrorism; including how they have gone about blocking terrorist finances as required by Resolution 1373.[53]

It is important to note that the UK's CTF strategy predates the introduction of the international legislative measures by both the UN and EU. The UK was unfortunately experienced in dealing with mainland terrorist attacks, well before the events of 9/11 although, unlike 9/11 and its associated attacks, these were restricted by territory (the UK) and politics (Irish Nationalism) rather than against a particular ideology or lifestyle, which can encompass many countries.[54] With the emergence of Northern Irish terrorist organizations such as the Irish Republican Army (IRA), their need for economic resources to continue their operations with estimated running costs of between £500,000 and £1.5 million per year,[55] the UK's legislation evolved to reflect the separate need to disrupt the flow of terrorist financing. For example, the Prevention of Terrorism Act 1974 enabled the courts

---

46   P. Binning, 'In Safe Hands? Striking the Balance Between Privacy and Security – Anti-Terrorist Finance Measures' (2002) *European Human Rights Law Review*, 6, 737–749.

47   See Cabinet Office, *The UK and the Campaign against International Terrorism – Progress Report* (Cabinet Office 2002, 24).

48   S.C. Res, 1373, U.N. SCOR, 56th Sess., 4385th Mtg. Article 1(a).

49   S.C. Res, 1373, U.N. SCOR, 56th Sess., 4385th Mtg. Article 1(b).

50   S.C. Res, 1373, U.N. SCOR, 56th Sess., 4385th Mtg. Article 1(c).

51   S.C. Res, 1373, U.N. SCOR, 56th Sess., 4385th Mtg. Article 1(5).

52   See A. Kruse, 'Financial and Economic Sanctions – From a Perspective of International Law and Human Rights' (2005) *Journal of Financial Crime*, 12(3), 217–220, 218.

53   The White House, *Progress Report on the Global War on Terrorism* (The White House 2003, 6).

54   For a good comparison between the IRA's and al-Qaeda's aims and objectives, see in general S. Greer, 'Human Rights and the Struggle Against Terrorism in the United Kingdom' (2008) *European Human Rights Law Review*, 2, 163–172, 165–167.

55   See in general L. Donohue, 'Anti Terrorist Finance in the United Kingdom and the United States' (2005–2006), *Michigan Journal of International Law*, 27, 303, 324 and 314–324.

to forfeit assets which were 'controlled by an individual convicted of membership, where such resources were intended for use in Northern Ireland terrorism.'[56]

The Prevention of Terrorism (Temporary Provisions) Act 1989 also introduced specific provisions under Part III to criminalize the financing of terrorism[57] and the control of terrorist finances[58] as well as imposing forfeiture and criminal penalties on those found guilty of this offence.[59] Using such legislation, the UK has achieved some success in Northern Ireland against the IRA by virtue of the offences created.[60] However, its effectiveness was still questioned and thus resulted in a review of the UK's terrorist policy by the Home Office in 1998. The consultation paper concluded that the terrorist financing provisions contained several weaknesses including the fact that there were only four terrorist financing convictions between 1978 and 1989.[61] Bell argued in 2003 that 'there have been no successful prosecutions for terrorist funding offences in Northern Ireland over the last 30 years and the forfeiture provisions under the Prevention of Terrorism (Temporary Provisions) Act 1989 have never been utilized.'[62] The Home Office thus recommended that the scope of the terrorist financing provisions should be extended to fund-raising for all terrorist purposes. The Criminal Justice Act 1993, therefore, added separate provisions to counteract terrorist financing under Part IV;[63] lowered the standard of proof from criminal to civil standards;[64] and brought the legislation more in line with anti-money laundering measures. Additionally, following the Omagh bombings in 1998, the Criminal Justice (Terrorism and Conspiracy) Act 1998 allowed courts to forfeit any property connected with proscribed terrorist organizations.[65] Therefore, it is evident that the UK already had a robust attitude towards disrupting terrorist finances and recognized it as a separate offence to money laundering, even before there was international action on the issue. This can be seen by the fact that the UK was one of the few Member States which signed and ratified the 1999 UN Convention on the Suppression of the Financing of Terrorism before 9/11. This was signed 10 January 2000 and ratified 7 March 2001.

---

56   L. Donohue, 'Anti Terrorist Finance in the United Kingdom and the United States' (2005-2006), *Michigan Journal of International Law*, 27, 303, 330.

57   Prevention of Terrorism (Temporary Provisions) Act 1989 (repealed) s 9.

58   Prevention of Terrorism (Temporary Provisions) Act 1989 (repealed) s 9; s 11.

59   Prevention of Terrorism (Temporary Provisions) Act 1989 (repealed) s 13.

60   For a more detailed discussion of terrorist funding in Northern Ireland see W. Tupman, 'Where Has All The Money Gone? The IRA as a Profit-Making Concern' (1998) *Journal of Money Laundering Control*, 1(4), 303–311.

61   W. Tupman, 'Where Has All the Money Gone? The IRA as a Profit-Making Concern' (1998) *Journal of Money Laundering Control*, 1(4), 303–311, 6.14.

62   R. Bell, 'The Confiscation, Forfeiture and Disruption of Terrorist Finances' (2003) *Journal of Money Laundering Control*, 7(2), 105–125, 113.

63   As amendments to the Northern Ireland (Emergency Provisions) Act 1991.

64   Criminal Justice Act 1993, s 37(2).

65   Criminal Justice (Terrorism and Conspiracy) Act 1998, s 4(3).

The subsequent legislation, the Terrorism Act 2000 was, and still is, the cornerstone of the UK's CTF strategy. Part III of the Act significantly extends provisions relating to terrorism to include international terrorism and persons residing outside the UK.[66] This allays previous criticism of UK legislation on the basis that it focused too heavily on Northern Ireland and other parts of the UK. The provisions therefore include, as noted above, offences of fund-raising[67] and money laundering,[68] and cover the issues of confiscation, seizure of cash during an investigation[69] and penalties of forfeiture if convicted.[70] Accordingly, the UK is one of the few countries which has properly separated CTF legislation and is thus one of the most advanced in the application of financial weapons against terrorist organizations. In 2002, HM Treasury published a report which outlined the important contribution made by the UK government towards targeting the sources of terrorist financing.[71] Building on this leadership, in 2007 the government also launched the financial challenge to crime and terrorism, which 'sets out for the first time how the public and private sector would come together to deter terrorists from using the financial system, detect them when they did, and use financial tools to disrupt them.'[72] In 2010, HM Treasury stated that 'the government's aim is to deprive terrorists and violent extremists of the financial resources and systems needed for terrorist-related activity, including radicalization.'[73] In terms of CTF legislation, the UK is therefore a world leader.

Financial Institutions and Regulatory Bodies

HM Treasury

HM Treasury is the leading CTF government department in the UK and is responsible for the execution of the UN's financial sanctions regime.[74] Explained in more detail below, HM Treasury in association with the Home Office implements the UK's terrorist financing policy. This is further evidence of how the Coalition

66   Terrorism Act 2000, s1(4)(a)(c)(d).

67   Terrorism Act 2000, s 15.

68   Terrorism Act 2000, s 18.

69   Terrorism Act 2000, ss 24–26.

70   Terrorism Act 2000, s 23.

71   HM Treasury, *Combating the Financing of Terrorism. A Report on UK Action* (HM Treasury 2002, 11).

72   HM Treasury, *The Financial Challenge to Crime and Terrorism* (London: HM Treasury, 2007).

73   HM Treasury, *The Financial Challenge to Crime and Terrorism* (London: HM Treasury, 2007, 5).

74   Financial Action Task Force, *Third Mutual Evaluation Report Anti-Money Laundering and Combating the Financing of Terrorism – United Kingdom* (Financial Action Task Force, 2007, 24).

government has extended the remit of the Home Office to tackle all aspects of financial crime including money laundering and fraud. This is especially so since the creation of the National Crime Agency. Nonetheless, the objective of HM Treasury, as highlighted in Chapter 2 is to safeguard 'the integrity of the financial system from exploitation by criminals and terrorists. It does this by deploying financial tools to deter, detect and disrupt crime and security threats. The approach taken is effective and proportionate to the risks posed as well as engaging with business, law makers and law enforcers.'[75] This is clearly illustrated by the publication of its CTF strategy document in 2007 which outlined how the government intended to tackle the financing of terrorism.[76] In an attempt to achieve these objectives, HM Treasury has created the Asset Freezing Unit. This is responsible for,

- domestic legislation on financial sanctions;
- the implementation and administration of domestic financial sanctions;
- domestic designations under the Terrorist Asset-Freezing etc. Act 2010;
- providing advice to Treasury Ministers;
- the implementation and administration of international financial sanctions in the UK;
- working in conjunction with the Foreign and Commonwealth Office on the design of individual financial sanctions regimes and listing decisions at the UN and EU;
- working with international partners to develop the international frameworks for financial sanctions; and
- licensing exemptions to financial sanctions.[77]

Furthermore, the Unit,

- issues Notices and notifications advising of the introduction, amendment, suspension or lifting of financial sanctions regimes with a view to making bodies and individuals likely to be affected by financial sanctions aware of their obligations;
- provides, on the financial sanctions home page of the Treasury website, a consolidated list of financial sanctions targets which consists of the names of individuals and entities that have been listed by the UN, EU and/or the UK under legislation relating to a specific financial sanctions regime;

---

75 HM Treasury, *The Financial Challenge to Crime and Terrorism* (London: HM Treasury, 2007, 11).

76 HM Treasury, *Combating the Financing of Terrorism. A Report on UK Action* (HM Treasury 2002, 11).

77 HM Treasury, 'Asset Freezing Unit' <http://www.hm-treasury.gov.uk/fin_san ctions_afu.htm> accessed 14 March 2012.

- provides, on the financial sanctions home page of the Treasury website, an investment ban list in relation to the EU measures against Burma/Myanmar;
- processes applications for licences to release frozen funds or to make funds available to designated/restricted persons; and
- responds to reports and queries from financial institutions, companies and members of the public concerning financial sanctions.[78]

Home Office

The Home Office is responsible for i) managing the police in England and Wales; ii) the Serious Organised Crime Agency (SOCA); and iii) tackling organized crime, counter terrorism, crime and immigration. The Coalition government published its counter terrorism strategy, or CONTEST, as it was referred to by the Home Office, in 2011.[79] This is administered and coordinated by the Home Office's Office for Security and Counter-Terrorism. In particular, this office is responsible for supporting the Home Secretary and other government departments in relation to CONTEST; is required to deliver certain parts of the counter terrorism strategy; must supervise the UK Security Service; and, coordinates counter-terrorism crisis management.[80] The strategy has four important objectives listed under the sound bites of pursue, prevent, protect and prepare. It therefore aims to i) Pursue: to stop terrorist attacks; ii) Prevent: to stop people becoming terrorists or supporting terrorism; iii) Protect: to strengthen our protection against a terrorist attack; and, iv) Prepare: to mitigate the impact of a terrorist attack. Despite these laudable aims, the strategy fails to provide any significant detail as to how the Home Office actually intends to combat and prevent the financing of terrorism.

Foreign and Commonwealth Office

The Foreign and Commonwealth Office is responsible for the implementation of several UN money laundering legislative provisions. It performs the same function in relation to CTF policy and is responsible for the ratification of UN Treaties and the implementation of UN Security Council Resolutions. In relation to the UK's counter terrorism strategy the Foreign and Commonwealth Office organizes the delivery of CONTEST overseas.

---

78   HM Treasury, 'Asset Freezing Unit' <http://www.hm-treasury.gov.uk/fin_sanc tions_afu.htm> accessed 14 March 2012.

79   The Home Office, *The United Kingdom's Strategy for Countering Terrorism* (London, 2011).

80   The Home Office, *The United Kingdom's Strategy for Countering Terrorism* (London, 2011, 123).

Serious Organised Crime Agency

SOCA is the UK's Financial Intelligence Unit (FIU) and as such administers the reporting obligations under the Proceeds of Crime Act 2002.[81] It also manages the reporting of suspected instances of terrorist financing from a wide range of financial services bodies and other relevant professions. SOCA was created by the Serious Organised Crime and Police Act 2005 as a major part of the then government's organized crime strategy.

Financial Intelligence

As with other financial crimes, financial intelligence is extremely important if the CTF policy is to be effective. Schedule 2, Part III, of the Anti-terrorism, Crime and Security Act 2001 therefore inserts section 21A into the Terrorism Act 2000 and creates the offence of failing to disclose in the regulated sector. A person commits an offence under this section if three conditions are met: i) the accused knows or suspects, or has reasonable grounds for knowing or suspecting that a person has committed an offence under sections 15–18 of the Terrorism Act 2000;[82] ii) the information or other matter upon which the accused has based his knowledge or suspicion, or which gives reasonable grounds for such knowledge or suspicion, came to him in the course of a business that operates within the regulated sector;[83] and, iii) the accused does not disclose the information or other matter to a constable or nominated officer (normally a money laundering reporting officer) as soon as practicable after he received the information.[84] A person does not commit an offence if he/she had a reasonable excuse for not disclosing the information or other matter or he is a professional legal adviser and the information or other matter came to him in privileged circumstances.[85] Lord Carlile argues that these reporting obligations are 'still [an] under-publicized duty, to which the only major statutory exception is genuine legal professional privilege.'[86] Since the introduction of the new section 21A, there have been no trials in which this new section has been tested.[87]

---

81   However, it is important to note that it is likely this role will transfer to the National Crime Agency during the next parliamentary year.

82   Terrorism Act 2000, s 21A(2).

83   Terrorism Act 2000, s 21A(3).

84   Terrorism Act 2000, s 21A(4).

85   Terrorism Act 2000, s 21A.

86   Home Office, *Report on the Operation in 2004 of the Terrorism Act 2000* (Home Office, 2004, 24).

87   Home Office, *Report on the Operation in 2004 of the Terrorism Act 2000* (Home Office, 2004, 18).

Furthermore, the Anti-terrorism, Crime and Security Act 2001 amends the Terrorism Act 2000 by inserting a further defence of protected disclosures.[88] In order for this to be utilized, three conditions must be met. The first condition is that the information or other matter disclosed came to the person making the disclosure (the discloser) in the course of a business in the regulated sector.[89] The second condition is that the information or other matter causes the discloser to know or suspect, or gives him reasonable grounds for knowing or suspecting, that a person has committed an offence as outlined above under sections 15-18 of the Terrorism Act 2000.[90] The third and final condition is that the disclosure is made to a constable or a nominated officer as soon as is practicable after the information or other matter comes to the discloser.[91]

An individual or organization who suspects that an offence has been committed under the Terrorism Act 2000 is required to complete a suspicious activity report (SAR), which is then sent to SOCA for processing. Lord Carlile, in his annual report on the operation of the Terrorism Act 2000 commented that 'there are concerns in the business sector about difficulties of compliance and the serious consequences that may flow from this.'[92] In 2005, the Lander Review noted that,

> ... just under 2,100 of the total SARs (1%) were judged by the FIU terrorism team to be of potential interest in a terrorist context, of which about 650 were passed on to the National Terrorist Financial Investigation Unit for more detailed investigation. There was a slight peak of reports of interest following the events of 7 and 21 July 2005.[93]

The number of terrorist related SARs submitted between 2007 and 2008 was 956.[94] This decreased slightly to 703 between 2008 and 2009.[95] The usefulness of SARs in relation to terrorist financing was highlighted by SOCA who took the view that,

> ... although the numbers continue to be small in proportion to the total numbers of SARs, their value can be significant, as has been demonstrated in previous years in which major terrorist incidents have taken place. All UK counter-terrorism

---

88   Terrorism Act 2000, s 21B.

89   Terrorism Act 2000, s 21B(2).

90   Terrorism Act 2000, s 21B(3).

91   Terrorism Act 2000, s 21B(4).

92   Home Office, *Report on the Operation in 2004 of the Terrorism Act 2000* (Home Office, 2004, 19–20).

93   Serious Organised Crime Agency, *Review of the Suspicious Activity Reports Regime.* (Serious Organised Crime Agency 2006, 13).

94   Serious Organised Crime Agency, *The Suspicious Activity Reports Regime Annual Report 2008.* (Serious Organised Crime Agency 2008, 42).

95   Serious Organised Crime Agency, *The Suspicious Activity Reports Regime Annual Report 2009.* (Serious Organised Crime Agency 2010, 14).

investigations have a financial aspect to them, and the UK FIU Terrorist Finance Team has continued to provide support to these over the year [2009].[96]

Sentencing and Recovery

A defendant who has been found guilty of any of the four principal terrorist financing offences, as outlined above, is liable to a maximum term of 14 years' imprisonment and/or an unlimited fine;[97] the same as that for the offence of money laundering. Despite this penalty and the devastating effects of the crime, there have been very few UK prosecutions for terrorist financing. Between 11 September 2001 and 31 December 2007, only 74 CTF charges were made in Great Britain, making up only 17 per cent of all charges made under the Terrorism Act 2000.[98] Furthermore, in 2007, the Crown Prosecution Service prosecuted only three defendants, under section 17 of the Terrorism Act 2000 and in 2008, only four defendants under section 15.[99] Between September 2001 and 2009, only 11 people were convicted under sections 15–19 of the Terrorism Act 2000.[100] As Robinson claims, terrorist money laundering prosecutions in Great Britain have 'mostly failed'.[101]

It is unclear why the prosecution rate has been so low, although one reason may be because, in order to prove the offences under Part III of the Terrorism Act 2000, the prosecution has to prove the terrorist element. For instance, for a section 17 offence it is necessary to prove that the defendant not only became involved in a funding arrangement but that he knew or suspected that the proceeds of the arrangement were for the purposes of terrorism. While the defendant may have suspected that the arrangement was illegal in some way, it is harder to prove that the suspicion was one of actual terrorism rather than drug trafficking, human trafficking or some other crime.[102] Due to the small numbers involved, there are no sentencing guidelines for these offences and no published cases relating to

---

96   Serious Organised Crime Agency, *The Suspicious Activity Reports Regime Annual Report 2009.* (Serious Organised Crime Agency 2010, 17).

97   Terrorism Act 2000, s 22.

98   P. Sproat, 'Counter-Terrorist Finance in the UK: A Quantitative and Qualitative Commentary Based on Open-Source Materials' (2010) *Journal of Money Laundering Control*, 315–335, 318.

99   House of Lords, 'Money Laundering and the Financing of Terrorism: European Union Committee' (2009) <http://www.publications.parliament.uk/pa/ld200809/ldselect/ldeucom/132/9031811.htm> accessed 24 June 2011.

100   HC Deb, 5 February 2010, c586w.

101   P. Sproat, 'Counter-Terrorist Finance in the UK: A Quantitative and Qualitative Commentary Based on Open-Source Materials' (2010) *Journal of Money Laundering Control*, 315–335, 320.

102   R. Alexander, 'Money Laundering and Terrorist Financing: Time for a Combined Offence' (2009) *Company Lawyer*, 30(7), 200–204, 202.

sentencing practice. The only guidance, to the authors' knowledge, is contained in section 30 of the Counter-Terrorism Act 2008, which states that if an offence has a terrorist connection, the court must treat that as an aggravating factor and sentence accordingly.

Examples of sentencing for section 15 offences include two Algerian men, Benmerzouga and Meziane, who were sentenced in 2003 to 11 years' imprisonment for raising over £200,000 for purposes of terrorism through a credit card fraud.[103] Similarly, in 2007, Hassan Mutegombwa received 10 years for inviting someone to provide money for the purposes of terrorism,[104] indicating that the judges involved thought that these two offences were serious enough to warrant lengthy terms of incarceration. Despite these examples, more normal sentences would appear to be much shorter. For example in 2008 Abu Izzadeen was sentenced to four and a half years for inciting terrorism and terrorist fundraising; Shah Jala Hussain received two years and three months for terrorist fundraising; while Simon Keeler received two and a half years and Abdul Muhid two years' imprisonment for the same offence.[105] More recently, in March 2011, Rajib Karim was sentenced to three years imprisonment for an offence under section 15(3) of the Terrorism Act 2000.[106] These would therefore suggest that the usual sentence for a fundraising offence is between two and three years' imprisonment.

Despite the lack of sentencing guidelines, there does appear to be more emphasis placed on recovery. This is not surprising when we bear in mind that the overall aim of CTF legislation is to prevent the funding of terrorism. It is perhaps predictable, then, that there has been a glut of initiatives and orders which enable the recovery of money and/or property intended for use in terrorism. For example, the Terrorism Act 2000, as amended by the Counter-Terrorism Act 2008, states that if a person is convicted of an offence under sections 15–19, any property connected with the offence can be the subject of a criminal forfeiture order.[107] The court also has the option of a confiscation order under the Proceeds of Crime Act (PCOA) 2002 (see Chapter 2), although if the court has the choice between the two, it may be better to opt for the forfeiture order as this deprives the defendant

---

103   The Telegraph, 'Two al-Qa'eda Terrorists Jailed for 11 Years' (2003) <http://www.telegraph.co.uk/news/1426290/Two-al-Qaeda-terrorists-jailed-for-11-years.html> accessed 28 June 2011.

104   Metropolitan Police, 'Operation Overamp. Hassan Mutegombwa' (Metropolitan Police Press Release, 2010) <http://www.powerbase.info/images/6/6c/Metropolitan_Police_Service_Press_Release_on_Conviction_of_Hassan_Mutegombwa.pdf> accessed 28 June 2011.

105   BBC News, 'Arrogant Muslim Preacher Jailed' (18 April 2008) <http://news.bbc.co.uk/1/hi/uk/7354397.stm> accessed 28 June 2011.

106   Metropolitan Police, 'Man Jailed for 30 Years for Terrorism Offences' (Metropolitan Police Press Release 2011) <http://content.met.police.uk/News/Man-jailed-for-30-years-for-terrorism-offences/1260268719101/1257246745756> accessed 28 June 2011.

107   Terrorism Act 2000, s 23.

of the title of designated assets, while a confiscation order is only an order to pay a sum of money and is enforced as if it were a fine. A person subject to a forfeiture order is required to give to a police officer all property which is specified in the order.[108] The Terrorism Act 2000 also allows for Orders in Council, which have the effect of giving foreign forfeiture orders recognition in England and Wales.

Furthermore, the Anti-terrorism, Crime and Security Act 2001 authorizes the seizure of terrorist cash anywhere in the UK;[109] the freezing of funds at the start of a terrorist related investigation;[110] and, the monitoring of suspected accounts.[111] It is worth noting that the Anti-Terrorism, Crime and Security Act 2001 received Royal Assent on 14 December 2001, only 94 days after the 9/11 attacks in New York and Washington and thus could be described as being rushed through Parliament. Nevertheless, the first recovery mechanism is provided for under Part I of the Act which allows for the civil seizure and forfeiture of terrorist cash. For the purposes of the Act, terrorist cash is defined to include cash which '(a) is intended to be used for the purposes of terrorism; (b) consists of resources of an organization which is a proscribed organization; or (c) is, or represents, property obtained through terrorism.'[112] The cash must have been found in the UK and can include coins and notes in any currency, postal orders, bankers' drafts, cheques of any kind, bearer bonds and bearer shares.[113] The Act permits the authorized officer to seize cash, if he has reasonable grounds for suspecting that it is terrorist cash.[114] Initially this is only for a period of 48 hours, but can be extended by a Magistrates' Court, acting in a civil capacity, to a maximum of two years.[115] If the period of seizure is for longer than 48 hours, then the cash must be placed in an interest-bearing account. Any interest earned on the sum will be added to the capital either when the money is forfeited or released.[116] Between 2001 and 31 January 2007, £469,000 worth of cash was seized under terrorism legislation and £1.4 million of terrorist funds under the POCA 2002.[117]

Additionally, Part II of the Anti-Terrorism, Crime and Security Act 2001 allows HM Treasury to freeze the assets of known or suspected terrorists. These are known as freezing orders, although are sometimes referred to as asset freezing

---

108   Terrorism Act 2000, schedule 4.
109   Anti-terrorism, Crime and Security Act 2001, Schedule 1, Part 2.
110   Anti-terrorism, Crime and Security Act 2001, ss 4–16.
111   Anti-terrorism, Crime and Security Act 2001, Schedule 2, Part 1.
112   Anti-terrorism, Crime and Security Act 2001, s 1(1).
113   Anti-terrorism, Crime and Security Act 2001, Schedule 1 paragraph 1.
114   Anti-terrorism, Crime and Security Act 2001, Schedule 1 paragraph 2
115   Anti-terrorism, Crime and Security Act 2001, Schedule 1 paragraph 3.
116   Anti-terrorism, Crime and Security Act 2001, Schedule 1 paragraph 4.
117   P. Sproat, 'Counter-Terrorist Finance in the UK: A Quantitative and Qualitative Commentary Based on Open-Source Materials' (2010) *Journal of Money Laundering Control*, 315–335, 324.

orders, freezing injunctions or Mareva[118] orders. An order can be made, if two statutory requirements are met. First, HM Treasury must reasonably believe that action threatening the UK's economy or the life or property of UK nationals or residents has taken place or is likely to take place. Interestingly, the Act provides that HM Treasury is not required to prove actual detriment in order to be able to freeze the assets of a suspected terrorist, but that a threat alone is sufficient. There is no condition that there should be a suspicion of criminal activity, nor a condition that any criminal activity exists. The second element is that the persons involved in the action are resident outside of the UK or are an overseas government.[119] Under the Act, a freezing order prohibits the person from making funds available to, or for the benefit of, a person or persons specified in the order,[120] which can include people in and outside of the UK.[121] The order is an interim order and as such must be kept under constant review by the Treasury.[122] It can last for no longer than two years[123] and, interestingly, binds not just the person named in the order but also third parties with knowledge of it.[124] White argues that while the order is powerful, it is generally regarded by the courts as draconian and therefore is only used in exceptional circumstances.[125] An example of such an order, however, is The Landsbanki Freezing Order 2008.[126] This was made in October 2008 against the Icelandic bank, Landsbanki after it was revealed that local councils in the UK had deposited approximately £800 million in the failing bank during the credit crunch.[127] The order froze funds owned, held and controlled by the bank and lasted until 15 June 2009.[128] Furthermore, following 9/11, HM Treasury and the Bank of England froze the assets of over 100 organizations and 200 individuals, including over £100 million of Taliban and al-Qaeda assets.[129]

---

118   See *Mareva Compania Naviera SA v International Bulkcarriers SA* [1980] 1 All E.R. 213.

119   Terrorism Act 2000, s 4(1)(a)(b).

120   Anti-terrorism, Crime and Security Act 2001, s 5(1).

121   Anti-terrorism, Crime and Security Act 2001, s 5(2).

122   Anti-terrorism, Crime and Security Act 2001, s 7.

123   Anti-terrorism, Crime and Security Act 2001, s 8.

124   S. White, 'Freezing Injunctions. A Procedural Overview and Practical Guide' (2005) <http://www.parkcourtchambers.co.uk/seminar-handouts/16.11.05%20Commercial-Chancery%20_S%20White_.pdf> accessed 24 June 2011.

125   S. White, 'Freezing Injunctions. A Procedural Overview and Practical Guide' (2005) <http://www.parkcourtchambers.co.uk/seminar-handouts/16.11.05%20Commercial-Chancery%20_S%20White_.pdf> accessed 24 June 2011.

126   The Landsbanki Freezing Order 2008, S.I. 2008/2668.

127   For an excellent discussion of the use of the powers under the Anti-terrorism, Crime and Security Act 2001 see G. Lennon and C. Walker, 'Hot Money in a Cold Climate' (2009) *Public Law*, January, 37–42.

128   HM Treasury, 'The Landsbanki Freezing Order' (2011) <http://www.hm-treasury.gov.uk/fin_stability_landsbanki.htm> accessed 24 June 2011.

129   HM Treasury, *Combating the Financing of Terrorism. A Report on UK Action* (HM Treasury 2002, 9).

The UK has additionally implemented the Terrorism (United Nations Measures) Order 2006 to give legal effect to Security Council Resolution 1373.[130] The Order also gives effect to the enforcement of EC Regulation 2580/2001, and permits the 'designation' of certain people thus increasing those whose funds, financial assets and economic resources can be frozen. HM Treasury took the view that the aim of the Order was enhanced to provide further restrictions on making funds, economic resources and financial services available to anyone who has been 'designated' in the UK by the Treasury as a person suspected of committing, attempting to commit, participating in or facilitating acts of terrorism. By virtue of Article 4 of the Order, HM Treasury has been given the power to 'designate' a person if four conditions are met. These are that HM Treasury has reasonable grounds to suspect that a person is or may be (a) a person who commits, attempts to commit, participates in or facilitates the commission of acts of terrorism; (b) a person named in the Council Decision; (c) a person owned or controlled, directly or indirectly, by a designated person; or (d) a person acting on behalf, or at the direction, of a designated person. Under Article 5 of the Order, HM Treasury is required to make appropriate measures to publicize the direction or to notify specific people and to inform the person identified in the direction.

Furthermore, under Article 7 of the 2006 Order, a person is prohibited from 'Dealing with funds, financial assets and economic resources of anyone who commits, attempts to commit, participates in or facilitates the commission of acts of terrorism; designated persons; anyone owned or controlled by them or anyone acting on their behalf or at their direction.' The article makes it a criminal offence to contravene this prohibition. Article 8 of the Order additionally prohibits making funds, financial assets, economic resources or financial services available to anyone in respect of whom Article 7 applies. Similarly, contravention of this prohibition is also a criminal offence.

The legality of the Terrorism (United Nations Measures) Order 2006 was challenged in *A v HM Treasury*.[131] Here, the appellants required orders from the court to quash the freezing of their assets under the aforementioned Order.[132] Collins J. decided that the orders granted should be set aside, against five of the applicants, on three grounds: i) parliamentary approval should have been sought; the orders should not have been made by Order in Council; ii) it was impossible to determine how the test adopted by HM Treasury (that it had reasonable grounds for suspecting the applicants were committing terrorists acts) could represent a necessary means of applying the relevant UN Resolution; and iii) the 2006 Order created criminal offences that contravened the principle of legal certainty. The interpretation of the phrase economic resources was crucial in the case, and the

---

130   S.I 2006/2657.

131   [2008] EWHC 869.

132   One of the applicants unsuccessfully argued that an order granted against himself by the Al-Qaeda and Taliban (United Nations Measures) Order 2006, S.I. 2006/2952 should be set aside.

Court decided that the definition of this phrase meant that the family members of the applicants did not know if they were breaching the Order or if they needed a licence from HM Treasury.[133] HM Treasury appealed to the Court of Appeal,[134] who considered four issues:

1. Was the 2006 Terrorism Order unlawful and should it be quashed?
2. What was impact of the lack of procedural safeguards in the 2006 Order?
3. Did the offences created under Articles 7 and 8 of the Order satisfy the principles of legal certainty and proportionality?
4. Whether the Al-Qaeda and Taliban (UN Measures) Order 2006 was unlawful because a person placed on the UN Sanctions Committee list had no appeal mechanism against that decision.

The Court of Appeal held that the reasonable ground test adopted by HM Treasury did not go beyond the ambit of Resolution 1373, but the requirement in the 2006 Order of 'or may be' did go further than the Resolution. Therefore, it determined that the directions granted by HM Treasury were quashed. The Court of Appeal further stated that the courts must be relied on to guarantee that satisfactory procedural protection is upheld for applicants under the Order[135] and that the provisions of the licensing system under the Order were proportionate and legally certain. Finally, it held that the Al-Qaeda and Taliban (UN Measures) Order 2006 was lawful.

In response, the government has introduced the Terrorism (UN Measures) Order 2009,[136] which provides that a direction will cease to have effect 12 months after it was made; although HM Treasury still has the ability to renew a direction.[137] The Order revises the prohibition on making funds, economic resources and financial services available for the benefit of a 'designated' person so that they only apply if the 'designated' person obtains, or is able to obtain, a significant financial benefit. The ban on making funds, economic resources and financial assets available directly to a 'designated person', as outlined above, is unaltered. Furthermore, the 2009 Order changes the prohibition on making economic resources available to a 'designated' person by providing a defence to that person if they did not know, and had no reasonable cause to suspect, that the economic resources which they provided to a 'designated' person would be likely to be exchanged or used in exchange for funds, goods or services. The Financial Services Secretary to the Treasury, Lord Myners, took the view that 'overall, these changes will improve the

---

133   For a more detailed discussion of this issue see *M v HM Treasury* [2008] UKHL 26.

134   *A v HM Treasury* [2008] EWCA Civ 1187.

135   The Court of Appeal stated that the method adopted should be comparable with that adopted in *Secretary of State for the Home Department v MB* [2008] 1 A.C. 440.

136   S.I. 2009/1747.

137   S.I. 2009/1747, article 5.

operation of the asset-freezing regime, ensure that it remains fair and proportionate and help facilitate effective compliance by ensuring that prohibitions are more tailored and clearer in how they apply.'[138] The matter finally came before the Supreme Court who considered the legitimacy of the Terrorism (UN Measures) Order and the Al-Qaeda and Taliban (UN Measures) Order 2006. Despite what had been said by the Court of Appeal, the Supreme Court determined that both of the Orders were *ultra vires* and HM Treasury swiftly responded by implementing the Draft Terrorist Asset Freezing Bill (2010) and implementing the Terrorist Asset-Freezing (Temporary Provisions) Act 2010.

Future Recommendations

The terrorist attacks of 9/11 galvanized the international response towards tackling terrorist financing. President Bush instigated the financial war on terror and declared that his administration would stifle terrorist funds wherever they were held in the world. The response of the UN was the implementation of several Security Council Resolutions, which had an immediate impact. Countries across the world began to freeze the assets of known and suspected terrorists. However, the position of the UK can be contrasted with the majority of other countries, largely due to the terrorist activities of the IRA and other paramilitary organizations. The UK had in place an effective CTF policy and achieved several notable successes against the IRA, but this position changed to counteract the threat posed by Islamic terrorist groups following 9/11. One of the main weapons used by the UK has been its ability to freeze the assets of suspected terrorist organizations. However, this ability has been restricted since the decision of the Supreme Court in *A v HM Treasury*. The position has become even more difficult due to the large number of increasingly sophisticated financial tools utilized by terrorists to fund their operations and any legislative and policy developments in this area will always be reactive. Therefore, irrespective of any legislation, improved methods of investigation, new powers for financial regulatory agencies or even an increased level of international co-operation, there is always the threat of a well-organized and self-funded terrorist cell, which operates under the radar of anti-terrorist financial legislation, and is capable of a terrorist attack, as graphically illustrated in London in July 2005.

Further Reading

Alexander, R. 'Money Laundering and Terrorist Financing: Time for a Combined Offence' (2009) *Company Lawyer*, 30(7), 200–204.
Bell, R. 'The Confiscation, Forfeiture and Disruption of Terrorist Finances' (2003) *Journal of Money Laundering Control*, 7(2), 105–125.

---

138   HC Debates 15 July 2009: Column WS96.

Binning, P. 'In Safe Hands? Striking the Balance Between Privacy and Security – Anti-Terrorist Finance Measures' (2002) *European Human Rights Law Review*, 6, 737–749.

Gallant, M. 'Promise and Perils: The Making of Global Money Laundering, Terrorist Finance Norms' (2010) *Journal of Money Laundering Control*, 13(3), 175–183.

Ramage, S. '2008 Amendments of the Proceeds of Crime Act 2002 and Other Legislation that Combats Terrorist Financing' (2008) *Criminal Lawyer*, 182, 1–5.

Ryder, N. 'A False Sense of Security? An Analysis of Legislative Approaches Towards the Prevention of Terrorist Finance in the United States and the United Kingdom' (2007) *Journal of Business Law*, November, 821–850.

Sproat, P. 'Counter-Terrorist Finance in the UK: A Quantitative and Qualitative Commentary Based on Open-Source Materials' (2010) *Journal of Money Laundering Control*, 13(4), 315–335.

Tupman, W. 'Ten Myths About Terrorist Financing' (2009) *Journal of Money Laundering Control*, 12(2), 189–205.

Chapter 4
Fraud

Introduction

International efforts to tackle financial crime have in the most part concentrated on money laundering and terrorist financing, as outlined in the two previous chapters. This is largely due to the United States of America (USA)-led war on drugs and the financial war on terrorism. Fraud, however, is another financial crime of epic proportions and as noted by Wright is 'becoming the crime of choice for organized crime and terrorist funding.'[1] This chapter therefore identifies the anti-fraud measures adopted in the United Kingdom (UK). Its primary focus will be to consider the strategic goals of the National Fraud Strategy and attempt to quantify the extent of the problem. The chapter will then consider background to the policy of criminalizing and regulating fraud, plus an evaluation of the financial institutions and regulatory bodies involved. Finally, we look at how the proceeds of fraudulent activity are recovered, including a brief analysis of sentencing options and practices.

What is the Offence of Fraud?

As outlined below and since 15 January 2007, there is now a single primary offence of fraud, contained in section 1 of the Fraud Act 2006. The offence can be committed in three different ways: by a false representation;[2] by a failure to disclose information when there is a legal duty to do so;[3] and, by abuse of position.[4] There are also a number of secondary offences including the possession or control of articles for use either in the course of or in connection with frauds;[5] the making, adapting, supplying or offering to supply articles for use in frauds;[6] participating in fraudulent trading as a sole trader;[7] and, obtaining services dishonestly where

---

1   R. Wright, 'Developing Effective Tools to Manage the Risk of Damage Caused by Economically Motivated Crime Fraud' (2007) *Journal of Financial Crime*, 14(1), 17–27, 18.

2   Fraud Act 2006, s 2.

3   Fraud Act 2006, s 3.

4   Fraud Act 2006, s 4.

5   Fraud Act 2006, s 6.

6   Fraud Act 2006, s 7.

7   Fraud Act 2006, s 9.

the defendant either intends not to pay at all or not to pay in full.[8] For reasons of space, only the primary offence will be discussed in detail.

Fraud by false representation section 2 Fraud Act 2006

To make out an offence under section 2 of the Fraud Act 2006, the defendant must have not only dishonestly made a false representation but to have also intended, by making that representation, to either make a gain (for himself or any other person) or to cause or expose an individual to the risk of a loss. The offence is entirely offender focused; as long as a false representation is actually made and the requisite dishonest intention (mens rea) element exists, the offence is made out. There is no need, therefore, to prove that an actual gain or loss was achieved, making this offence a conduct crime rather than a result crime and arguably much wider than the offences under the Theft Acts of 1968 and 1978. The second major change in the legislation is that the concept of deception has been removed entirely. Ormerod therefore argues that it 'is overbroad, based too heavily on the ill-defined concept of dishonesty, too vague to meet the obligation under Art. 7 of the ECHR [European Convention on Human Rights], and otherwise deficient in principle.'[9]

For reasons of clarity, a representation is stated to be 'any representation as to fact or law, including a representation as to the state of mind of (a) the person making the representation, or (b) any other person.'[10] This can be either expressed or implied[11] and achieved through both words and conduct, including body language, identity and items of clothing.[12] A representation made by implied conduct, for example, would include the dishonest use of a credit card, in the sense that the individual is falsely representing the fact that they have the authority to use the card.[13] A representation can also be made through an omission. Interestingly, the representation does not have to be made to a person and includes the situation where information is submitted to a 'system or device designed to receive, convey or respond to communications (with or without human intervention).'[14] This would include CHIP and PIN devices or ATM machines. If the representation is made to a machine, for practical purposes the offence can only be made out where the representation has been submitted; so in the case of using an email, when the email is actually sent. Representations are deemed to be false when they are either misleading or untrue and the defendant knows or thinks this to be the case.[15] To

---

8   Fraud Act 2006, s 11.

9   D. Ormerod, 'The Fraud Act 2006 – Criminalising Lying?' (2007) *Criminal Law Review*, 193–219, 219.

10   Fraud Act 2006, s 2(3).

11   Fraud Act 2006, s 2(4).

12   Crown Prosecution Service, 'The Fraud Act 2006' (2008) <http://www.cps.gov.uk/legal/d_to_g/fraud_act/> accessed 8 June 2011.

13   See *R v Lambie* [1982] AC 449.

14   Fraud Act 2006, s 2(5).

15   Fraud Act 2006, s 2(2).

aid in the interpretation of this, the concept of knowledge has been defined by the House of Lords (now Supreme Court) in *R v Montila (Steven William)*,[16]

> A person may have reasonable grounds to suspect that property is one thing (A) when in fact it is something different (B). But that is not so when the question is what a person knows. A person cannot know that something is A when in fact it is B. The proposition that a person knows that something is A is based on the premise that it is true that it is A. The fact that the property is A provides the starting point. Then there is the question whether the person knows that the property is A.[17]

This would suggest a fairly stringent test, although the Crown Prosecution Service believes that in practice it will be no more burdensome than proving the nature of deception in previous 'obtaining by deception' cases. For example it claims that 'where a debit or credit card has been used fraudulently, evidence of the rightful owner and that he or she did not carry out the transaction' will suffice.[18]

In terms of mens rea (guilty mind) the prosecution has to show that the defendant dishonestly made the false representation. As with the offence of theft under section 1 of the Theft Act 1968, dishonesty, if denied by the defendant, is defined by the Ghosh Test,[19] although the situations where the defendant is not dishonest under section 2 Theft Act 1968 do not apply. The prosecution must also prove that there was an intention to make a gain or intent to cause a loss (or risk the causing of a loss). Both gain and loss are defined in section 5 of the Fraud Act 2006. A gain includes 'keeping what one has, as well as a gain by getting what one does not have'[20] and a loss includes 'getting what one might get, as well as a loss by parting with what one has.'[21] Both refer to money and other property[22] and additionally include losses and gains which are temporary or permanent.[23] Interestingly, however, the term gain does not have to mean

---

16   [2004] UKHL 50.

17   *R v Montila (Steven William)* [2004] UKHL 50.

18   Crown Prosecution Service, 'The Fraud Act 2006' (2008) <http://www.cps.gov.uk/legal/d_to_g/fraud_act/> accessed 8 June 2011.

19   [1982] 1 QB 1053: in determining whether the prosecution had proved that a defendant was acting dishonestly, a jury had first of all to decide whether according to the ordinary standards of reasonable and honest people what was done was dishonest; if it was not dishonest by those standards, that was the end of the matter and the prosecution failed. If, however, it was dishonest by those standards, then the jury had to consider whether the defendant himself had to have realized that what he was doing was by those standards dishonest.

20   Fraud Act 2006, s 5(3).

21   Fraud Act 2006, s 5(4).

22   Defined as real, personal, things in action and other intangible property – Fraud Act 2006, s 5(2).

23   Fraud Act 2006, s 5(2) (b).

profit and can include the situation where a person obtains money which he was actually entitled to receive.[24]

Fraud by failing to disclose information – section 3 Fraud Act 2006

Fraud by failing to disclose information, under section 3 of the Fraud Act 2006, is essentially a crime of lying by omission. The defendant must have dishonestly failed to disclose to another person information which he was under a legal duty to disclose and, by this failure, intended to make a gain for himself or another, or cause a loss or the risk of a loss to another. As with the offence under section 2 above, the offence is offender focused with it being unnecessary to prove either that someone was misled or that a loss or gain was actually made. Once more this makes the offence easier to prove than the deception offences it replaces. The extent and nature of the legal duty is not defined in the Act, although the Explanatory Notes do provide examples of when a duty might exist, including the intentional failure to disclose a heart condition when applying for life insurance. It could also encompass the situation as in *R v Firth*[25] where a consultant failed to inform a hospital that he was using NHS facilities for private patients. Furthermore, the Law Commission stated,

Such a duty may derive from statute (such as the provisions governing company prospectuses), from the fact that the transaction in question is one of the utmost good faith (such as a contract of insurance), from the express or implied terms of a contract, from the custom of a particular trade or market, or from the existence of a fiduciary relationship between the parties (such as that of agent and principal).

For this purpose there is a legal duty to disclose information not only if the defendant's failure to disclose gives the victim a cause of action for damages, but also if the law gives the victim a right to set aside any change in his or her legal position to which he or she may consent as a result of the non-disclosure. For example, a person in a fiduciary position has a duty to disclose material information when entering into a contract with his or her beneficiary, in the sense that a failure to make such disclosure will entitle the beneficiary to rescind the contract and to reclaim any property transferred under it.[26]

The information which is not disclosed does not have to be material or relevant; there is no *de minimis* provision and it is not a defence to claim ignorance of the

---

24   *Attorney General Reference (no. 1 of 2001)* [2002] 3 All E.R. 840, CA.

25   (1990) 91 Cr App R 217.

26   The Law Commission, 'Fraud. Report on a Reference Under Section 3(1) (e) of the Law Commissions Act 1965' Law Commission Report No 276, Cm 5560 (2002), para 7.28 and 7.29.

duty or incompetence in supplying information.[27] For any of these issues to make a difference the defendant would have to prove that the failure was not carried out dishonestly. Other terms under the offence have the same meaning as those previously discussed above.

Fraud by abuse of position – section 4 Fraud Act 2006

The third and final way in which fraud can be committed under section 1 of the Fraud Act 2006 is by abuse of position. For the offence to have been committed the defendant must occupy a position 'in which he is expected to safeguard, or not act against, the financial interests of another person';[28] he must dishonestly abuse this position; and through this abuse intend to either make a gain for himself or another or cause a loss or risk the causing of a loss.[29] Similar to the other provisions, this can also be carried out through omission rather than by a positive act.[30] Also, as with the other two offences, this too is offender focused. With regard to the position which the defendant must occupy, the Law Commission has stated,

> The necessary relationship will be present between trustee and beneficiary, director and company, professional person and client, agent and principal, employee and employer, or between partners. It may arise otherwise, for example, within a family, or in the context of voluntary work, or in any context where the parties are not at arm's length. In nearly all cases where it arises, it will be recognized by the civil law as importing fiduciary duties, and any relationship that is so recognized will suffice. ... The question whether the particular facts alleged can properly be described as giving rise to that relationship will be an issue capable of being ruled on by the judge and, if the case goes to the jury, of being the subject of directions.[31]

While this position is a position of trust, it arguably falls short of 'one where there is a legal duty or an entitlement to single minded loyalty';[32] making it more of a moral rather than a legal obligation. The Crown Prosecution Service has therefore put together a non-exhaustive list of examples including,

---

27   Crown Prosecution Service, 'The Fraud Act 2006' (2008) <http://www.cps.gov. uk/legal/d_to_g/fraud_act/> accessed 8 June 2011.

28   Fraud Act 2006, s 4(1)(a).

29   Fraud Act 2006, s 4.

30   Fraud Act 2006, s 4(2).

31   The Law Commission, 'Fraud. Report on a Reference Under Section 3(1) (e) of the Law Commissions Act 1965' Law Commission Report No 276, Cm 5560 (2002), para 7.38.

32   Crown Prosecution Service, 'The Fraud Act 2006' (2008) <http://www.cps.gov. uk/legal/d_to_g/fraud_act/> accessed 8 June 2011.

- an employee of a software company who uses his position to clone software products with the intention of selling the products on his own behalf;
- where a person is employed to care for an elderly or disabled person and has access to that person's bank account but abuses that position by removing funds for his own personal use;
- an Attorney who removes money from the grantor's accounts for his own use. The Power of Attorney allows him to do so but when excessive this will be capable of being an offence under section 4;
- an employee who fails to take up the chance of a crucial contract in order that an associate or rival company can take it up instead;
- an employee who abuses his position in order to grant contracts or discounts to friends, relatives and associates;
- a waiter who sells his own bottles of wine passing them off as belonging to the restaurant;
- a tradesman who helps an elderly person with odd jobs, gains influence over that person and removes money from their account; and,
- the person entrusted to purchase lottery tickets on behalf of others.[33]

Despite this guidance on the term position, there is no aid as to the meanings of abuse or financial interests, which presumes that they should take their ordinary meaning. Other terms including dishonesty and intending to make a loss or gain have the same interpretation as discussed above.

The Extent of Fraud

The international profile of fraud has increased significantly during the last two decades;[34] this is due, in part, to instances of global corporate fraud relating to the collapse of the Bank of Credit and Commerce International,[35] Barings Bank,[36]

---

33   Crown Prosecution Service, 'The Fraud Act 2006' (2008) <http://www.cps.gov.uk/legal/d_to_g/fraud_act/> accessed 8 June 2011.

34   For an interesting discussion of the historical development of fraud see G. Robb, *White-Collar Crime in Modern England – Financial Fraud and Business Morality 1845–1929* (Cambridge University Press 1992).

35   For an excellent discussion see A. Arora, 'The Statutory System of the Bank Supervision and the Failure of BCCI' (2006) *Journal of Business Law*, August, 487–510.

36   For a general commentary of the collapse of Barings Bank L. see Proctor, 'The Barings Collapse: A Regulatory Failure, or a Failure of Supervision?' (1997) *Brooklyn Journal of International Law*, 22, 735–767.

Enron[37] and WorldCom.[38] Additionally, there have been a number of fraudulent schemes that have targeted individuals including the Ponzi fraud scheme by Bernard Madoff.[39] Large-scale fraud has also occurred in the European Union (EU) following the collapse of Parmalat and Vivendi,[40] and Jerome Karivels fraudulent investments that cost SocGEN £3.7 billion.[41] The USA has witnessed high profile frauds including Adelphia Communications, Qwest Communications International Inc, America Online, Xerox and Tyco International.[42] Furthermore, as a result of the recent global financial crisis, mortgage fraud has become another major worldwide concern. For example, the Federal Bureau of Investigation, citing research by The Prieston Group, has estimated that the annual level of mortgage fraud in the USA is between $4–6 billion.[43] Additionally, the USA has also seen an increase in the number of ponzi fraud schemes including Bernard Madoff and Alan Stanford.[44] In 2008, Bernard Madoff was arrested by federal agents after being accused of orchestrating one of the largest ponzi frauds ever encountered in the USA. The impact of the fraud is extensive as noted by Nunziato 'it [the fraud] is estimated that thousands of investors lost somewhere between twenty and sixty-five billion dollars. Madoff purported to invest the savings of some four thousand clients, and these investors spanned across forty-eight of the fifty states, as well as throughout Europe, Latin America, and Asia.'[45] The UK has also experienced

---

37   Generally see T. Hurst, 'A Post-Enron Examination of Corporate Governance Problems in the Investment Company Industry' (2006) *Company Lawyer*, 27(2), 41–49.

38   See J. Sidak, 'The Failure of Good Intentions: The WorldCom Fraud and the Collapse of American Telecommunications After Deregulation',(2003) *Yale Journal on Regulation*, 20, 207–261.

39   It has been reported that the total amount of losses in the Madoff scandal could have exceeded $50bn. See T. Anderson, H. Lane and M. Fox, 'Consequences and Responses to the Madoff Fraud' (2009) *Journal of International Banking and Regulation*, 24(11), 548–555, 548.

40   M. Abarca, 'The Need for Substantive Regulation on Investor Protection and Corporate Governance in Europe: Does Europe Need a Sarbanes-Oxley?' (2004) *Journal of International Banking Law and Regulation*, 19(11), 419–431, 419.

41   J. Haines, 'The National Fraud Strategy: New Rules to Crack Down on Fraud' (2009) *Company Lawyer*, 30(7), 213.

42   M. Lunt, 'The Extraterritorial Effects of the Sarbanes-Oxley Act 2002' (2006) *Journal of Business Law*, May, 249–266, 249.

43   Federal Bureau Investigation (n/d), 'Mortgage Fraud' <http://www.fbi.gov/hq/mortgage_fraud.htm> accessed 22 April 2010.

44   For a more detailed discussion of these cases see R. Bale and T. Volpe, 'Ponzi schemes and financial fraud regulation' (2011) *Brief*, Summer, 40, 8.

45   M. Nunziato, 'Aiding and abetting, a Madoff family affair: why secondary actors should be held accountable for securities fraud through the restoration of the private right of action for aiding and abetting liability under the federal security laws' (2010) *Albany Law Review*, 73, 603–643 at 603–604.

large scale instances of fraud with examples including, Polly Peck,[46] Independent Insurance,[47] the Mirror Group Pension Scheme,[48] the Guinness share-trading fraud[49] and the collapse of Barlow Clowes.[50]

Despite this collection of large-scale frauds, the calculation of global and/or national fraud, like other types of financial crime, is fraught with methodological difficulties.[51] Indeed, the Fraud Review stated that 'there are no reliable estimates of the cost of fraud to the economy as a whole',[52] although it has been argued that 'in monetary terms, fraud is on a par with Class A drugs.'[53] In 2005, the cost of fraud was conservatively suggested to amount to £13.9 billion in the UK.[54] More recently, the National Fraud Authority noted that the figure was nearer £73 billion.[55] The threat of fraud can therefore not be underestimated and, with suggestions that terrorists are increasingly using it to fund their illegal activities,[56] it is imperative that we have effective anti-fraud policies and procedures.

Policy Background – From Where did the Offence Originate?

The UK's fraud policy can be contrasted with its money laundering and terrorist financing policies due to the lack of international legislative measures from the

---

46   J. Gallagher, J. Lauchlan and M. Steven, 'Polly Peck: The Breaking of an Entrepreneur?' (1996) *Journal of Small Business and Enterprise Development*, 3(1), 3–12. It is important to note that Azil Nadir was convicted of stealing £29m from Polly Peck and subsequently sentenced to ten years imprisonment. See BBC News (23 August 2012), 'Asil Nadir jailed for ten years for Polly Peck thefts' <http://www.bbc.co.uk/news/uk-19352531> accessed 26 September 2012.

47   *R v Bright* [2008] 2 Cr. App. R. (S.) 102.

48   R. Sarker, 'Maxwell: Fraud Trial of the Century' (1996) *Company Lawyer*, 17(4), 116–117.

49   R. Sarker, 'Guinness – Pure Genius' (1994) *Company Lawyer*, 15(10), 310–312.

50   A. Doig, *Fraud* (Willan Publishing 2006, 9–12).

51   Attorney General's Office, *Fraud Review – Final Report* (Attorney General's Office 2006, 21). For a more detailed examination of the problems associated with determining extent of fraud see M. Levi and J. Burrows, 'Measuring the Impact of Fraud in the UK: A Conceptual and Empirical Journey' (2008) *British Journal of Criminology*, 48(3), 293–318.

52   M. Levi and J. Burrows, 'Measuring the Impact of Fraud in the UK: A Conceptual and Empirical Journey' (2008) *British Journal of Criminology*, 48(3), 293–318, 297.

53   R. Sarker, 'Fighting Fraud – A Missed Opportunity?' (2007) *Company Lawyer*, 28(8), 243–244, 243.

54   M. Levi, J. Burrows, M. Fleming and M. Hopkins, *The Nature, Extent and Economic Impact of Fraud in the UK* (ACPO 2007, iii).

55   National Fraud Authority, *Annual Fraud Indicator* (National Fraud Authority 2012, 3).

56   N. Ryder, 'A False Sense of Security? An Analysis of Legislative Approaches to the Prevention of Terrorist Finance in the United States of America and the United Kingdom' (2007) *Journal of Business Law*, November, 821–850, 825.

United Nations and the EU. Both institutions have developed anti-fraud policies that concentrate on their own finances but they have tended to steer away from initiating a global legislative regime. Since 2006, fraud became a major policy goal of the previous Labour government and is now a major concern for the Coalition government. This is due to the publication of the Fraud Review,[57] which was asked to recommend ways to reduce the threat posed by fraud. In particular, the Fraud Review was asked to identify the extent of fraud, what role the government should play to tackle fraud and how it could obtain value for money.[58] Unsurprisingly and in light of our comments above, the Review was unable to accurately outline the extent of fraud. In relation to its second task, however, it concluded that the government has two functions: i) to protect public money from fraudsters; and ii) to protect consumers and businesses against fraud. The Review recommended that the government should adopt a holistic approach towards fraud and develop a national strategy. Furthermore, it recommended the creation of the NFA to develop and implement the strategy. It also suggested that a National Fraud Reporting Centre should be created so that businesses and individuals could report fraud. The National Fraud Intelligence Bureau (NFIB) is the agency dedicated to analysing and assessing fraud, employing analysts from both law enforcement and the private sector. The Review also suggested that a national-led police authority should be established based on the City of London Police Force.[59]

In an attempt to carry forward these aims, the NFA was given three objectives:[60] i) to create a criminal justice system that is sympathetic to the needs of the victims of fraud by ensuring that the system operates more effectively and efficiently;[61] ii) to attempt to discourage organized criminals from committing fraud in the UK; and, iii) to increase the public's confidence in the response to fraud.[62] A significant measure introduced by the NFA to achieve this was the publication of the National Fraud Strategy.[63] This provides the NFA with five objectives including, tackling the

---

57   The government announced that it intended to introduce a radical overhaul of the laws on fraud in its 2005 general election manifesto. Labour Party, *Labour Party Manifesto – Britain Forward Not Back* (Labour Party: 2005).

58   Labour Party, *Labour Party Manifesto – Britain Forward Not Back* (Labour Party: 2005, 4–5).

59   Attorney General's Office, *Fraud Review – Final Report* (Attorney General's Office 2006, 10).

60   National Fraud Strategic Authority, *The National Fraud Strategy – A New Approach to Combating Fraud* (National Fraud Strategic Authority 2009, 10).

61   For a more detailed discussion of how this is to be achieved see The Attorney General's Office, *Extending the Powers of the Crown Court to Prevent Fraud and Compensate Victims: A Consultation* (Attorney General's Office 2008).

62   National Fraud Strategic Authority, 'UK Toughens up on Fraudsters With New Anti-Fraud Authority' <http://www.attorneygeneral.gov.uk/NewsCentre/Pages/UK ToughensUpOn%20FraudstersWithNewAnti-FraudAuthority.aspx> accessed 2 October 2008.

63   National Fraud Strategic Authority, *The National Fraud Strategy – A New Approach to Combating Fraud* (National Fraud Strategic Authority 2009, 3).

threat of fraud, acting effectively to pursue fraudsters and holding them to account, improving the support available to victims, reducing the UK's exposure to fraud and targeting action against fraud more effectively.[64] Parallels can, therefore, be drawn between the UK's fraud, money laundering and counter-terrorist financing policies due to the publication of this strategy document.

Prior to the Fraud Act 2006, the UK's legislative framework concerning fraudulent activity comprised of eight statutory deception offences in the Thefts Act of 1968 and 1978 and the common law offence of conspiracy to defraud.[65] The deception offences created by the Theft Acts were difficult to enforce[66] and as stated by Ormerod 'were notoriously technical. Although overlapping, they were over-particularized, creating a hazardous terrain for prosecutors who, in charging, could be tripped up by something as subtle as the fraudster's method of payment. The interpretive difficulties were substantial.'[67] This led to the introduction of the Theft Act 1978, although unfortunately, this did little to rectify the problems.[68] The Home Office noted that it 'is not always clear which offence should be charged, and defendants have successfully argued that the consequences of their particular deceptive behaviour did not fit the definition of the offence with which they have been charged.'[69] In 1998, the then Home Secretary Jack Straw MP asked the Law Commission to examine the law on fraud. Specifically, the Law Commission was asked,

> to examine the law on fraud, and in particular to consider whether it: is readily comprehensible to juries; is adequate for effective prosecution; is fair to potential defendants; meets the need of developing technology including electronic means of transfer; and to make recommendations to improve the law in these respects with all due expedition. In making these recommendations, to consider whether a general offence of fraud would improve the criminal law.[70]

---

64   National Fraud Strategic Authority, *The National Fraud Strategy – A New Approach to Combating Fraud* (National Fraud Strategic Authority 2009, 3).

65   The Theft Act 1986 was the creation of the Criminal Law Revision Committee Theft and Related Offences, Cmnd. 2977, May 1966. Other noteworthy attempts to tackle fraud before the Theft Act were the Prevention of Fraud (Investments) Act 1958 and the Financial Services Act 1986.

66   See generally P. Kiernan and G. Scanlan, 'Fraud and the Law Commission: The Future of Dishonesty' (2003) *Journal of Financial Crime*, 10(3), 199–208.

67   D. Ormerod, 'The Fraud Act 2006 – Criminalising Lying?' (2007) *Criminal Law Review*, 193–219, 200.

68   For a useful discussion of the law of theft see A. Doig, *Fraud* (Willan Publishing 2006, 22–35).

69   A. Doig, *Fraud* (Willan Publishing 2006, 22–35). For a more detailed illustration of this problem see generally *R v Preddy* [1996] AC 815, 831.

70   HC Debates 7 April 1998 c.176-177WA.

In 1999 it published a Consultation Paper which distinguished between two types of fraudulent offences – dishonesty and deception.[71] The Law Commission concluded that while the concerns expressed about the existing law were valid they could be met by extending the existing offences in preference to creating a single offence of fraud.[72] The Law Commission published its final report in 2002 which culminated in the Fraud Bill.[73] The Fraud Act came into force on 15 January 2007[74] and as explained above overhauls and widens the criminal offences available in respect of fraudulent and deceptive behaviour.[75] Dennis argued that the Act 'represents the culmination of a law reform debate that can be traced back more than 30 years.'[76] Scanlan takes the view that the Fraud Act 2006 'provides prosecutors with a broad range offence of fraud which is dishonesty based and which can be committed in a number of ways.'[77] This clearly represents a significant improvement on the statutory offences of the Theft Acts and the common law offences of conspiracy to defraud.

Financial Institutions and Regulatory Bodies

Serious Fraud Office

As with other financial crime offences, there are also a broad range of regulatory agencies that attempt to combat fraud, with the most prominent being the Serious Fraud Office (SFO). This was established following an era of financial deregulation in the 1980s; an era that resulted in London attracting 'foreign criminals, including "mademen" from the US Mafia, the "Cosa Nostra", who were now in London taking advantage of the new climate of enterprise, offering securities scams,

71   The Law Commission, *Legislating the Criminal Code Fraud and Deception – Law Commission Consultation Paper No 155* (Law Commission 1999).

72   The Law Commission also published an informal discussion paper in 2000. See Law Commission, *Informal Discussion Paper: Fraud and Deception – Further Proposals From the Criminal Law Team* (Law Commission 2000).

73   For an analysis of the Law Commission's report see P. Kiernan and G. Scanlan, 'Fraud and the Law Commission: The Future of Dishonesty' (2003) *Journal of Financial Crime*, 10(3), 199–208.

74   The Fraud Act 2006 (Commencement) Order 2006, S.I. 2006/3500.

75   NB: not all of the offences under the Theft Act 1968 have been abolished. For example false accounting (Theft Act 1968, s 17), the liability of company directors (Theft Act 1968, s 18), false statements by company directors (Theft Act 1968, s 19) and dishonest destruction of documents (Theft Act 1968, s 20(1)).

76   I. Dennis, 'Fraud Act 2006' (2007) *Criminal Law Review*, January, 1–2, 1.

77   G. Scanlan, 'Offences Concerning Directors and Officers of a Company: Fraud and Corruption in the United Kingdom – The Present and the Future' (2008) *Journal of Financial Crime*, 15(1), 22–37, 25.

commodity futures trading frauds and other forms of investment rip-offs.'[78] Bosworth-Davies noted that 'almost overnight, London became the fraud capital of Europe and every con-man, snake-oil, salesman, grafter and hustler turned up.'[79] To tackle these problems the government decided to create an independent governmental department which had both investigative and prosecutorial powers.[80] This was achieved through the Criminal Justice Act 1987 which was influenced by the Fraud Trials Committee Report, commonly known as the Roskill Report. The Roskill Committee, set up in 1983, considered the introduction of more effective means of fighting fraud through changes to the law and criminal proceedings. The Committee was asked to 'consider in what ways the conduct of criminal proceedings in England and Wales arising from fraud can be improved and to consider what changes in existing law and procedure would be desirable to secure the just, expeditious and economical disposal of such proceedings.'[81] In its assessment of that situation it criticized the staffing levels of the agencies policing fraud and argued that there was a great deal of overlap between them. Roskill concluded that 'co-operation between different investigating bodies in the UK was inefficient, and the interchange of information or assistance between our law enforcement authorities was unsatisfactory.'[82] The Committee made 112 recommendations, of which all but two were implemented.[83] Its main recommendation was the creation of a new unified organization responsible for the detection, investigation and prosecution of serious fraud cases.

The result was the SFO, which has jurisdiction in England, Wales and Northern Ireland, but not Scotland.[84] It is headed by a director, who is appointed and accountable to the Attorney General. Under the Criminal Justice Act, the SFO has the ability to search property and compel persons to answer questions and produce documents provided they have reasonable grounds to do so.[85] In 2009–10 the SFO had an annual budget of £44.6 million, employed 303 staff and was

---

78   R. Bosworth-Davies, 'Investigating Financial Crime: The Continuing Evolution of the Public Fraud Investigation Role – A Personal Perspective' (2009) *Company Lawyer*, 30(7), 195–199, 196.

79   R. Bosworth-Davies, 'Investigating Financial Crime: The Continuing Evolution of the Public Fraud Investigation Role – A Personal Perspective' (2009) *Company Lawyer*, 30(7), 195–199, 196.

80   See generally R. Wright, 'Fraud after Roskill: A View From the Serious Fraud Office' (2003) *Journal of Financial Crime*, 11(1), 10–16.

81   Roskill, *Fraud Trials Committee Report* (HMSO 1986, 8).

82   Roskill, *Fraud Trials Committee Report* (HMSO 1986, 8).

83   For a detailed commentary of the Roskill Commission see M. Levi, 'The Roskill Fraud Commission Revisited: An Assessment' (2003) *Journal of Financial Crime*, 11(1), 38–44.

84   Criminal Justice Act 1987, s 1.

85   Criminal Justice Act 1987, s 2. It is important to note that the SFO has other investigative and prosecutorial powers under the Fraud Act 2006, the Theft Act 1968, the Companies Act 2006, the Serious Crime Act 2007, the Serious Organised Crime and

working on 86 active cases.[86] Interestingly, its annual budget for 2011–2012 fell to £36.8 million.[87]

It sees its mission as protecting 'society from extensive, deliberate criminal deception which could threaten public confidence in the financial system. We investigate fraud and corruption that requires our investigative expertise and special powers to obtain and assess evidence to successfully prosecute fraudsters, freeze assets and compensate victims.'[88] In determining whether or not to investigate an allegation of fraud, the SFO use the following list of criteria:

1. Does the value of the alleged fraud exceed £1 million?
2. Is there an international element to the fraud?
3. Is it likely to cause widespread public concern?
4. Does the case require specialized knowledge?
5. Does the SFO need to use its investigative powers?

The SFO also considers the seriousness of the case and its complexity and will investigate investment fraud, bribery and corruption, corporate fraud and public sector fraud.

Following a number of high profile failed prosecutions, the effectiveness of the SFO has, however, been questioned. Mahendra, for example, describes the notorious failures of the SFO as reminiscent of 'watching the England cricket team – a victory being so rare and unexpected that it was a cause of national rejoicing.'[89] Indeed, Wright notes that 'because the SFO operates in the spotlight, the beam falls on the unsuccessful as well as the victorious. Indeed it shines with blinding brightness on the ones that get away.'[90] The prosecutorial inadequacies of the SFO were also highlighted by the Review of the Serious Fraud Office.[91] The Review compared the performance of the SFO with the US Attorney's Office for the Southern District of New York and the Manhattan District Attorney's Office and concluded that 'the discrepancies in conviction rates are striking.'[92] The Review noted that between 2003 and 2007 the SFO's average conviction rate was

---

Police Act 2005, the Proceeds of Crime Act 2002 and the Regulation of Investigatory Powers Act 2000.

86 Serious Fraud Office, *Achievements 2009–2010* (Serious Fraud Office 2010, 3).

87 Serious Fraud Office (n/d), 'Our performance' <http://www.sfo.gov.uk/our-work/our-performance.aspx> accessed 26 September 2012.

88 Serious Fraud Office, *SFO Budget 2009–2010* (Serious Fraud Office 2010, 3).

89 B. Mahendra, 'Fighting Serious Fraud' (2002) *New Law Journal*, 152(7020), 289.

90 R. Wright, 'Fraud after Roskill: A View From the Serious Fraud Office' (2003) *Journal of Financial Crime*, 11(1), 10–16, 10.

91 J. de Grazia, *Review of the Serious Fraud Office – Final Report* (Serious Fraud Office 2008).

92 J. de Grazia, *Review of the Serious Fraud Office – Final Report* (Serious Fraud Office 2008, 3–4).

61 per cent, while the conviction rates in the two aforementioned cases studies were 91 per cent and 97 per cent respectively.[93]

In an attempt to try and allay some of this criticism and in the wake of the collapse of the Jubilee Line fraud trial,[94] in March 2005 the Crown Prosecution Service, two and a half years later, announced the creation of the Fraud Prosecution Unit. This is now referred to as the Fraud Prosecution Division.[95] The Division limits its involvement to those suspected cases involving the corruption of public officials, fraud on government departments, fraud on overseas governments, complicated money laundering cases and any other matter that it feels is within its remit. Such cases must also exceed £750,000.[96] In October 2008, HM Crown Prosecution Service Inspectorate concluded there 'has been a positive direction of travel in terms of successful outcomes (convictions), which stood at a creditable 85% of the defendants proceeded against in 2007–2008; underlying casework quality, which is characterized by strong legal decision-making and active case progression; and the development of management systems and leadership profile.'[97] Bosworth Davies has therefore taken the view that 'it [the SFO] was not the great success that Roskill envisaged, and its activities were marked out by 20 years of professional jealousy and internal squabbling among its component teams.'[98] Conversely, the performance of the SFO is hampered by the complexity of the crimes it investigates.[99] Raphael notes that the SFO is 'always kept short of resources and instead of being a unified fraud office, was just another, more sophisticated, prosecution agency.'[100]

---

93   J. de Grazia, *Review of the Serious Fraud Office – Final Report* (Serious Fraud Office 2008).

94   J. Masters, 'Fraud and Money Laundering: The Evolving Criminalisation of Corporate Non-Compliance' (2008) *Journal of Money Laundering Control*, 11(2), 103–122, 104.

95   Crown Prosecution Service, 'DPP Announces New Head of Fraud Prosecution Division' (2009) <http://www.cps.gov.uk/news/press_releases/136_09/> accessed 22 January 2010.

96   Crown Prosecution Service, 'DPP Announces New Head of Fraud Prosecution Division' (2009) <http://www.cps.gov.uk/news/press_releases/136_09/> accessed 22 January 2010.

97   HM Crown Prosecution Service Inspectorate, *Review of the Fraud Prosecution Service* (HM Crown Prosecution Service Inspectorate 2008, 5).

98   R. Bosworth-Davies, 'Investigating Financial Crime: The Continuing Evolution of the Public Fraud Investigation Role – A Personal Perspective' (2009) *Company Lawyer*, 30(7), 195–199, 198.

99   R. Wright, 'Fraud after Roskill: A View From the Serious Fraud Office' (2003) *Journal of Financial Crime*, 11(1), 10–16, 10.

100   R. Wright, 'Fraud after Roskill: A View From the Serious Fraud Office' (2003) *Journal of Financial Crime*, 11(1), 10–16, 10.

Financial Services Authority

In addition to the SFO, a secondary agency that tackles fraud is the Financial Services Authority (FSA).[101] Its fraud policy can be divided into four parts: i) a direct approach;[102] ii) increased supervisory activity;[103] iii) promoting a more joined up approach;[104] and iv) FSA Handbook modifications.[105] The FSA, for example, requires senior management to take responsibility for managing their own risk of fraud by having in place effective controls and instruments that are proportionate to the risks they face.[106] It also works to improve whistle-blowing arrangements, amend the financial crime material contained within the FSA Handbook and ensure that the financial services sector, trade associations and the government continue to communicate the risk of fraud to their customers and consumers.[107]

To implement this policy the FSA has been given an extensive array of enforcement powers, some of which it has utilized to combat fraud. It is a prosecuting authority for both money laundering, and certain fraud related offences,[108] and has the power to impose a financial penalty where it establishes that there has been a contravention by an authorized person of any requirement.[109] For example, the FSA fined Capita Financial Administration Limited £300,000

---

101 Financial Services Authority, *Developing Our Policy on Fraud and Dishonesty – Discussion Paper 26* (Financial Services Authority 2003).

102 This would have seen the FSA focusing its efforts on specific types of fraud or dishonesty which constitute the greatest areas of concern, and where they can make a difference.

103 This would include, for example, considering the firms' systems and controls against fraud in more detail in terms of supervisory work, including how firms collect data on fraud and dishonesty.

104 The third approach would involve the FSA liaising closely with the financial sector and other interested parties in order to achieve a more effective approach towards fraud prevention in the financial services sector.

105 The final proposed method would include codification and clarification of the relevant fraud risk management provisions of the Handbook.

106 Financial Services Authority, 'The FSA's New Approach to Fraud – Fighting Fraud in Partnership', speech by Philip Robinson, 26 October 2004 <http://www.fsa.gov. uk/library/communication/speeches/2004/sp208.shtml> accessed 3 August 2011.

107 Financial Services Authority, 'The FSA's New Approach to Fraud – Fighting Fraud in Partnership', speech by Philip Robinson, 26 October 2004 <http://www.fsa.gov. uk/Pages/Library/Communication/Speeches/2004/SP208.shtml> accessed 3 August 2011.

108 For example, in 2008 the FSA successfully prosecuted William Radclyffe for offences under the Theft Acts, the Financial Services Act 1986 and the Financial Services and Markets Act 2000. Financial Services Authority, 'Fake Stockbroker sentenced to 15 months' <http://www.fsa.gov.uk/pages/Library/Communication/PR/2008/011.shtml> accessed 28 March 2010.

109 Financial Services and Markets Act 2000, s 206 (1).

for poor anti-fraud controls in 2006,[110] and in May 2007 fined BNP Paribas Private Bank £350,000 for weaknesses in its systems and controls which allowed a senior employee to fraudulently transfer £1.4 million out of the firm's clients' accounts without permission.[111] Furthermore it has fined the Nationwide Building Society £980,000 for 'failing to have effective systems and controls to manage its information security risks',[112] and Norwich Union Life, £1.26 million for not 'having effective systems and controls in place to protect customers' confidential information and manage its financial crime risks.'[113]

In addition to fining, the FSA also has the power to ban authorized persons and firms from undertaking any regulated activity.[114] For example, in 2008 the FSA fined and/or banned 12 mortgage brokers for submitting false mortgage applications, prohibited another 24 brokers from working and issued fines in excess of £500,000.[115] In the first half of 2009, the level of fines imposed by the FSA had already exceeded this figure. In addition to imposing sanctions on fraudsters, the FSA has also enabled victims of fraud to recover losses suffered at the hands of companies involved in share fraud activity. For example, in February 2010 the FSA recovered £270,000 for defrauded investors who were advised to buy shares in Eduvest plc.[116] Although historically the FSA has concentrated is financial crime policy on money laundering, largely at the expense of fraud, in order to meet its statutory objective to reduce financial crime, its recent efforts to tackle fraud, especially mortgage fraud, have been fast tracked.

---

110   Financial Services Authority, 'FSA Fines Capita Financial Administrators Limited £300,000 in First Anti-Fraud Controls Case' <http://www.fsa.gov.uk/pages/Library/Communication/PR/2006/019.shtml> accessed 16 March 2006.

111   Financial Services Authority, *Financial Services Authority Annual Report 2007/2008* (Financial Services Authority 2008, 23).

112   Financial Services Authority, 'FSA Fines Nationwide £980,000 for Information Security Lapses' <http://www.fsa.gov.uk/pages/Library/Communication/PR/2007/021.shtml> accessed 14 February 2007.

113   Financial Services Authority, 'FSA Fines Norwich Union Life £1.26m' <http://www.fsa.gov.uk/pages/Library/Communication/PR/2007/130.shtml> accessed 4 November 2009.

114   Financial Services and Markets Act 2000, s 56.

115   National Fraud Strategic Authority, *The National Fraud Strategy – A New Approach to Combating Fraud* (National Fraud Strategic Authority 2009, 16).

116   Financial Services Authority, 'FSA Returns £270,000 to Victims of Share Fraud' <http://www.fsa.gov.uk/pages/Library/Communication/PR/2010/032.shtml> accessed 21 March 2010.

National Fraud Authority

The most recent agency created to tackle fraud is the NFA.[117] The objectives of the NFA are threefold: i) creating a criminal justice system that is sympathetic to the needs of fraud victims by ensuring that the system operates more effectively and efficiently;[118] ii) discouraging organized criminals from committing fraud in the UK; and iii) increasing the public's confidence in the response to fraud.[119] Professor Barry Rider states that the NFA,

> ... has an impressive list of strategic aims: tackling the key threats of fraud that pose the greatest harm to the United Kingdom; the pursuit of fraudsters effectively, holding them to account and improving victim support; the reduction of the UK's exposure to fraud by building, sharing and acting on knowledge; and securing the international collaboration necessary to protect the UK from fraud.[120]

The NFA's Interim Chief Executive Sandra Quinn has boldly claimed that 'we can respond quickly and effectively to the fraud threat.'[121] This level of optimism was not shared by Bosworth-Davies who stated that the NFA 'will last about as long as the unlamented Asset Recovery Agency.'[122] Despite this pessimism, an important measure introduced by the NFA was the publication of the National Fraud Strategy, which is an integral part of the government's fraud policy.[123] Under this strategy the NFA is required to,

1. tackle the threats presented by fraud;
2. act effectively to pursue fraudsters and hold them to account;
3. improve the support available to victims;

---

117   National Fraud Strategic Authority, *The National Fraud Strategy – A New Approach to Combating Fraud* (National Fraud Strategic Authority 2009, 10).

118   For a more detailed discussion of how this is to be achieved see The Attorney General's Office, *Extending the Powers of the Crown Court to Prevent Fraud and Compensate Victims: A Consultation* (Attorney General's Office 2008).

119   National Fraud Strategic Authority, 'UK Toughens up on Fraudsters With New Anti-Fraud Authority' <http://www.attorneygeneral.gov.uk/NewsCentre/Pages/UK ToughensUpOn%20FraudstersWithNewAnti-FraudAuthority.aspx> accessed 2 October 2008.

120   B. Rider, 'A Bold Step?' (2009) *Company Lawyer*, 30(1), 1–2 at 1.

121   National Fraud Strategic Authority, *The National Fraud Strategy – A New Approach to Combating Fraud* (National Fraud Strategic Authority 2009, 16).

122   R. Bosworth-Davies, 'Investigating Financial Crime: The Continuing Evolution of the Public Fraud Investigation Role – A Personal Perspective' (2009) *Company Lawyer*, 30(7), 195–199, 199.

123   National Fraud Strategic Authority, *The National Fraud Strategy – A New Approach to Combating Fraud* (National Fraud Strategic Authority 2009, 3).

4. reduce the UK's exposure to fraud by building on the nation's capability to prevent it; and,

5. target action against fraud more effectively by building, sharing and acting on knowledge and securing the international collaboration necessary to protect the UK from fraud.[124]

Despite the fanfare announcement by the government that it had created the NFA, the one fundamental question which must be asked, is, will it actually make any difference to the overall effectiveness of the UK's fraud policy. If we are to believe that the extent of fraud in the UK is somewhere between £14–£30 billion, how is it possible for one agency to make any valuable dent in this statistic if it only has a budget of £29 million over a three year period. More resources are therefore urgently required.

Office of Fair Trading

Another secondary agency is the Office of Fair Trading (OFT) which 'is chiefly concerned with the protection of consumers. It also regulates competition amongst businesses but this is approached from a consumer protection perspective.'[125] The OFT has three regulatory objectives: i) investigation of whether markets are working well for consumers; ii) enforcement of competition laws; and iii) enforcement of consumer protection laws. The OFT has its own fraud policy,[126] which is aimed at informing and protecting consumers from fraudulent scams.[127] Furthermore, the OFT works and co-operates with other agencies such as the SFO,[128] and liaises with overseas agencies.[129] Other secondary agencies include the Serious Organised Crime Agency which acts as the UK's Financial Intelligence Unit, and plays an

---

124   National Fraud Strategic Authority, *The National Fraud Strategy – A New Approach to Combating Fraud* (National Fraud Strategic Authority 2009, 16).

125   P. Kiernan, 'The Regulatory Bodies Fraud: Its Enforcement in the Twenty-First Century' (2003) *Company Lawyer*, 24(10), 293–299, 295.

126   Office of Fair Trading, *Prevention of Fraud Policy* (Office of Fair Trading).

127   See for example Office of Fair Trading, *Scamnesty 2010 Campaign Strategy* (Office of Fair Trading 2009).

128   See for example Office of Fair Trading, *Memorandum of Understanding Between the Office of Fair Trading and the Director of the Serious Fraud Office* (Office of Fair Trading 2003).

129   See for example Office of Fair Trading, 'OFT and Nigerian Financial Crime Squad Join Forces to Combat Spam Fraud' (2005) <http://www.oft.gov.uk/news-and-updates/press/2005/210-05> accessed 2 August 2010.

integral part in the fight against financial crime and HM Revenue and Customs who deals with issues such as VAT fraud, alcohol fraud[130] and oil fraud.[131]

Effectiveness

In the UK, for example, there is a considerable degree of overlap between the SFO and the FSA, with both having extensive investigative and prosecutorial powers that seek to achieve the same objective. The failures of the SFO are well documented, while the FSA's effectiveness must be questioned because of its obsession with combating money laundering. It is therefore recommended that a single financial crime agency should be established to co-ordinate the UK's fraud policy with extensive investigative and prosecutorial powers. Such an idea was mooted by Fisher who recommended the creation of a 'single "Financial Crimes Enforcement Agency" to tackle serious fraud, corruption and financial market crimes.'[132] This recommendation has been supported by the Conservative Party while in opposition before the 2010 General Election, who suggested the establishment of an Economic Crime Agency (ECA) that would do the work of the SFO, the Fraud Prosecution Service and the OFT. In 2010, the then Shadow Chancellor George Osborne MP stated 'we are very, very bad at prosecuting white-collar crime. We have six different government departments, eight different agencies and the result is that these crimes go unpunished.'[133] Following the 2010 general election, the coalition government outlined its desire to create a single agency to tackle financial crime, stating, as mentioned in Chapter 2, 'We take white collar crime as seriously as other crime, so we will create a single agency to take on the work of tackling serious economic crime that is currently done by, among others, the Serious Fraud Office, Financial Services Authority and Office of Fair Trading.'[134] While such rhetoric sounds promising, the financial crisis could have scuppered the government's plans to create such an agency.[135] The Fraud Advisory Panel writing in March 2010 took the view that, due to the current climate, the time

---

130   See for example HM Revenue and Customs, 'Renewal of the "Tackling Alcohol Fraud" Strategy' (HM Revenue and Customs 2009).

131   See HM Customs and Excise, *Oils Fraud Strategy: Summary of Consultation Responses Regulatory Impact Assessment* (HM Customs and Excise 2002).

132   J. Fisher, *Fighting Fraud and Financial Crime: A New Architecture for the Investigation and Prosecution of Serious Fraud, Corruption and Financial Market Crimes* (Policy Exchange 2010, 3).

133   Times Online 'Conservatives Confirm Plans for Single Economic Crime Agency' <http://timesonline.typepad.com/law/2010/04/conservatives-confirm-plans-for-single-economic-crime-agency.html> accessed 26 April 2010.

134   HM Government, *The Coalition: Our Programme for Government* (HM Government 2010, 9).

135   D. Leigh and R. Evans, 'Cost of New Economic Crime Agency Could Prove Prohibitive' <http://www.guardian.co.uk/business/2010/jun/02/economic-crime-agency-scheme-cost> accessed 12 July 2010.

is just not right for an ECA.[136] However, as highlighted in Chapter 2, the Coalition government has announced its intention to create the National Crime Agency that will oversee and manage the UK's fight against financial crime. Therefore, the anti-fraud agencies discussed in this chapter face an extremely uncertain future.[137]

Financial Intelligence

The UK has a strong history of utilizing financial intelligence as part of its broader financial crime strategy, a point clearly illustrated by the anti-money laundering reporting provisions of the Proceeds of Crime Act (POCA) 2002 and the duty to report any suspected instances of terrorist financing under the Terrorism Act 2000. The Fraud Review noted that,

> Fraud is massively underreported. Fraud is not a police priority, so even when reports are taken, little is done with them. Many victims therefore, don't report at all. So the official crime statistics display just the tip of the iceberg and developing a strategic law enforcement response is impossible because the information to target investigations does not exist.[138]

If a suspected fraud is committed against a bank it is reported to its Money Laundering Reporting Officer (MLRO). Successful frauds are reported to SOCA. Conversely, it is the decision for individual banks to determine whether or not to report the fraud to the police. In 2007, the Home Office announced that victims of credit card, cheque and online banking fraud are able to report the matter to their banks and other financial institutions.[139] However, although still important, the obligation to report allegations of fraud is not as straight forward. The primary statutory obligation for reported instances of fraud is contained under the POCA 2002.[140] It is a criminal offence under the Act to fail to disclose via a Suspicious Activity Report (SAR) where there is knowledge, suspicion or reasonable grounds to know or suspect, that a person is laundering the proceeds of criminal conduct. Successful fraud is defined as money laundering for the purpose of this Act.[141] Furthermore, the Act specifies that members of the regulated sector are required to

---

136   See generally Fraud Advisory Panel, *Roskill Revisited: Is There a Case for a Unified Fraud Prosecution Office?* (Fraud Advisory Panel 2010).

137   The legislative proposals to create the NCA were published Crime and Courts Bill 2012. This is not expected to receive Royal Assent until 2013.

138   Attorney General's Office, *Fraud Review – Final Report* (Attorney General's Office 2006, 7).

139   Home Office, 'Fraud' <http://www.crimereduction.homeoffice.gov.uk/fraud/fraud17.htm> accessed 7 December 2009.

140   Proceeds of Crime Act 2002, s 330.

141   It is important to note that the Proceeds of Crime Act 2002 applies to serious crime, which includes fraud.

report their suspicions as soon as reasonably practical to SOCA via their MLRO. There is no legal obligation to report unsuccessful or attempted frauds to the authorities because any attempted frauds will not give rise to any legal criminal proceedings, and therefore fall outside the scope of the mandatory reporting obligations under the POCA 2002. Ultimately, the decision whether or not an investigation will be conducted lies with the police. The Home Office has advised that the police should only investigate where there are good grounds to believe that a criminal offence has been committed.[142]

Furthermore, members of the regulated sector are obliged to report fraud to the FSA in the following circumstances:

1. it becomes aware that an employee may have committed a fraud against one of its customers; or
2. it becomes aware that a person, whether or not employed by it, may have committed a fraud against it; or
3. it considers that any person, whether or not employed by it, is acting with intent to commit a fraud against it; or
4. it identifies irregularities in its accounting or other records, whether or not there is evidence of fraud; or
5. it suspects that one of its employees may be guilty of serious misconduct concerning his honesty or integrity and which is connected with the firm's regulated activities or ancillary activities.[143]

In determining whether or not the matter is significant, the firm must consider:

1. the size of any monetary loss or potential monetary loss to itself or its customers (either in terms of a single incident or group of similar or related incidents);
2. the risk of reputational loss to the firm; and
3. whether the incident or a pattern of incidents reflects weaknesses in the firm's internal controls.[144]

Such notifications are required 'as the FSA needs to be aware of the types of fraudulent and irregular activity which are being attempted or undertaken, and to act, if necessary, to prevent effects on consumers or other firms.'[145] To help with this endeavour, each notification 'should provide all relevant and significant details of the incident or suspected incident of which the firm is aware.'[146] Furthermore,

---

142   Home Office, *Home Office Circular 47/2004 Priorities for the Investigation of Fraud Cases* (Home Office 2004).
143   SUP 15.3.17R.
144   SUP 15.3.18G.
145   SUP 15.3.19G.
146   SUP 15.3.19G.

if the firm has suffered significant financial losses as a result of the incident, or may suffer reputational loss, the FSA will question 'whether the incident suggests weaknesses in the firm's internal controls.'[147] If the fraud is committed by an FSA Approved Person,[148] the FSA has the power to withdraw its authorization and the possibility of prosecution becomes real.

It can therefore be seen that the UK's policy towards fraud has gained momentum. This has been evidenced by both the previous government and a willingness shared by the new coalition administration to continue with such endeavors. However, there is still scope for improvement in the initiatives that have been introduced to tackle fraud. For example, the effectiveness of the criminalization of fraud has been limited by the inadequacies of the Theft Acts and the common law offences, a position that has been improved by the introduction of the Fraud Act. However, concerns still remain about the enforcement of these offences by the SFO and the Crown Prosecution Service, following the collapse of several high profile instances of fraud. While it is simply too early to determine if the Fraud Act has made any difference to the prosecution of fraudsters, the coalition government must be commended for recognizing the need to create a single ECA as long as this does actually happen. In addition to the creation of such an agency the government also needs to tackle the reporting of instances of suspicious fraudulent activities, which is fragmented with a number of different reporting mechanisms available, causing yet more confusion and delay.

Sentencing and Recovery

Under section 1(3) of the Fraud Act 2006, the maximum term of imprisonment for a fraud offence is 10 years. This can be contrasted with the USA, where for securities fraud, mail fraud and wire fraud the maximum is 20 years' imprisonment.[149] As with other financial offences an offender can also receive an unlimited fine. Between 2008 and 2009 there were 14,238 prosecutions in the UK under sections 1-4 of the Fraud Act 2006; resulting in 11,133 convictions and a conviction rate of 78.2 per cent.[150] Furthermore, in 2010/11 the SFO took 17 complex fraud cases to trial achieving at least one conviction in every case. This included 31 defendants (both individual and corporate) and amounted in a conviction rate of 84 per cent.[151]

---

147   SUP 15.3.20G.

148   An approved person is an individual who has been approved by the FSA to perform controlled functions, which relates to the carrying on of a regulated activity by a firm. See Financial Services and Markets Act 2000, s 59.

149   Australian Government and Australian Institute of Criminology, *Charges and Offences of Money Laundering* Transnational Crime Brief No. 4 (Australian Institute of Criminology 2008).

150   HL Deb, 18 May 2011, c338W.

151   HC Deb, 24 May 2011, c775.

When contrasted with the 50 per cent conviction rate for money laundering (see Chapter 2), this is significantly better.

The court also has the ability to use the Ancillary Orders of confiscation (see Chapter 2), compensation (the payment of monies to the victims involved), financial reporting and disqualification. A financial reporting order is found under sections 76–79 of the Serious Organised Crime and Police Act 2005 and requires the offender to make regular reports to the authorities about his financial affairs for up to 20 years.[152] Failure to provide the necessary reports or the inclusion of false or misleading information can lead to a separate criminal conviction and a further custodial term.[153] Furthermore, if the offence was in connection with 'the promotion, formation, management, liquidation or striking off of a company, with the receivership of the company's property or with his being an administrative receiver of a company',[154] the court can disqualify the offender from acting as a director of a company for a specified period of time. The disqualification, found under the Company Directors Disqualification Act 1986, prevents the offender from acting as a company director, even if the job title is different, or from instructing others to act on his behalf. While the offender can work for a company, without the court's permission, he cannot be concerned in the promotion, formation or management of the company; act as an insolvency practitioner; act as a receiver of a company's property; or take part in the promotion, formation or management of a limited liability partnership. Disqualification can last for a maximum period of 15 years and is thus a clear example of incapacitating the offender to prevent further offending behaviour. Anyone found to be in contravention of the order is liable for an additional criminal offence with a maximum imprisonment period of two years.[155]

Unlike the financial crimes previously considered, a fair amount of judicial guidance does exist in relation to deciding what length of sentence should be imposed for the offence of fraud. Originally, this was provided in the form of Court of Appeal guideline judgments.[156] For example in *R v Feld*[157] factors held to be relevant to sentencing fraud included,

- The amount involved and the manner in which the fraud is carried out.
- The period over which the fraud is carried out and the degree of persistence with which it is carried out.

152　If the person was given life imprisonment. Otherwise, the maximum period is 15 years – Serious Organised Crime and Police Act 2005, s 76.

153　Serious Organised Crime and Police Act 2005, s 79.

154　Company Directors Disqualification Act 1986, s 2.

155　Company Directors Disqualification Act 1986, s 13.

156　See *R v Barrick* [1985] 7 Cr. App. Rep. (S) 142; *R v Stewart* [1987] 2 All E.R. 383; *R v Clark* [1988] 2 Cr. App. Rep. (S) 95; *R v Stevens and others* [1993] 14 Cr. App. R. (S) 372; *R v Palk and Smith* [1997] 2 Cr. App R. (S) 167; *R v Feld* [1999] 1 Cr. App. R. (S) 1; and, *R v Roach* [2002] 1 Cr. App. R. (S) 12.

157　[1999] 1 Cr. App. R. (S) 1.

- The position of the accused within the company and his measure of control over it.
- Any abuse of trust which is revealed.
- The consequences of the fraud.
- The effect on public confidence in the City and the integrity of commercial life.
- The loss to small investors, which will aggravate the fraud.
- The personal benefit derived by a defendant.
- The plea.
- The age and character of the defendant.[158]

Moreover in *R v Barrick*,[159] Lane L.C.J. set out a number of factors which should be taken into account when sentencing professional people for offences of fraud,

- The quality and degree of trust reposed in the offender including his rank.
- The period over which the fraud or the thefts have been perpetrated.
- The use to which the dishonestly taken money or property was put;
- The effect upon the victim.
- The impact of the offences on the public and public confidence.
- The effect on fellow-employees or partners.
- The effect on the offender himself.
- His own history.
- Those matters of mitigation special to himself such as illness; being placed under great strain by excessive responsibility or the like; where, as sometimes happens, there has been a long delay, say over two years, between his being confronted with his dishonesty by his professional body or the police and the start of his trial; finally, any help given by him to the police.[160]

Interestingly, Lane L.C.J. also warned how 'professional men should expect to be punished as severely as others: in some cases, more severely'[161] and gave some recommendations as to appropriate sentencing starting points,[162] which were subsequently updated in *R v Clark*:[163]

---

158   [1999] 1 Cr. App. R. (S) 4.
159   [1985] 7 Cr. App. Rep. (S) 142.
160   [1985] 7 Cr. App. Rep. (S) 147.
161   [1985] 7 Cr. App. Rep. (S) 143; this was also supported in the later case of *R v Stewart* [1987] 2 All E.R. 383.
162   'Where the amounts involved could not be described as small but were less than £10,000 or thereabouts, terms of imprisonment ranging from the very short up to about eighteen months were appropriate. Cases involving sums of between about £10,000 and £50,000 would merit a term of about two or three years' imprisonment. Where greater sums were involved, for example those over £100,000, then a term of three and a half to four years would be justified'. [1985] 7 Cr. App. Rep. (S) 143–144.
163   [1988] 2 Cr. App. Rep. (S) 95.

- Where the amount is not small, but is less than £17,500, terms of imprisonment from the very short up to 21 months will be appropriate;
- Cases involving sums between £17,500 and £100,000, will merit two to three years;
- Cases involving sums between £100,000 and £250,000, will merit three to four years;
- Cases involving between £250,000 and £1 million will merit between five and nine years;
- Cases involving £1 million or more will merit 10 years or more.
- Where the sums involved are exceptionally large, and not stolen on a single occasion, or the dishonesty is directed at more than one victim or group of victims, consecutive sentences may be called for.[164]

Other guideline judgments relevant to fraud include *R v Palk and Smith*[165] (fraudulent trading); *R v Stevens and others*[166] (mortgage fraud); and *R v Roach*[167] (obtaining a money transfer by deception).

In addition to these judgments, and since 25 October 2009, a Sentencing Council Guideline[168] also exists and in accordance with *R v Tongue (Ross)* 'once guidelines have been issued it should be the exception rather than the rule to cite previous cases.'[169] As with the majority of offences, the first and primary consideration when sentencing fraud offences is the seriousness of the offending behaviour. This is measured by looking at both the culpability of the offender and the level of harm caused or at risk of being caused. While, as discussed above, the primary offence of fraud does not require a result to have occurred, i.e. that a loss or gain was actually achieved, the larger the loss or gain the more serious the offence will be considered to be. Other factors which will be taken into account include 'the degree of planning [and] the determination with which the offender carried out the offence';[170]

- The impact of the offence on the victim;
- Harm to persons other than the direct victim;
- Erosion of public confidence;

---

164   [1988] 2 Cr. App. Rep. (S) 100.

165   [1997] 2 Cr. App. R. (S) 167.

166   [1993] 14 Cr. App. R. (S) 372.

167   [2002] 1 Cr. App. R. (S) 12.

168   Sentencing Guidelines Council, *Sentencing for Fraud – Statutory Offences Definitive Guideline* (Sentencing Guidelines Secretariat 2009).

169   [2007] EWCA Crim 561.

170   Sentencing Guidelines Council, *Sentencing for Fraud – Statutory Offences Definitive Guideline* (London: Sentencing Guidelines Secretariat, 2009, 5).

- Any physical harm or risk of physical harm to the direct victim or another person;
- Difference between loss intended and resulting loss; and
- Legitimate entitlement to part or all of the amount obtained.[171]

The Council has also identified four factors which it believes are particularly relevant when undertaking a sentencing decision for a fraud offence, including: i) the number of people involved in the offence and the role of the offender; ii) whether or not it involved the use of another person's identity; iii) whether or not the offending was carried out over a significant period of time; and, iv) whether there was a lasting effect on the victim.[172]

Finally, the guideline provides starting points and sentencing ranges for a number of fraudulent offences. For example, in the case of banking and insurance fraud and obtaining credit through fraud, where the offence was 'fraudulent from the outset, professionally planned *and either* fraud carried out over a significant period of time *or* multiple frauds' [emphasis in original],[173] the starting point,[174] whereby the amount of money obtained was £500,000 or more, is five years in custody; with the range set at four to seven years. Bearing in mind that the Court of Appeal in *R v Clark* recommended five to nine years for amounts ranging from £250,000 to £1 million the Guideline would thus appear to be more lenient than judicial suggestions. Conversely at the other end of the spectrum, where the offence is one of a 'single fraudulent transaction, not fraudulent from the outset',[175] and involves a monetary amount of less that £5,000, the starting point[176] is a financial penalty; with the range identified as being from a fine to a low level community order. Sentencing ranges and starting points are also provided for confidence frauds; possessing, making or supplying articles for use in fraud; revenue fraud (against HM Revenue and Customs) and benefit fraud.

Sentencing examples for fraud range from the infamous cases as cited above, to the more mundane. For instance, in the Independence Insurance fraud, Michael Bright was sentenced to two terms of seven years for two counts of conspiracy to defraud, with each term to run concurrently and disqualified from being a director for 12 years. As the offences took place before The Fraud Act 2006 existed, the 10 year sentence, as mentioned above, was not open to the sentencing judge in terms of the fraud, although the maximum sentence available for conspiracy to defraud

---

171   Sentencing Guidelines Council, *Sentencing for Fraud – Statutory Offences Definitive Guideline* (London: Sentencing Guidelines Secretariat, 2009, 6–7).

172   Sentencing Guidelines Council, *Sentencing for Fraud – Statutory Offences Definitive Guideline* (London: Sentencing Guidelines Secretariat, 2009, 8).

173   Sentencing Guidelines Council, *Sentencing for Fraud – Statutory Offences Definitive Guideline* (London: Sentencing Guidelines Secretariat, 2009, 24).

174   based on a value of £750,000.

175   Sentencing Guidelines Council, *Sentencing for Fraud – Statutory Offences Definitive Guideline* (London: Sentencing Guidelines Secretariat, 2009, 24).

176   Based on a value of £2,500.

was, nevertheless, 10 years.[177] Despite this term being available, and the fact that the sentencing judge said that the offence committed by Bright was 'so grave' and 'altogether beyond the scope that Parliament could have had in mind when fixing such a maximum' and 'if any offence should attract the maximum penalty, it is this one';[178] the maximum term was not given. This was because it was decided that while the conspiracy charge was the most appropriate for trial purposes, the lesser charge of fraudulent trading fully covered the substance of the offences in question, and thus it should only be this maximum (seven years[179]) which should be available. Notwithstanding this, upon receiving the lesser sentence, Bright appealed,[180] arguing that it was unjust to use the full maxima and that mitigating factors of old age, good character and poor health had not been taken into account. The Court of Appeal dismissed the appeal, arguing that the crime had been one of 'utmost gravity',[181] but interestingly also stated that the sentencing court had been wrong in limiting the original sentence to one of seven years. While the court had the power to increase the sentence, it remained unchanged and arguably Bright was lucky that this increase was not imposed, especially when as per the guidelines above, his crime included professional offending; was a planned offence; was committed with a high level of culpability; and caused a vast amount of harm. This leniency is further supported by *R v Clark*, which not only states that 10 years' imprisonment is appropriate where the case involves amounts of £1 million or more but also suggests that the use of consecutive sentencing may have been more appropriate than the use of concurrent sentences. A more just sentence, therefore, would arguably have been in the region of 14 to 20 years.

In contrast to money laundering there would therefore appear to be greater reluctance by the courts to impose the maximum available sentence in fraud cases. This is further supported by the fact that the perpetrators in the Guinness share-trading fraud case received sentences of five years[182] (Ernest Saunders), 30 months[183] (Anthony Parnes), 12 months and a fine of £5 million (Gerald Ronson) and a fine of £4 million (Jack Lyons). Other cases include Carl Cushnie (former Chairman of Versailles) who, for a £150 million[184] fraud, was jailed for six years and disqualified from being a director for 10 years; Fred Clough (Finance Director of

---

177   Criminal Justice Act 1987, s 12(3).

178   M. Leroux, 'Michael Bright Gets Maximum Seven Years From Independent Insurance Fraud' (*The Times*, 25 October) <http://business.timesonline.co.uk/tol/business/industry_sectors/banking_and_finance/article2733660.ece> accessed 10 June 2011.

179   Although this has now been increased to 10 years – Companies Act 2006, s 993.

180   *R v Bright* [2008] 2 Cr. App. R. (S) 102.

181   In October 2008, Michael Bright also paid £1,258,467.04 pursuit to a confiscation order – *R v Bright* [2008] EWCA Crim 462, para 33.

182   Although this was halved on appeal.

183   This was reduced on appeal to 21 months.

184   Although was sentenced on the basis of a loss of £20 million.

Versailles) who received five years' imprisonment[185] and a 15 year disqualification and Abbas Gokal (connected with the fall of BCCI[186]) who received 14 years. This leniency to large-scale fraud can however be compared to the USA where Jeffrey Skilling (Enron) was sentenced to 24 years and four months' imprisonment and ordered to pay $26 million towards restoring the Enron pension fund and Bernard Madoff who received 150 years' imprisonment and a criminal forfeiture order of $100 million for his massive Ponzi scheme.

More mundane examples include Jacinta Kibunyi,[187] who in 2009 was sentenced to 12 months' imprisonment following a plea of guilty to possessing a false identity document, as she had used a false passport to open a bank account. While using false passports is obviously serious, the sentence here could be argued to be on the excessive side, especially when compared to the facts and amount of money involved in the Bright case and the court's acknowledgment that she may have been a victim of trafficking. Furthermore is the case of John and Anne Darwin, who were sentenced to six years three months and six years six months respectively, for six convictions of fraud and nine of money laundering. By faking John Darwin's death, the couple received nearly £680,000 in benefits; with John Darwin also being convicted of dishonestly obtaining a passport.[188] Anne Darwin additionally agreed to pay £591,838.25 under the terms of the POCA 2002 and due to him having no realizable financial assets; John Darwin agreed to pay a nominal sum of £1.[189] Finally, there is the case of Guy Pound,[190] whose initial sentence of three years' imprisonment was increased to six for defrauding a charitable trust for a period of 11 years and making a gain of £2 million. Bearing in mind his level of planning, breach of trust, abuse of power and high culpability, the low level of his sentence would also appear appropriate.

From an analysis of the cases above, it would, therefore, be useful for sentencing judges if a pattern had emerged and it was possible to devise a table whereby the amount of the financial benefit achieved or loss caused could be equated with the length and severity of the sentence, equating to a weighing scale notion of just

---

185   He had cooperated with the authorities and pleaded guilty and therefore received a 50 per cent discount off his sentence.

186   For more information on the collapse of BCCI see N. Passas, 'The Genesis of the BCCI Scandal' (1996) *Journal of Law and Society*, 23(1), 57; J. Beaty and S.C. Gwynne, *The Outlaw Bank: A Wild Ride to the Secrets of BCCI* (Beard Books 2004).

187   *R v Jacinta Kibunyi*, Court of Appeal Criminal Division, 14 January 2009, unreported.

188   N. Bunyan and R. Edwards, 'Canoe Wife Trial: Darwin's Jailed for More Than Six Years' (*The Daily Telegraph* 23 July 2008) <http://www.telegraph.co.uk/news/2448044/ Canoe-wife-trial-Darwins-jailed-for-more-than-six-years.html> accessed 10 June 2011.

189   The Times Online, 'Canoe Fraudster Anne Darwin to Repay Nearly £600,000' (*The Times* 11 November 2009) <http://www.timesonline.co.uk/tol/news/uk/article6912213. ece> accessed 10 June 2010.

190   *R v Pound (Guy); Attorney General's Reference (No. 59 of 2004)*, [2004] EWCA 2488.

deserts. Practice, displayed in these few cases does not appear, however, to be able to offer this. Although Bright received seven years for a fraud costing the FSA £357 million, a sentence of one year less was given where the amounts were £250,000 (John Darwin) £2 million (Pound) and £20 million (Cusnie). While it is acknowledged that the harm caused, or risked being caused, is not the only factor for the sentencing judge to take into account, it is one which has been identified by the Criminal Justice Act 2003, the relevant sentencing guideline and the guideline judgments of *R v Barrick* and *R v Clark*. All of these offenders showed high levels of culpability and so the length of their sentences should arguably have been more diverse to show the differences in seriousness and harm caused. It is also surprising, if not shocking, that offences involving millions of pounds, do not initiate the maximum sentence of 10 years and provides evidence that we are in desperate need of sentencing guidelines to provide for not just more consistent sentencing, but also sentencing at the higher end of the sentencing scale. Bearing in mind that current sentencing guidelines on fraud only cover amounts up to £500,000 it is suggested that not only do we need the guidelines but that they also need to be extended to include amounts ranging up to millions of pounds and sentencing ranges and starting points to include the legislative maxima. While *R v Clark* includes guidelines where cases involve £1 million or more, the cases above would suggest that sentencing judges are not paying much attention to these.

Future Recommendations

The UK's fraud policy has gathered pace following the publication of the Fraud Review, the introduction of the Fraud Act 2006 and the creation of the NFA. However, the policy is now in a state of flux due to a series of measures introduced by the Coalition Government. The Fraud Act, seen by many as an improvement on the offences created by the Theft Acts (1968-1996) criminalized different types of fraudulent activities and provides prosecutors with new powers to tackle fraud. However, despite promises and reassurances from the Coalition government to create a single ECA, there are still too many agencies that perform the same function, a position that has deteriorated following the creation of the NCA. For example, HM Treasury has been charged with developing and implementing the UK's policies towards money laundering and terrorist financing, yet it has very little to do with the UK's fraud policy. Furthermore, the Home Office, who has been charged with tackling the problems associated with organized crime, now appears to manage the fraud policy.

It is therefore recommended that a single government department be given the task of tackling all types of financial crime, with it seeming to be logical that this task is given to HM Treasury, given its experience with money laundering and terrorist financing. Additionally, it is strongly suggested that a single financial crime agency be created so as to avoid the current overlap between the SFO and the FSA. The UK government should develop a unitary financial crime agency that incorporates the functions of the agencies outlined above. The primary legislation that imposes reporting obligations is the POCA 2002, under which fraud is reported to SOCA. However, in some circumstances allegations of fraud are reported to banks, the police and, in the regulated sector, such reports are made to the FSA ... There is still no legal obligation to report instances of fraud, which can be contrasted with the approach adopted in the USA, where all allegations of fraud are reported to the Financial Crime Enforcement Network, or FinCEN. It is therefore suggested that the UK should adopt a similar reporting strategy. The system needs clarification and it is suggested that all allegations of fraud should be reported to the Serious Organised Crime Unit, the UKs Financial Intelligence Unit.

Further Reading

Bosworth-Davies, R. 'Investigating Financial Crime: The Continuing Evolution of the Public Fraud Investigation Role – A Personal Perspective' (2009) *Company Lawyer*, 30(7), 195–199.

de Grazia, J. *Review of the Serious Fraud Office – Final Report* (Serious Fraud Office 2008).

Doig, A. *Fraud* (Willan Publishing 2006).

Fraud Advisory Panel, *Roskill Revisited: Is There a Case for a Unified Fraud Prosecution Office?* (Fraud Advisory Panel 2010).

Kiernan, P. and G. Scanlan, 'Fraud and the Law Commission: The Future of Dishonesty' (2003) *Journal of Financial Crime*, 10(3), 199–208.

Levi, M. 'The Roskill Fraud Commission Revisited: An Assessment' (2003) *Journal of Financial Crime*, 11(1), 38–44.

Masters, J. 'Fraud and Money Laundering: The Evolving Criminalization of Corporate Non-Compliance' (2008) *Journal of Money Laundering Control*, 11(2), 103–122.

Ormerod, D. 'The Fraud Act 2006 – Criminalising Lying?' (2007) *Criminal Law Review*, Mar, 193–219.

Ormerod, D. and D. Williams, *Smith's Law of Theft* (Oxford University Press 2007).

Rider, B. 'A Bold Step?' (2009) *Company Lawyer*, 30(1), 1–2.

Scanlan, G. 'Offences Concerning Directors and Officers of a Company: Fraud and Corruption in the United Kingdom – The Present and the Future' (2008) *Journal of Financial Crime*, 15(1), 22–37.

Wright, R. 'Fraud After Roskill: A View from the Serious Fraud Office' (2003) *Journal of Financial Crime*, 11(1), 10–16.

Wright, R. 'Developing Effective Tools to Manage the Risk of Damage Caused by Economically Motivated Crime Fraud' (2007) *Journal of Financial Crime*, 14(1), 17–27.

Chapter 5
Insider Dealing

Introduction

Insider dealing is the illegal trading in shares or securities by someone, or at the instigation of someone, with inside knowledge of unpublished business data or information that would affect the price of shares being bought or sold.[1] It has been defined by Alexander as:

> trading in organized securities markets by persons in possession of material non-public information, and has been recognized as a widespread problem that is extremely difficult to eradicate. Some of the insider dealing is based on corporate information, that is, information about a company's finances or operations.[2]

Due to the desirability of having a clean market in the United Kingdom (UK) a policy of criminalizing the activity with an additional civil recovery route has been introduced. The primary focus of this chapter will therefore be to analyse these initiatives including also an attempt at quantifying the extent of the problem. The chapter will then consider background to the policy of criminalizing and regulating insider dealing, plus an evaluation of the financial institutions and regulatory bodies involved. Finally we look at the success of criminal and civil sentencing options and practices.

What is the Offence of Insider Dealing?

The offence of insider dealing is contained in section 52 of the Criminal Justice Act 1993, which came into force on 1 March 1994.[3] This states that it is an offence for an individual who has information as an insider, to deal in securities on a regulated market on the basis of such information. A regulated market is defined

---

1   Serious Fraud Office (2010) *Insider Dealing* <http://www.sfo.gov.uk/media/99234/insider%20dealing%20web%201.pdf> accessed 4 October 2011.

2   K. Alexander, *Insider Dealing and Market Abuse: The Financial Services and Markets Act 2000* – ESRC Centre for Business Research, University of Cambridge, Working Paper No. 222 (Cambridge, University of Cambridge, 2001) at p. 4.

3   For an excellent discussion of the offences under the Criminal Justice Act 1993, see E. Lomnicka, 'The New Insider Dealing Provisions: Criminal Justice Act 1993, Part V' (1994) *Journal of Business Law*, March, 173–188.

as any 'market, however operated, which, by an order made by the Treasury, is identified (whether by name or by reference to criteria prescribed by the order) as a regulated market'.[4] An individual who has inside information is also guilty of an offence if he encourages another person to deal in securities or, he discloses such inside information otherwise than in accordance with the proper functions of his employment.[5] In short the three available offences are known as dealing, encouraging another to deal and disclosing information.[6] For all three offences, it is important to prove that there is the existence of inside information. This is defined by section 56 of the Act as information which:

a. relates to particular securities or to a particular issuer of securities or to particular issuers of securities and not to securities generally or to issuers of securities generally;
b. is specific or precise;
c. has not been made public; and
d. if it were made public would be likely to have a significant effect on the price of any securities.[7]

This definition is largely based on that adopted by the Insider Dealing Directive which stated that inside information is that 'which has not been made public of a precise nature relating to one or several issuers of transferable securities or to one or several transferable securities, which, if it were made public, would be likely to have a significant effect on the price of the transferable security or securities in question'.[8] In this context, it is therefore important to ascertain whether or not the said information has been made public. The definition of 'made public' according to section 58 of the Act is therefore if the information has been:

•   published for the purpose of informing investors and their professional advisers;
•   contained in records which are open to inspection by the public;
•   is readily acquired by those likely to deal in any securities; or,
•   derived from information which has been made public.

The information in question does not have to have been communicated to the public at large, as long as a section of the public are made aware of it; does not have to have been published in the UK; can be acquired on an observation only basis; can attract a fee; and, can be acquired only by those exercising expertise

---

4   Criminal Justice Act 1993, s 60.
5   Criminal Justice Act 1993, s 52(2).
6   Serious Fraud Office above, n 1.
7   Criminal Justice Act 1993, s 56(1).
8   Insider Dealing Directive, Council Directive 89/592/EEC, Article 1(1).

or diligence.[9] A person will be classed as being an insider, for the purposes of the Act, if the relevant information has been gained through him being a director, employee or shareholder or he has access to such information through the course of his office, profession or employment.[10] A person therefore has information as an insider 'if and only if it is, and he knows it is, inside information, and he has it, and knows that he has it, from an inside source.'[11] Once again, this definition is largely based on the definition adopted by the Directive which provided that a person can be identified as an insider if:

> by virtue of his membership of the administrative, management or supervisory bodies of the issuer – by virtue of his holding in the capital of the issuer – or because he has access to such information by virtue of the exercise of his employment, profession or duties, possesses inside information from taking advantage of that information with full knowledge of the facts by acquiring or disposing of for his own account or for the account of a third party, either directly or indirectly, transferable securities of the issuer or issuers to which that information relates.[12]

Welch et al. noted that 'Member States tended to divide into two camps: those which treated anyone holding inside information as an insider and those which required some link with the company or issuer before a person in possession of inside information became subject to the prohibition on insider dealing. The Insider Dealing Directive was a minimum harmonization directive and required Member States to prohibit insider dealing only by insiders with a link to the company, known as primary insiders.'[13]

In accordance with the Act, a person is therefore not deemed to have information as an insider just because it is inside information and gained from an inside source. Rather it must be proven that he had actual knowledge of both of these aspects.[14] Securities for the purpose of the offence relate to price-affected securities, with the inside information in question needing to have a 'significant effect on the price [or value] of the securities'[15] involved; thus making the inside information price sensitive. Examples of relevant securities include shares, debt securities, warrants, depositary receipts, options, futures and contracts for differences.[16] The Insider Dealing Directive stated that securities included:

---

9 Criminal Justice Act 1993, s 58(3).

10 Criminal Justice Act 1993, s 57(2).

11 Criminal Justice Act 1993, s 57(1).

12 Insider Dealing Directive, Council Directive 89/592/EEC, Article 2(1).

13 J. Welch, M. Pannier, E. Barrachino et al., *Comparative Implementation of EU Directives (I) – Insider Dealing and Market Abuse* (The British Institute of International and Comparative Law: London, 2005) at p. 9.

14 Serious Fraud Office above, n 1.

15 Criminal Justice Act 1993, s 56(2).

16 Criminal Justice Act 1993, Schedule 2.

(a) shares and debt securities, as well as securities equivalent to shares and debt securities; (b) contracts or rights to subscribe for, acquire or dispose of securities referred to in (a); (c) futures contracts, options and financial futures in respect of securities referred to in (a); (d) index contracts in respect of securities referred to in (a), when admitted to trading on a market which is regulated and supervised by authorities recognized by public bodies, operates regularly and is accessible directly or indirectly to the public.[17]

Furthermore, a regulated market is one which has been identified as such for the purposes of the Act by HM Treasury,[18] with one example being the London Stock Exchange.[19] For the offence to be made out the prosecuting authority also needs to show that the individual was within the UK at the time of the dealing; the regulated market is one which has been defined as regulated in the UK by HM Treasury; if the offence involved a professional intermediary, he too was within the UK at the time of the dealing; and finally, if the offence involves encouraging another to deal, the discloser and recipient of the information and/or encouragement are within the UK when the information or encouragement is given and received.[20]

Dealing

As stated above, the first offence is committed if a person using inside information deals in price-affected securities on a regulated market. The person involved can either be relying on a professional intermediary or acting as a professional intermediary themselves.[21] Dealing in securities is defined by section 55 of the Act as either acquiring or disposing of securities or procuring (directly or indirectly) an acquisition or disposal of the securities by another person.[22] Acquiring includes entering into a contract in order to create a security or making an agreement that a security will be acquired.[23] Furthermore, disposing involves bringing to an end such a contract or entering into an agreement that a security will be disposed of.[24] Interestingly, there is no requirement to establish a causal link between the held information and the dealing; although as detailed below, it is a defence if the trader can prove that he would have dealt in the same way regardless of the inside information. Examples of this behaviour include where the inside information is that a publicly-listed company is about to be taken over, which would usually result in the price of its shares increasing. By buying shares before this information

---

17   Insider Dealing Directive, Council Directive 89/592/EEC, Article 1(2).
18   Criminal Justice Act 1993, s 60.
19   Serious Fraud Office above, n 1.
20   Criminal Justice Act 1993, s 62.
21   Criminal Justice Act 1993, s 52(1) and s 52(3).
22   Criminal Justice Act 1993, s 55(1).
23   Criminal Justice Act 1993, s 55(2).
24   Criminal Justice Act 1993, s 55(3).

is made public the likely result is a large profit for the insider. Conversely, the inside information could be that a publicly-listed company is about to issue a profit warning and before this information is widely known the insider sells his shares to avoid losses.[25]

Encouraging another to deal

This offence covers the situation whereby the person with the inside information encourages another to deal with securities on any regulated market on the basis of this information and the insider knows or has reasonable cause to believe that such dealing will take place. It is worth noting that the offence of encouraging another to deal is not a result crime and thus will take place as soon as the encouragement is given, even if no subsequent dealing occurs.

Disclosing information

The final offence is committed where an individual who has inside information discloses this to another person and he has reasonable cause to believe that they will use this information to deal in price affected securities on any regulated market or as a professional intermediary or through a professional intermediary. The offence is only carried out when the disclosure occurs outside of the individual's 'proper performance of the functions of his employment, office or profession'[26] and although can be made in writing, is more likely to be made orally.[27]

Defences

There are, however, a number of defences to the three offences, all contained within section 53 and Schedule 1 of the Criminal Justice Act 1993. For example, the offence will not have been committed if the person in question can show that at the time of the dealing he either did not expect to make a profit (which also includes the avoidance of a loss);[28] had reasonable grounds for believing that the information on which the dealing was based was widely known; or, that he would have acted in the way that he did even if he had not known about the insider information.[29] For this latter excuse, the defendant would have to prove that 'he had a compelling reason for dealing in the securities in question and that he would have done so on that basis regardless of the inside information.'[30] If the offence

---

25   P. Barnes, 'Insider Dealing and Market Abuse: The UK's Record on Enforcement' (2011) *International Journal of Law, Crime and Justice*, 39, 174–189 at 176.

26   Criminal Justice Act 1993, s 52(2)(b).

27   Serious Fraud Office above, n 1.

28   Criminal Justice Act 1993, s 53(6).

29   Criminal Justice Act 1993, s 53(1).

30   Serious Fraud Office above, n 1.

is based on an individual encouraging another to deal in securities using insider information, the same three defences, outlined above, also apply.[31] Furthermore, if a person discloses insider information, he is not guilty of an offence under section 52 Criminal Justice Act 1993, if he can show that either he did not expect anyone to deal in securities based on that information; or, if there was such an expectation, he did not expect the dealing to result in a profit.[32]

In addition to these defences, a number of so called 'special defences' also exist within Schedule 1 of the Act. The first of these is acting in good faith as a market maker, with a market maker described as 'a person who holds himself out at all normal times in compliance with the rules of a regulated market or an approved organization as willing to acquire or dispose of securities; and is recognized as doing so under those rules.'[33] Furthermore, under paragraph 2, it is a defence if an individual can show that the inside information was 'market information' and it was 'reasonable for an individual in his position to have acted as he did despite having such information as an insider at the time.'[34] For this purpose, market information is information consisting of one or more of the following facts:

a. that securities of a particular kind have been or are to be acquired or disposed of, or that their acquisition or disposal is under consideration or the subject of negotiation;
b. that securities of a particular kind have not been or are not to be acquired or disposed of;
c. the number of securities acquired or disposed of or to be acquired or disposed of or whose acquisition or disposal is under consideration or the subject of negotiation;
d. the price (or range of prices) at which securities have been or are to be acquired or disposed of or the price (or range of prices) at which securities whose acquisition or disposal is under consideration or the subject of negotiation may be acquired or disposed of;
e. the identity of the persons involved or likely to be involved in any capacity in an acquisition or disposal.[35]

Moreover, a person has not committed the offence of insider dealing if he can prove: that he acted in connection with a disposal or acquisition which was already subject to negotiation or under consideration; that he did so with a view to facilitating this disposal or acquisition; and, that the insider information was market information and was acquired by his involvement in the disposal or

---

31 Criminal Justice Act 1993, s 53(2)
32 Criminal Justice Act 1993, s 53(3).
33 Criminal Justice Act 1993, Schedule 1, para 1.
34 Criminal Justice Act 1993, Schedule 1, para 2.
35 Criminal Justice Act 1993, Schedule 1, para 4.

acquisition.[36] The above meaning of market information also applies here. Finally, it is a defence if the person involved can show that he acted in accordance with 'price stabilization rules'.[37] These are defined as rules made under section 144(1) of the Financial Services and Markets Act 2000. Whichever defence is relied upon, the burden of proof, on the balance of probabilities, is on the defence to prove that such a situation existed.[38]

The Extent of Insider Dealing

The difficulties of estimating the extent of financial crime have been noted throughout this book with such difficulties even more so apparent with insider dealing. This is largely for two reasons, one because a large amount of insider dealing is thought to take place on a relatively low level basis. A person may obtain some inside information, and deals on this basis, but does not deal in a sufficient amount of securities to raise any alarm bells. Additionally, through the use of 'rings' there can be so many people involved and so many links between the dealer and the insider that it is almost impossible to link the two together. Barnes therefore explains how the only official estimate of insider dealing comes from a report to the House of Commons in May 1990 from the Trade and Industry Committee. This states that between May 1988 and 1990, 240 investigations were conducted into possible insider dealing cases. Moreover, between 1985 and 1990, 101 cases had been investigated and transferred to the Department of Trade and Industry, which resulted in 19 prosecutions and 10 convictions.[39] More recently, Dubow and Monteiro looked at market cleanliness by assessing the rise and fall of share prices two days before information was released to the public. Significant changes in share prices were seen as evidence of some level of insider dealing. Between 2000 and 2005, they found between 25 and 33 per cent of all merger bids involved statistically significant price changes in a two day window prior to the information being publicly known, thus indicating some insider dealing activity.[40] Barnes, however, claims that the figure is much higher than this. Taking two months prior to announcement as the measuring point, he found that in more than 90 per cent of cases, there was some evidence of insider dealing.[41] Barnes therefore estimates, on the basis of 50 profit warnings and 150 takeover bid announcements per year, that there are approximately 1,000 instances of insider dealing each year.

---

36 Criminal Justice Act 1993, Schedule 1, para 3.
37 Criminal Justice Act 1993, Schedule 1, para 5.
38 Serious Fraud Office above, n 1.
39 Barnes above, n 26 at 186.
40 B. Dubow, and N. Monteiro, 'Measuring Market Cleanliness' (2006) FSA Occasional Paper, March 2006, London: Financial Services Authority.
41 P. Barnes, *Stock Market Efficiency, Insider Dealing and Market Abuse* (Gower 2009).

When this is compared to the low level of prosecution as outlined below, he argues that there is only a one in 500 chance of being caught.[42]

Policy Background

The UK's insider dealing policy, like its strategies towards money laundering and counter-terrorist financing, has been influenced by the measures introduced by the European Union (EU). However, there is some uncertainty as to the commencement of the EU's policy towards insider dealing. For example, some commentators have suggested that the EUs regulation of insider dealing was influenced by 'insider trading' regulations in the United States of America (USA) that were introduced as a result of the 'Wall Street Crash' in 1929.[43] The origins of insider dealing can be found in the USA, who criminalized insider trading via the Securities Exchange Commission Act 1934. Furthermore, its insider dealing policy was also influenced by the fact that several European Countries had already introduced laws to tackle insider dealing.[44] In 1987, the EU published its draft Insider Dealing Council Directive,[45] which was finally introduced in 1989.[46] The final draft entitled the 'Directive Coordinating Regulations on Insider Dealing' was accepted in November, 1989.[47] Duderstadt took this view:

> That this was at all possible in such a short time was due mainly to three factors: first, the suction arising from the programme for the completion of a Single Market, secondly, the annexing of the draft Directive with those measures which, since they served to complete the common market, could be adopted by a majority vote; and, thirdly, the fact that the German financial market, the main opposition to legislation, increasingly appeared in an unfavourable light internationally because of its supposedly inadequate insider dealing regulation.[48]

---

42   Barnes above, n 26 at 186.

43   J. Hansen, 'The New Proposal for a European Union Directive on Market Abuse' (2002) *University of Pennsylvania Journal of International Economic Law*, 23, 241–268 at 250.

44   This included for example France, Sweden, Denmark, Norway and the United Kingdom.

45   The original Directive was published in May 1987 (Directive 7310/87) and amended in October 1988 (Directive 8810/88).

46   Council Directive 89/592/EEC.

47   85/592. See I. Duderstadt, 'Implementation of the Insider Dealing Directive in the UK and Germany' (1996) *Journal of Financial Crime*, 4(2), 105–116 at 107.

48   Ibid.

The aim of the proposal was to 'ensure equality of opportunity to all investors.'[49] Furthermore, the Directive sought to 'provide minimum standards for insider dealing laws throughout the Community.'[50] The first attempt to introduce insider dealing laws in the UK occurred in 1977 and 1978.[51] Finally, the then new Conservative government introduced the Companies Act 1980 that created a criminal offence for certain persons to deal in 'securities when they had unpublished price sensitive information.'[52] These provisions were amended by the Company Securities (Insider Dealing) Act 1985 which provided that:

> Persons who had access to material non-public information by virtue of their position with a company (including directors, officers, employees, and various kinds of agents of the company) from trading in the securities of the company while in possession of such information. These insiders were also prohibited from making selective disclosure of such information to others ("tipping"); and it prohibited their tippees from trading on the basis of such inside information. The Act also prohibited persons in possession of non-public information about a proposed takeover of a company from trading in that company's stock.[53]

However, the provisions of the Company Securities (Insider Dealing) Act 1985 were very ineffective. A point clearly illustrated by the fact that no successful prosecutions were brought under the Act. Nonetheless, McVea stated that:

> The present British legislation, enshrined in the Company Securities (Insider Dealing) Act 1985 as supplemented by the Companies Act 1985 and the Financial Services Act 1986, is a much more advanced and thorough body of legislation than the proposed EEC measures. Consequently the UK Government will have little to do by way of compliance with its provisions.[54]

The Directive was implemented in the UK via the Criminal Justice Act 1993, and it contained a number of provisions that have influenced the UK's policy toward insider dealing. For example, Article 3 'requires a prohibition on insiders possessing inside information from (a) disclosing that information to any third person unless such disclosure is made in the normal course of the exercise of his employment, profession or duties; or (b) recommending or procuring a third

---

49   F. Cantos, 'EEC Draft Directive on Insider Dealing' (1989) *Journal of International Banking Law*, 4(4), N174–176 at 174.

50   M. Ashe, 'The Directive on Insider Dealing' (1992) *Company Lawyer*, 13(1), 15–19 at 15.

51   Welch et al. above, n 15 at 18.

52   Companies Act 1980, part V.

53   Company Securities (Insider Dealing) Act 1985, ss. 1–8.

54   H. McVea, 'Plans for Compulsory Insider Dealing Legislation by the EEC' (1987) *Company Lawyer*, 8(5), 223–224 at 223.

party, on the basis of inside information, to acquire or dispose of transferable securities.' Additionally, the EU introduced the Market Abuse Directive in 2003,[55] which was instigated via the Financial Services and Markets Act.[56] The Market Abuse Directive 'prohibits abusive behaviour such as insider dealing and market manipulation. It creates obligations aimed at deterring abuses, such as insiders lists, suspicious transaction reporting, and disclosure of trades by managers of issuers. It also requires issuers to disclose inside information.'[57] Importantly, the Directive requires member states to 'require that any person professionally arranging transactions in financial instruments who reasonably suspects that a transaction might constitute insider dealing or market manipulation shall notify the competent authority without delay.'[58] The use of suspicious transaction reports has become an integral part of the UK's insider dealing policy and is managed by the Financial Services Authority.

Financial Institutions and Regulatory Bodies

The regulation of insider dealing, like the other types of financial crime discussed in this book, has been governed by a wide range of government departments, financial regulatory and law enforcement bodies. The principal or primary government department that manages the UK's insider dealing policy was the then Department of Trade and Industry (DTI). Article 8 of the Insider Dealing Directive provided that each Member State shall nominate an authority to make certain that the provisions of the Directive are complied with. Hannigan noted that 'the appropriate competent authorities in the UK would be the DTI and the Stock Exchange which currently bear the brunt of insider dealing regulation although the Securities and Investments Board (SIB) might also be nominated as

---

55   Market Abuse Directive 2003/6 ([2003] OJ L96/16). The European Commission published the proposed Directive 'on insider dealing and market manipulation (market abuse) on 30 May 2001'. See M. McKee, 'The Proposed EU Market Abuse Directive'(2001) *Journal of International Financial Markets*, 3(4), 137–142 at 137. In 2009, the EU Commission instigated a call for evidence as part of its ongoing review of the effectiveness of the Market Abuse Directive. See European Commission (2009) 'Call for Evidence Review of Directive 2003/6/EC on Insider Dealing and Market Manipulation (Market Abuse Directive)' <http://ec.europa.eu/internal_market/consultations/docs/2009/market_abuse/call_for_evidence.pdf> accessed 12 August 2010.
56   Financial Services and Markets Act 2000, s 118–118C. For a more detailed discussion of the Market Abuse Directive and its impact in the United Kingdom see Chapter 6.
57   Ed. 'Commission Seeks Evidence in Review of Market Abuse Directive' (2009) *Company Law Newsletter*, 252, 4–5 at 4.
58   Market Abuse Directive 2003/6 ([2003] OJ L96/16), Article 6(9).

its role develops.'[59] Therefore, the DTI was given a wide range of investigatory powers under the Financial Services Act 1986 to counter the threat posed by insider dealing.[60] In particular, the DTI were permitted to appoint investigators who would determine if an offence of insider dealing had been committed to the DTI.[61] The Financial Services Act 1986 also provides the investigators with a broad range of investigatory powers.[62] This was a welcome addition to the arsenal of UK law enforcement agencies as these powers were unique and not contained in the previous legislative framework and were described as a 'major deficiency which was not remedied promptly.'[63] The DTI delegated most of its insider dealing functions to the SIB and was created following the publications of the seminal recommendations of Professor Gower in 1984.[64] The subsequent White Paper envisaged two-practitioner bodies, the SIB, covering the regulation of securities and investments, and the Marketing of Investment Boards (MIB), covering the marketing of investments. After the publication of the White Paper, the MIB was established in the form of an organizing committee, but it was subsequently decided that it should merge to form a single body, the SIB. Lomnicka took the view that 'the SIB was incorporated in … anticipation of the FSA 1986.'[65] The SIB exercised both legislative and administrative functions, and was described as an 'umbrella organization'.[66] The SIB's Core Rule 28 dealt with insider dealing and 'prohibiting firms from knowingly effecting transactions that would contravene the statutory restrictions, whether for their own account or for a customer.'[67] Core Rule 28 provided that:

> a firm is prohibited from carrying out a transaction (either in the UK or elsewhere) for its own account (or on the account of an associate acting on its own account), when it knows of circumstances which mean that it, its associate,

59   B. Hannigan, 'Regulating Insider Dealing – The EEC Dimension' (1989) *Journal of International Banking Law*, 4(1), 11–14 at 14.

60   Financial Services Act 1986, s 177.

61   Financial Services Act 1986, s 177(1).

62   Financial Services Act 1986, s 105.

63   G. Brazier, *Insider Dealing: Law and Regulation* (Cavendish Publishing 1996) at p. 166.

64   *Financial Services in the UK: A New Framework for Investor Protection*, Cmnd. 9432.

65   E. Lomnicka, 'Making the Financial Services Authority Accountable' (2000) *Journal of Business Law*, 65–81 at 66.

66   Ibid. at 67.

67   M. White, 'The Implications for Securities Regulation of New Insider Dealing Provisions in the Criminal Justice Act 1993' (1995) *Company Lawyer*, 16(6), 163–171 at 169.

or an employee of either, is prohibited from effecting the transaction by virtue of the CJA (Part V) 1993.[68]

If a firm breached Core Rule 28, the Financial Services Act 1986 provided that the SIB could pursue a civil action for breach of a statutory duty where a business had 'failed to comply with the regulatory standards required of it under the FSA [1986].'[69] Gray noted that:

> Section 62 conferred on an investor a right of action if he suffered loss as a result of an investment business's contravention of any of the matters mentioned in s 62(1), primarily any of the SIB rules and regulations governing the conduct of investment business or those of an SRO or Recognized Professional Body where applicable to that investment business.[70]

It is important to note that the effectiveness of the enforcement measures contained in the Financial Services Act 1986, the regulatory performance of the SIB and DTI has been questioned by several commentators. For example, Welch et al., writing for the British Institute of International and Comparative Law concluded that:

> It proved extremely difficult to prosecute cases of insider dealing successfully under the criminal law. In addition, the powers of the regulatory bodies under the Financial Services Act 1986 in relation to activities which fell short of criminal behaviour extended only to authorized persons and, in some cases, key employees.[71]

One of the primary regulatory agencies that tackles insider dealing is the Financial Services Authority (FSA). As previously mentioned in an earlier chapter of this book, the FSA has a statutory obligation to reduce financial crime by virtue of the Financial Services and Markets Act 2000.[72] Under the Act, financial crime has been given a very broad definition that includes fraud, dishonesty, misconduct, or misuse of information relating to a financial market and handling the proceeds of crime.[73] The FSA perceive insider dealing as a significant threat to its statutory objectives and it is also viewed as being 'the highest profile aspect' of its market

---

68   H. McVea, 'Fashioning a System of Civil Penalties for Insider Dealing: Sections 61 and 62 of the Financial Services Act 1986' (1996) *Journal of Business Law*, July 344–361 at 355.

69   J. Gray, 'Financial Services Act 1986 Reforms: Part 2' (1991) *International Banking Law*, 9(9), 412–416 at 412.

70   Ibid. at 414.

71   Welch et al. above, n 15 at 20.

72   Financial Services and Markets Act 2000, s 6.

73   Financial Services and Markets Act 2000, s 6(3).

abuse regime.[74] Filby took the view that 'the FSA has now been responsible for enforcing the insider dealing regulations under both Acts since late 2001. This responsibility ranges from detecting insider dealing, through to investigating suspected instances, to applying sanctions.'[75] It is therefore fair to assume that insider dealing falls within the regulatory remit of the FSA under its financial crime statutory objective. The FSA has adopted a 'preventative' approach towards tackling insider dealing which means that 'market participants' are expected to have in place the following mechanisms:

1. appropriate and effective systems and controls to prevent insider dealing;
2. an insider list that is as short as possible and based on need-to-know;
3. a willingness to undertake a thorough internal review following a leak;
4. effective and targeted training of staff including support staff;
5. monitoring of staff personal account dealing;
6. robust controls when dealing with third parties;
7. effective information technology controls; and
8. an awareness of the limitation of code words as an effective tool to keep information confidential, especially if used in isolation.[76]

An essential part of this preventive stance is the use of suspicious transaction reports. As will be explained in the next chapter (market abuse), authorized firms are required to report suspicious transactions of insider dealing activity to the FSA, even if the transaction does not occur. This was one of the innovative parts introduced in the UK following the implementation of the Market Abuse Directive in 2005. The FSA Handbook provides that a regulated firm must report any suspicious activity to the FSA and failure to comply with this requirement could result in a breach and punishment.[77] For example, in 2009 the FSA fined Mark Lockwood £20,000 for failing to identify a transaction and for not reporting the transaction to the FSA which allowed the firm to be used for the purpose of an insider dealing transaction.[78] Furthermore, in January 2012, the FSA fined Caspar Agnew £65,000 for failing to identify and act on a suspicious order that allowed

---

74   Financial Services Authority, Speech by Margaret Cole, Director of Enforcement, American Bar Association, 4 October 2007 <http://www.fsa.gov.uk/pages/Library/Communication/Speeches/2007/1004_mc.shtml> accessed 9 November 2011.

75   M. Filby, 'The Enforcement of Insider Dealing Under the Financial Services and Markets Act 2000' (2003) *Company Lawyer*, 24(11), 334–341 at 334.

76   Financial Services Authority, Speech by Margaret Cole, Director of Enforcement, American Bar Association, 4 October 2007 <http://www.fsa.gov.uk/pages/Library/Communication/Speeches/2007/1004_mc.shtml> accessed 9 November 2011.

77   FSA Handbook 'Supervision', SUP 15.10 <http://fsahandbook.info/FSA/html/handbook/SUP/15/10> accessed 10 November 2011.

78   Financial Services Authority, 'FSA Fines Broker for Failing to Prevent Insider Dealing' (2009) 2 September 2009 <http://www.fsa.gov.uk/pages/Library/Communication/PR/2009/115.shtml> accessed 9 November 2011.

his firm to be used to facilitate an insider dealing transaction.[79] The importance of the suspicious transaction reports was emphasized by the FSA who noted that 'some 95% of these [suspicious transaction reports] relate to potential insider dealing. We cannot overestimate the importance of these reports and the role of market participants in detecting and preventing market abuse.'[80] There are three other ways in which the FSA becomes aware of allegations of insider dealing – supervision, market surveillance, and whistleblowing.

One of the most significant powers that the FSA has employed against insider dealing is its investigative and enforcement powers. The FSMA 2000 provides the FSA with extensive investigatory powers. The FSA has the ability to require information from firms,[81] to appoint investigators,[82] to obtain the assistance of overseas financial regulators[83] and provide appointed investigators with additional powers.[84] If the FSA suspect a case involves insider dealing they have the power to investigate and request information.[85] Under FSMA 2000, the FSA is able to conduct a general investigation[86] and an investigation into particular cases.[87] Furthermore, the 2000 Act provides that the FSA is permitted to appoint more investigators 'where there are circumstances suggesting that insider dealing in the CJA sense has occurred.'[88] As will be discussed in the following section of this chapter, the FSA has begun to use its enforcement and investigative powers with greater frequency. For example, writing in its Financial Crime Newsletter in 2010, Margaret Cole, the FSA's Director of Enforcement, stated that:

> We are determined to deliver a strong deterrent message, and a year on from our first ever insider dealing criminal case, we have secured two further convictions. Last month also saw our largest ever fine on an individual, Simon Eagle for £2.8 million, for deliberate market abuse. Through such enforcement actions we aim to change behaviour so that markets are cleaner, fairer and more orderly, and retail customers get a fairer deal. We continue to work successfully in partnership with other key organizations and this has been highlighted in our recent enforcement successes. This year we carried out our

---

79   Financial Services Authority, 'Former Compliance Officer at Greenlight Capital and JP Morgan Cazenove Trader Fined' (2012) 27 January 2012 <http://www.fsa.gov.uk/library/communication/pr/2012/007.shtml> accessed 3 February 2012.

80   Ibid.

81   Financial Services and Markets Act 2000, ss 165–166.

82   Financial Services and Markets Act 2000, ss 167–168.

83   Financial Services and Markets Act 2000, s 169.

84   Financial Services and Markets Act 2000, s 172.

85   Filby above, n 76 at 336.

86   Financial Services and Markets Act 2000, s 167.

87   Financial Services and Markets Act 2000, s 168.

88   Financial Services and Markets Act 2000, s 168(2)(a).

largest ever operation against suspected insider dealing where we worked in joint operation with the Serious Organised Crime Agency.[89]

The FSA retains the power to bring criminal prosecutions for insider dealing under the CJA; however, it is arguable that the authority has been slow in progressing down this route, attracting criticism, preferring to use financial penalties as its main enforcement mechanism, with some commentators wondering if the FSA would ever get around to commencing criminal prosecutions for insider dealing at all. In the early days of the FSA there seemed to be a culture of reluctance on the part of the authority's senior management to acknowledge that one of its tasks was to reduce the incidence of financial crime and combat market abuse, after so long as a self-regulating club. There does, however, now seem to be some evidence that the FSA is beginning to get tougher with insider dealers and more criminal prosecutions are likely in the future. Alexander notes the increasing FSA intensity in referring to a speech by Margaret Cole, Director of the FSA's Enforcement Division, where she emphasized that the FSA would be seeking to increase the number of criminal prosecutions it brings,[90] with others within the FSA calling it '… one of the most significant changes in our approach' and that shortly after this speech the FSA obtained its first conviction for insider dealing. This increase in intensity and focus toward criminal prosecutions has borne fruit with the first criminal conviction for insider dealing brought by the FSA in which a solicitor was sentenced to eight months for passing on information to his father-in-law about an impending takeover. Additionally the courts have recently given a green light to the FSA to use their prosecutorial powers in confirming that the FSA is able to bring prosecutions under the CJA without recourse to the Secretary of State or Director of Public Prosecutions. It is also clear that the reach of the FSA is expanding as a result of its more aggressive approach to dealing with market abuse stretching out beyond traditional securities markets and into the debt markets.

Sentencing and Recovery

Although it is recognized by a number of prosecuting authorities that insider dealing exists, the majority of cases which end in a successful prosecution are minimal. Indeed, Barnes argues that on average there are only one or two criminal prosecutions per year, with only 30 successful criminal convictions existing between 1987 and 2010.[91] Furthermore, Filby took the view that 'prosecutions for insider dealing under section 56 of the Criminal Justice Act 1993 (CJA) for

---

89   Financial Services Authority 'Financial Crime Newsletter' (2010) July, Issue 14 at 1.

90   R. Alexander, 'Corporate Crimes: Are the Gloves Coming Off?' (2009) *Company Lawyer*, 30(11), 321–322.

91   Barnes above, n 26 at 183.

insider dealing have been few and far between. The legislation itself has been criticised for restricting what is a highly technical fraud to the criminal arena.'[92] This has however increased over the last few years, with the FSA having secured 10 convictions of insider dealing since 2009 and in August 2011,were in the process of prosecuting another 13 individuals.[93] For the financial year of 2010/11 the FSA achieved 'five criminal convictions for insider dealing, with sentences ranging from 12 months to three years and four months [and] five confiscation orders against individuals totalling £1,705,285.76.'[94] The maximum sentence on conviction on indictment for insider dealing in England and Wales is seven years' imprisonment, an unlimited fine, or both.[95] Additionally, the Financial Services Act 1986 'provides a right of action for certain breaches of the regulatory framework established by the FSA.'[96] Additionally, it is important to point out that there are two other grounds for liability for insider dealing under the common law – breach of fiduciary duty and breach of confidence.[97] Examples of these criminal prosecutions include Christopher McQuoid[98] who was given an eight month custodial term for using inside information to make a profit of almost £50,000. In addition to the term of imprisonment, a confiscation order was made to retrieve all of the benefit and he was ordered to pay £30,000 in prosecution costs. In an appeal against sentence, which was dismissed, the Court of Appeal confirmed that those involved in insider dealing were criminals,[99] that it was a species of fraud and hence was cheating.[100] Margaret Cole stated:

> By pursuing a criminal prosecution in this case, the FSA has shown that we will take tough action to achieve our aim of credible deterrence in the financial markets … Anyone engaging in similar acts should see this as a clear warning that the FSA intends to bring all its powers to bear to protect the integrity of our markets.[101]

Despite what some may have seen as a warning that insider dealing would be classed as a serious offence and commensurate with an immediate custodial term,

---

92   Filby above, n 76 at 336.

93   Financial Service Authority (2011) *Investment Banker and Two Associates Charged with Insider Dealing* (2011) Press Release, 4 August 2011 <http://www.fsa.gov.uk/pages/Library/Communication/PR/2011/069.shtml> accessed 6 October 2011.

94   Financial Services Authority, *Annual Report 2010/11* (Financial Services Authority 2011) at p. 60.

95   Criminal Justice Act 1993, s 61.

96   Financial Services Act 1986, s 62.

97   McVea, above, n 69 at 344.

98   *Regina v Christopher McQuoid* [2009] EWCA Crim 1301.

99   Ibid. at para. 8.

100   Ibid. at para. 9.

101   Financial Services Authority, 'An Update from the Financial Crime and Intelligence Division' (2009) Financial Crime Newsletter, Issue 13, 1–7.

in March 2009, Timothy Power, former executive of the Belgo Group, received an 18 month jail sentence suspended for two years, for two counts of insider dealing amounting to a profit of £9.8 million.[102] While it is accepted that Power served 163 days in imprisonment while waiting for his trial, had pleaded guilty and his offences were old in nature (committed in 1997–1998), his suspended sentence would still appear to be lenient, especially when the sentencing judge described the offences as:

> Serious because they are a grave breach of trust by someone at the centre of a company which is going to cause sensitive movement on the Stock Exchange and upon which other people are relying for honesty and transparency.[103]

In December of the same year, however, father and son team, Neel and Matthew Uberoi were sentenced to prison terms of 24 and 12 months respectively for insider dealing trades worth a benefit of £288,050.05. In passing sentence, Judge Tester argued

> This offence is cheating and it is important for economic and social wellbeing to have clean markets. The public rightly recoils from the idea of people with inside information having a license to print money.[104]

While this was more punitive than previous cases, it is still fairly lenient when compared to the 2006 case of Asif Butt.[105] He was initially sentenced to five years' imprisonment for conspiracy to commit insider dealing. Using confidential information, over a period of three years and through 19 criminal transactions, Butt made £388,488 profit for his investment bank (Credit Suisse); equating to £237,000 in personal benefit (not too dissimilar to the £288,000 benefit mentioned above). Although describing his offence as serious, 'flagrant, calculated and deliberate',[106] the Court of Appeal did reduce the sentence to one of four years.

More recent cases include Malcolm Calvert who in 2010 was sentenced to 21 months in prison for five counts of insider dealing amounting to a profit of

---

102 P. Cheston, 'Former Belgo Chief Spared Prison for Insider Trading Deal' *London Evening Standard*, 2 March 2009 <http://www.thisislondon.co.uk/standard/article-23656323-former-belgo-chief-is-spared-prison-for-insider-trading-deal.do;jsessionid=A89 0C0DFCC53652272A3B0EA79225CFE>.

103 Ibid.

104 Financial Services Authority, *Corporate Broker Intern and His Father Receive 12 and 24 Month Prison Sentences Respectively for Insider Dealing* (2009) Press Release, 10 December 2010 <http://www.fsa.gov.uk/pages/Library/Communication/PR/2009/170. shtml> accessed 6 October 2011.

105 *R v Butt (Asif Nazir)* [2006] 2 Cr. App. R. (S) 44.

106 Ibid. at para. 25.

£103,883;[107] Neil Rollins whose sentence of 27 months was reduced by the Court of Appeal to 18 months' imprisonment for counts of insider dealing and money laundering;[108] and Christian Littlewood who in 2011 received a sentence of three years and four months in custody for eight counts of dealing AIM listed shares between 2000 and 2008. His co-defendant, Helmy Omar Sa'aid, received two years' imprisonment and a confiscation order of £640,000.[109] Profits were thought to be in the region of £590,000 on trading of shares worth over £2 million.[110]

In addition to criminal prosecutions there is also a civil recovery route carried out by the FSA. When successful prosecutions have occurred in this arena, the FSA has been relatively harsh in terms of using its sentencing powers. For example, in 2006 the FSA issued the largest fine that had ever been issued against an individual, fining the hedge fund manager of GLG Partners (GLG) and Philippe Jabre (former Managing Director) £750,000 each, for insider dealing and market abuse. Jabre was privy to confidential share information on 11 February 2003, which he agreed not to use until it had become public. The information was announced on 17 February, but on 12 and 13 February he breached the restriction by short selling approximately $16 million of ordinary shares.[111] More recently in 2009, the FSA fined Mark Lockwood, a trading desk manager, £20,000 for failing to prevent insider dealing. While he had reason to believe that a transaction was being conducted on the basis of insider dealing he failed to either prevent the trade or alert the FSA through the submission of an SAR.[112] What is interesting in this example is that Lockwood was fined for a failure to act rather than being positively involved in the offence. This was because it was acknowledged that his position included an obligation to notify the FSA of any suspicious behaviour, which in this case he obviously failed to do. Such examples suggest, in theory, that the FSA and the courts believe that insider dealing is a serious offence and is just as serious as other financial crimes. Although, this is arguably not being mirrored in practice, with some serious and dishonest offences being met with fairly low

---

107   Financial Services Authority, *Former Cazenove Broker Sentenced to 21 Months in Prison for Insider Dealing* (2010) Press Release, 11 March 2010 <http://www.fsa.gov.uk/pages/Library/Communication/PR/2010/043.shtml> accessed 6 October 2011.

108   Financial Service Authority, *Neil Rollins Update* (2011) Press Release 30 June 2011 <http://www.fsa.gov.uk/pages/Library/Communication/Statements/2011/neil_rollins.shtml> accessed 6 October 2011.

109   Financial Services Authority, *Investment Banker, His Wife and Family Friend Sentenced for Insider Dealing* (2011) Press Release, 2 February 2011 <http://www.fsa.gov.uk/pages/Library/Communication/PR/2011/018.shtml> accessed 6 October.

110   Financial Services Authority, *Annual Report 2010/11* (2011) London: FSA, p. 60.

111   Financial Services Authority, *FSA Fines GLG Partners and Philippe Jabre £750,000 Each for Market Abuse* Press Release, 1 August 2006 <http://www.fsa.gov.uk/pages/Library/Communication/PR/2006/077.shtml> accessed 6 October 2011.

112   Financial Services Authority, *FSA Fines Broker for Failing to Prevent Insider Dealing*, Press Release, 2 September 2009 <http://www.fsa.gov.uk/pages/Library/Communication/PR/2009/115.shtml> accessed 6 October 2011.

level responses or even suspended sentences. When the maximum penalty for the offence is seven years' imprisonment, how large must the benefit be before a reasonably serious sentence is passed?

Future Recommendations

The UK has adopted a very tough legislative stance towards preventing insider dealing. Its policy has been heavily influenced by the provision of the Insider Dealing Directive and the eagerness of US authorities to criminalize insider dealing activities in Europe. Despite the laudable intentions of the early insider dealing legislative provisions, their effectiveness was illustrated by the small number of successful prosecutions brought during the 1980s. It was hoped that the civil enforcement provisions in the Financial Services Act 1986 would be an effective weapon against insider dealing. However, these provisions were heavily underused by the SIB and that subsequently influenced the Labour Government in 1997 to announce the creation of the FSA, which would become the new financial regulatory agency to tackle insider dealing. The criminalization of insider dealing in the UK is largely seen as a failure as a result of the high burden of proof required in such difficult evidentiary cases. The attempt to address this perceived failure has come in the form of a civil regime enacted as part of FSMA 2000. It is certainly evident that the level of fines remains high and this coupled with a more aggressive approach taken by the FSA, particularly in respect of criminal prosecutions for insider dealing should allow it to claim success in its mission, at least in respect of market abuse. However, it is possible to argue that this is largely due to the decision by the coalition government to abolish the FSA by 2012.

Further Reading

Ashe, M. 'The Directive on Insider Dealing' (1992) *Company Lawyer*, 13(1), 15–19.

Barnes, P. *Stock Market Efficiency, Insider Dealing and Market Abuse* (Gower 2009).

Barnes, P. 'Insider Dealing and Market Abuse: The UK's Record on Enforcement' (2011) *International Journal of Law, Crime and Justice*, 39, 174–189.

Dubow, B. and N. Monteiro, 'Measuring Market Cleanliness' FSA Occasional Paper, March 2006 (Financial Services Authority 2006).

Filby, M. 'The Enforcement of Insider Dealing under the Financial Services and Markets Act 2000' (2003) *Company Lawyer*, 24(11), 334–341.

Gray, J. 'Financial Services Act 1986 Reforms: Part 2' (1991) *International Banking Law*, 9(9), 412–416.

Hannigan, B. 'Regulating Insider Dealing – The EEC Dimension' (1989) *Journal of International Banking Law*, 4(1), 11–14.

Hansen, J. 'The New Proposal for a European Union Directive on Market Abuse' (2002) *University of Pennsylvania Journal of International Economic Law*, 23, 241–268.

Lomnicka, E. 'The New Insider Dealing Provisions: Criminal Justice Act 1993, Part V' (1994) *Journal of Business Law*, March, 173–188.

McVea, H. 'Fashioning a System of Civil Penalties for Insider Dealing: Sections 61 and 62 of the Financial Services Act 1986' (1996) *Journal of Business Law*, July, 344–361.

McVea, H. 'Plans for Compulsory Insider Dealing Legislation by the EEC' (1987) *Company Lawyer*, 8(5), 223–224.

White, M. 'The Implications for Securities Regulation of New Insider Dealing Provisions in the Criminal Justice Act 1993' (1995) *Company Lawyer* 16(6), 163–171.

Chapter 6

Market Abuse

Introduction

The term market abuse covers both the use of inside information and market manipulation. Conduct which can amount to market abuse therefore includes: insider dealing, improper disclosure, market manipulation; behaviour giving rise to false and misleading impressions; misuse of information; and, behaviour that is likely to give rise to market distortion.[1] Policy in the United Kingdom (UK) is largely managed by the Financial Services Authority (FSA), although other bodies such as the Serious Fraud Office (SFO) also play an important role. The policy is threefold – the market abuse regime (MAR), the enforcement powers of the FSA and the reporting of suspicious transactions. The primary focus of this chapter will therefore be to analyse these initiatives, including also an attempt at quantifying the extent of the problem. The chapter will then consider background to the policy of criminalizing and regulating market abuse with particular emphasis on the civil MAR brought in by the Code of Market Conduct, plus an evaluation of the financial institutions and regulatory bodies involved. Finally we look at the success of criminal and civil sentencing options and practices.

What is the Civil Offence of Market Abuse?

Market abuse is defined both in statute and in a European Union (EU) Market Abuse Directive (MAD). Section 118 of the Financial Services and Markets Act (FSMA) 2000, defines the behaviour as including trading on the basis of inside information; disclosing inside information other than in the proper course of employment; using information which is not generally available to the market and which would lead regular users of the market to think that the dealer had fallen below the standard of behaviour reasonably expected of him; trading which gives misleading or false impressions; trading which uses deception or fictitious devices; the disclosing of information which leads to a misleading or false impression; and behaviour which is likely to distort the market.[2] In short, as outlined in the introduction, the abuse is made up of insider dealing and market manipulation.

---

1   S. Sheikh, 'FSMA Market Abuse Regime: A Review of the Sunset Clauses International' (2008) *Company and Commercial Law Review*, 19(7), 234–236.

2   Financial Services and Markets Act 2000, s 118.

In a similar vein, the MAD[3] also splits the behaviour into these two areas. Inside information is defined as 'information that is precise, non-public and likely to have a significant impact on the price of a financial instrument,'[4] while market manipulation is said to comprise three forms,

- transactions and orders to trade that give false or misleading signals or secure the price of a financial instrument at an artificial level;
- transactions or orders to trade that employ fictitious devices; and
- distribution of information likely to give false or misleading signals.

Under such definitions market abuse is not a criminal offence, although such offences do exist further on in the FSMA 2000. These consist of misleading statements and practices,[5] misleading the FSA[6] and misleading the Office of Fair Trading (OFT).[7] On the basis that insider dealing has been dealt with in Chapter 5, it will only be market manipulation which will be discussed further.

Misleading statements and practices

The offence under section 397 of the FSMA 2000 applies to three situations whereby a person either,

a. makes a statement, promise or forecast which he knows to be misleading, false or deceptive in a material particular;
b. dishonestly conceals any material facts whether in connection with a statement, promise or forecast made by him or otherwise; or
c. recklessly makes (dishonestly or otherwise) a statement, promise or forecast which is misleading, false or deceptive in a material particular.[8]

The offence is proven where the statement, forecast or promise made by the suspected abuser creates a misleading or false impression as to the price, value or market in a relevant investment; the statement, forecast or promise is made for the purpose of creating such an impression and induces another person to 'enter into, or to refrain from entering or offering to enter into a relevant agreement;

---

3   The Market Abuse Directive 2003/6/EC <http://www.fsa.gov.uk/pages/About/What/International/pdf/MAD.pdf> accessed 18 October 2011.

4   Ibid.

5   Financial Services and Markets Act 2000, s 397.

6   Financial Services and Markets Act 2000, s 398.

7   Financial Services and Markets Act 2000, s 399.

8   Financial Services and Markets Act 2000, s 397(1).

or to exercise, or refrain from exercising, any rights conferred by a relevant investment.'[9] Examples include,

- buying or selling qualifying investments at the close of the market with the effect of misleading investors who act on the basis of closing prices, other than for legitimate reasons;
- wash trades – that is, a sale or purchase of a qualifying investment where there is no change in beneficial interest or market risk, or where the transfer of beneficial interest or market risk is only between parties acting in concert or collusion, other than for legitimate reasons;
- painting the tape – that is, entering into a series of transactions that are shown on a public display for the purpose of giving the impression of activity or price movement in a qualifying investment; and
- entering orders into an electronic trading system, at prices which are higher than the previous bid or lower than the previous offer, and withdrawing them before they are executed, in order to give a misleading impression that there is demand for or supply of the qualifying investment at that price.[10]

For the purpose of such examples 'legitimate reasons' might include the situation whereby the transaction is being carried out due to a prior regulatory or legal obligation; the transaction is executed in such a way which takes into account the need for fair play in the market; or the transaction creates an exposure to market risk rather than removes it.[11]

Misleading the Authority/OFT

The FSMA 2000 also contains two misleading offences. The first is in relation to any dealings with the FSA under the Act and is made out where a person who is required to comply with an obligation under the Act recklessly or knowingly 'gives the Authority (i.e. the FSA) information which is false or misleading in a material particular.'[12] In many respects, this is a loophole offence, in the sense that it includes all those situations where 'no other provision of this Act'[13] applies. The second misleading offence refers to any action which misleads the OFT, although rather than creating a new offence, in essence all section 399 of the Act does is to bring into the FSMA 2000, section 44 of the Competition Act 1998. This states

---

9 Financial Services and Markets Act 2000, s 397(2).

10 Financial Services Authority (2005) Market Abuse Directive Instrument 2005, para 1.6.2 <http://ec.europa.eu/internal_market/finances/docs/actionplan/transposition/uk/d13.3-uk.pdf> accessed 20 October 2011.

11 Ibid. at para 1.6.6 E.

12 Financial Services and Markets Act 2000, s 398(1).

13 Financial Services and Markets Act 2000, s 398(2).

that a person is guilty of an offence if he/she knowingly or recklessly provides the OFT with information which is either misleading or false.[14]

For all market abuse activity, irrelevant of where it is defined, it must occur within the UK. For the purposes of market manipulation under section 118 of the Act it must be in relation to qualifying investments which are either 'admitted to trading on a prescribed market'[15] operating in the UK or 'which a request for admission to trading on such a prescribed market has been made.'[16] For these purposes, investments which are 'related investments' in such a prescribed market will also fall under such behaviour.[17] In this context, 'behaviour' is defined as 'action or inaction'[18] and so includes the situation where either the trader should have alerted the market to a problem and neglected to do so, or created a reasonable expectation that he would act in a particular way and again failed to do so. In relation to the criminal offences, the abuser must be within the UK and either the person who is induced must also be within the UK or the intended agreement would have been exercised within the UK.[19]

Defences

Defences for market abuse in the main rely on the suspected market manipulator proving that either he believed on reasonable grounds that his behaviour did not amount to market abuse, or he exercised all due diligence and took all reasonable precautions to avoid such abuse.[20] This will provide a defence to an unlimited fine, but will not prevent the FSA from informal or disciplinary proceedings. To be able to prove one of these defences, the suspected abuser must first show that he believed that he was not engaging in market abuse and that this belief was objectively reasonable, of which there must be sufficient evidence. The next stage is to convince the FSA that he took all reasonable precautions and exercised all due diligence in performing the transactions in question. Due to the fact that the test is *all* reasonable precautions and *all* due diligence, this sets a fairly high standard and *any* lack of care may be sufficient grounds for the FSA to disallow the defence. A defence can also be relied upon, if it can be proven that the disclosure in question was 'protected'. A protected disclosure must satisfy three conditions and if so proven will 'not be taken to breach any restriction on the disclosure of information'[21] misleading or otherwise. The first condition is where the discloser

---

14   Competition Act 1998, s 44(1).
15   Financial Services and Markets Act 2000, s 118A(1)(b)(i).
16   Financial Services and Markets Act 2000, s 118A(1)(b)(ii).
17   Financial Services and Markets Act 2000, s 118A(1)(b)(iii).
18   Financial Services and Markets Act 2000, s 130A(3).
19   Financial Services and Markets Act 2000, s 397(6).
20   Financial Services and Markets Act 2000, s 123(2).
21   Financial Services and Markets Act 2000, s 131A(1).

knows or suspects 'that another person has engaged in market abuse';[22] the information in question came to the discloser in the course of his profession, employment, trade or profession;[23] and, the disclosure is made to either the FSA or to a nominated officer as soon as practicable after the information came to light.[24]

For the purposes of the available criminal offences, such an offence will not be made out where the statement, forecast or promise was made in accordance with price stabilizing rules; control of information rules or 'the relevant provisions of Commission Regulation (EC) No 2273/2003 of 22 December 2003 implementing Directive 2003/6/EC of the European Parliament'[25] relating to the stabilization of financial instruments and buy-back programmes. The price stabilizing rules[26] relate to provisions put into place by the FSA which grant a defence or 'safe harbour'[27] against market manipulation, while control of information rules are enacted under section 147 of the FSMA 2000. Furthermore, it is also a defence if the suspected abuser can show 'that he reasonably believed that his act or conduct would not create an impression that was false or misleading.'[28]

The Civil Market Abuse Regime

As stated above market abuse under section 118 of the FSMA 2000 and the MAD is not criminal. Rather, under these instruments, a civil MAR has been developed. This is largely to bypass the high burdens of evidential proof which are needed in criminal cases, which arguably in the past have led to small numbers of prosecutions. The government's answer to the problem of the lack of convictions was to 'fill the regulatory gap.'[29] The new approach to tackling abuse is 'The MAR', arguably reflecting that the focus was not merely on insider dealing but the whole ambit of activities that could affect the probity of the financial markets. Indeed, one of the key aims of the MAR is to give the FSA maximum flexibility in its task by requiring a lower standard of proof than needed to secure a criminal conviction.[30] Additionally, unlike the criminal provisions of the Criminal Justice Act 1993, for insider dealing, the MAR does not require the 'prosecuting' authority to show

---

22   Financial Services and Markets Act 2000, s 131A(2).

23   Financial Services and Markets Act 2000, s 131A(3).

24   Financial Services and Markets Act 2000, s 131A(4).

25   Financial Services and Markets Act 2000, s 397(4).

26   Financial Services Authority (2000) *The Price Stabilising Rules, Annex A* <http://www.fsa.gov.uk/pubs/cp/cp78.pdf> accessed 18 October 2011.

27   Ibid.

28   Financial Services and Markets Act 2000, s 397(5).

29   See M. Filby, 'Part VIII Financial Services and Markets Act: Filling Insider Dealing's Regulatory Gaps' (2004) *Company Lawyer*, 23(12), 363–370.

30   E. Swan, 'Market Abuse: A New Duty of Fairness' (2004) *Company Lawyer*, 25(3), 67–68.

intent on the part of the market participant,[31] a cause for initial concern explained by the government on the basis that the MAR was not primarily about catching errant individuals but about providing clean and efficient financial markets.[32] As Swan notes, this leads to the potential of market abuse being committed by 'mistake' and as such it is clearly possible that the offence can be committed negligently,[33] although in a response to the Joint Committee on Financial Services and Markets, the FSA did note that they do not 'propose to prosecute people for accidental offences.'[34] This lack of intent requirement has now been confirmed by the Court of Appeal.[35]

The concept of a civil regime in the UK itself is not new, and was a hotly debated topic during the passage of the Criminal Justice Act 1993, but was obviously felt to be a step too far at that time.[36] The obvious lack of success of the criminal provision within the Criminal Justice Act 1993 put civil enforcement squarely back on the agenda. The overall aim of the FSMA 2000 was therefore to provide a comprehensive regulatory structure to oversee all financial services operations. To enable this to happen, it gives considerable power to the FSA to make rules in pursuit of its statutory objectives. The five objectives are maintaining market confidence,[37] ensuring financial stability,[38] promoting public awareness,[39] protecting consumers,[40] and reducing financial crime.[41] Arguably tackling market abuse covers three of the stated objectives, and if used innovatively can also help to promote public awareness. Therefore it is important not to read it in isolation, but to also include reference to the wider role of the FSA in keeping markets clean and efficient for investor confidence to blossom. This additionally protects individual consumers against misspelling and reduces the incidence of financial crime, in particular that of fraud on investors.[42]

---

31   MAR1.2.6G.

32   A. Alcock, 'Market Abuse – The New Witchcraft' (2001) *New Law Journal*, 151, 1398.

33   Swan above, n 30.

34   Joint Committee on Financial Services and Markets, First Report, para 265 <http://www.publications.parliament.uk/pa/jt199899/jtselect/jtfinser/328/32809.htm> accessed 8 July 2010.

35   *Winterflood Securities Ltd and others v Financial Services Authority* [2010] EWCA Civ 423; [2010] WLR (D) 101.

36   See Ed. 'Insiders Beware!' (1993) *Company Lawyer*, 14(11), 202.

37   Financial Services and Markets Act 2000, s 3.

38   Financial Services and Markets Act 2000, s 3A. This section was inserted by the Financial Services Act 2010 in response to the global financial crisis.

39   Financial Services and Markets Act 2000, s 4.

40   Financial Services and Markets Act 2000, s 5.

41   Financial Services and Markets Act 2000, s 6.

42   Note that during the preparation of this chapter the new Conservative/Liberal Democrat coalition announced major reforms to bank and financial services regulation, with much of the FSA's role in supervising banks and the maintenance of financial stability

Under the civil regime, the FSA is required to publish a code of conduct outlining what the FSA's responsibilities are in respect of guarding against market abuse.[43] The Code of Market Conduct (MAR) of the FSA Handbook is 'central'[44] to the operation of the Market Abuse Regime, described by others as the 'backbone' of the regime.[45] The original version only stated what behaviour *did not* amount to market abuse.[46] However, later versions have included examples of what *does* amount to market abuse, thus giving clear guidelines to market participants of the types of behaviour to avoid. The code is designed to provide assistance and guidance in ascertaining what behaviour amounts to market abuse.[47] The Code is quick to point out that it is not an exhaustive description of all types of behaviour amounting to market abuse,[48] nor is it an exhaustive description of all factors to be taken into account in the determination of whether such behaviour is market abuse.[49] The Code of market conduct also contains two so-called 'safe harbours', outlining behaviour that will not amount to market abuse, these being share buy-back schemes and price stabilization programmes associated with new issues.[50] While the Code of Market Conduct[51] plays a central role in controlling market abuse, reference must also be made to the Handbook generally, in particular the High Level Standards such as Principles of Business,[52] and Senior Management Arrangement, Systems and Controls,[53] and the specific Handbooks such as Supervision,[54] Decision Procedures and Penalties Manual,[55] Disclosure Rules and Transparency Rules[56] and the Listing Rules.[57]

What then amounts to behaviour that would be regarded as market abuse? In determining such behaviour we have to look to both the FSMA 2000 and the Code of Market Conduct to see what is and what isn't behaviour amounting

---

being moved to the Bank of England. The final outcome of the proposed reforms was published in January 2012 in the form of the Financial Services Bill 2012.

43   Financial Services and Markets Act 2000, s 119.

44   L. Linklater, 'The Market Abuse Regime: Setting Standards in the Twenty-First Century' (2001) *Company Lawyer*, 22(9), 267–272 at 269.

45   D. Sabalot and R. Everett, *Financial Services and Markets Act 2000* (2004) Butterworths New Law Guide LexisNexis, at 270.

46   These are termed 'safe harbours' in which the activity is not subject to the prohibition.

47   MAR1.1.2G; Note anything marked with a 'C' is behaviour that does not constitute market abuse – MAR1.1.4G.

48   MAR1.1.6G.

49   MAR1.1.7G.

50   MAR1.10 and Annex 1.

51   MAR.

52   PRIN.

53   SYSC.

54   SUP.

55   DEPP.

56   DTR.

57   LR.

to market abuse. Unsurprisingly the first of the seven is the classic offence of insider dealing,[58] requiring an 'insider' to deal, or try to deal on the basis of 'inside information.' The second form of behaviour caught by the regime is improper disclosure,[59] where the 'insider' discloses 'inside information' to another person without permission. The FSA gives the example of a company employee who, on finding out that his company has become the target of a takeover, buys or sells shares before that information becomes public.[60] The improper disclosure provision is designed to catch the 'insider' if he then tells a friend or work colleague. The classic example of the potential for market abuse surrounding takeovers and mergers has long been seen, and has been a primary concern for the FSA and its predecessor organizations. The FSA noted that while they felt that the statistics were improving, the levels of informed price movements ahead of takeover announcements were still causing concern.[61] However, the trend has, more recently, been a cause for concern again, with abnormal price movements seen in over 30 per cent of takeovers, the highest level for five years.[62] The third type of behaviour caught by the legislation is misuse of information[63] not generally available, which would have an effect on an investor's decision about the terms on which to deal. The FSA example for this type of behaviour is the employee who learns that his company is about to lose a significant contract that would have an overall effect on the price of securities of that company, such as a government order for an aircraft carrier which is to be cancelled.

This is the first of the two so-called super-equivalent provisions that have been specifically retained by the FSA even though it was not part of the Directive, and as such goes further than that which was required by the Directive. The super-equivalent provisions catch more potentially abusive practices as they retain the term 'behaviour' as opposed to the Directives more specific terminology,[64] with the Directive requiring some positive action by the market participant.[65] This provision utilizes the regular user test as a basis of ascertaining whether or not market abuse has been committed. It is clear from the examples in the Code of Market Conduct

---

58   Financial Services and Markets Act 2000, s 118(2).

59   Financial Services and Markets Act 2000, s 118(3).

60   Financial Services Authority, 'Why Market Abuse Could Cost You Money – The Revised Code of Market Conduct is Here to Help Protect You' (2008) <http://www.fsa.gov. uk/pubs/public/market_abuse.pdf> accessed 29 June 2010.

61   Financial Services Authority (2007) 'Market Watch. Market Division: Newsletter on Market Conduct and Transaction Reporting Issues' (2007) <http://www.fsa.gov.uk/pubs/ newsletters/mw_newsletter21.pdf> accessed 30 June 2010.

62   R. Wachman 'Suspicious Share Trading Before Takeover News at Five-Year High' (2010) <http://www.guardian.co.uk/business/2010/jun/10/fsa-takeover-suspicious-trading> accessed 30 June 2010.

63   Financial Service and Markets Act 2000, s 118(4)(a)(b).

64   Financial Services Authority, 'UK Implementation of EU Market Abuse Directive' (2004) <http://www.fsa.gov.uk/pubs/other/eu_mad.pdf> accessed 5 July 2010.

65   Sheikh above, n 1 at 236.

that this is a broader approach than the Directive required as there is no need for a person in possession of the information to be an 'insider'. The example given by the FSA is the situation whereby an 'insider' has lunch with a non-insider friend and tells him of a proposed takeover. Acting on this information, the friend then places a bet. In this situation, the friend will be liable to action by the FSA.[66] It is also worth noting that the information does not need to be 'inside information' either. Rather the focus is on relevant information not generally available, known by its acronym 'RINGA'. As this is retained from the pre-Directive regime, and extends further than the Directive's provisions, it is designed for use only in situations where the first two provisions do not apply, sweeping up behaviour that would slip through the remit of the MAD.[67] The super-equivalent provisions are subject to a sunset clause.[68] This was originally set to trigger on 30 June 2008,[69] was then subsequently increased to 31 December 2009[70] and then further extended to 31 December 2011.[71] This arguably shows that the UK authorities believe that maintaining the flexibility of these super-equivalent provisions is an important component of the MAR, at least until the EU has completed its review of the MAD. It could however also show mistrust in the possibility that the European minimum standard may not be sufficiently strong enough to deal with market abuse in a UK securities market context.

The fourth type of behaviour is manipulating transactions,[72] where trades or the placing of orders to trade give a false or misleading impression of the supply of, or demand for, one or more investments, thus raising the price of the investment to an artificial or abnormal level.[73] The fifth type of behaviour is manipulating devices,[74] where a person trades or places orders to trade, employing fictitious devices or any other form of deception. The sixth form of behaviour surrounds dissemination[75] where a person gives out information conveying a false or misleading impression about an investment or issuer of an investment knowing that this information is

---

66   MAR1.5.10E, Para(1).

67   A. Loke, 'From the Fiduciary Theory to Information Abuse: The Changing Fabric of Insider Trading Law in the UK, Australia and Singapore' (2006) *The American Journal of Comparative Law*, 54(1), 123–172.

68   Sheikh above, n 1.

69   Financial Services and Markets Act 2000 (Market Abuse) Regulations 2005 (SI 2005/381).

70   Financial Services and Markets Act 2000 (Market Abuse) Regulations 2008 (SI 2008/1439).

71   Financial Services and Markets Act 2000 (Market Abuse) Regulations 2009 (SI 2009/3128).

72   Financial Services and Markets Act 2000, s 118(5)(a)(b).

73   See for example *Queen v Securities and Futures Authority Ltd. Disciplinary Appeal Tribunal of the Securities and Futures Authority Limited, ex parte Bertrand Fleurose* [2001] EWHC Admin 292; [2001] 2 All ER (Comm) 481.

74   Financial Services and Markets Act 2000, s 118(6).

75   Financial Services and Markets Act 2000, s 118(7).

false and misleading. The final type of behaviour is distortion and misleading behaviour[76] that gives a false and misleading impression of either the supply of, or demand for, an investment; or behaviour that otherwise distorts the market in an investment. This is the second of the super-equivalent provisions, and while the first one deals with the misuse of information, the second is concerned with market manipulation and distortion in particular. Again, the objective regular user test is applied and again, these provisions are to be applied where the behaviour does not fall within the definition of the other sections dealing with market manipulation, misleading impressions and distortion.

A key element in the pre-Directive UK provision is the notion of the regular user. The original version of the legislation required that the behaviour in question, occurring in relation to qualifying investments satisfying one or more of the conditions set, had to be regarded by a 'regular user of that market who is aware of the behaviour as a failure on the part of the person or persons concerned to observe the standard behaviour reasonably expected of a person in his or their position in relation to the market.'[77] The regular user test sets up an objective and hypothetical standard against which market participants can be judged, and has been seen as a sophisticated financial services equivalent of the reasonable man standard used to judge whether a person has breached his/her duty of care in an action for negligence.[78] The regular user test was not included in the MAD, however, it has been retained by the FSA in support of the so-called super-equivalent provisions, albeit with the protection of a sunset clause, thus the regular user test now only applies to sections 118(4) and 118(8) FSMA 2000.

With reference to insider dealing and similar to criminal provisions, to be caught by the civil regime the information must be 'inside information' and be held by an 'insider'. Simply having inside information is not of itself sufficient. One clear improvement as a result of the MAD is that issuers of securities are now required to produce insider lists of people with access to 'inside information'.[79] What constitutes an 'insider' is contained in section 118B FSMA 2000 which lists a number of criteria which have to be taken into consideration. Thus to be an insider the person will have the 'inside information' as a result of being a director or shareholder of the issuer of the securities,[80] holding capital of an issuer,[81] having access to inside information as a result of their employment, profession or duties,[82] or as a result of criminal activities.[83] Additionally the person is an insider if he has

---

76   Financial Services and Markets Act 2000, s 118(8).
77   Financial Services and Markets Act 2000, s 118(1)(c), pre Market Abuse Directive.
78   See *Blyth v Birmingham Waterworks* [1856] 11 Ex Ch 781; see also *Hall v Brooklands Auto Racing Club* [1933] 1 KB 205.
79   See now DTR 2.8 FSA Handbook.
80   Financial Services and Markets Act 2000, s 118B(a).
81   Financial Services and Markets Act 2000, s 118B(b).
82   Financial Services and Markets Act 2000, s 118B(c).
83   Financial Services and Markets Act 2000, s 118B(d).

obtained by other means that which he knows or could reasonably be expected to know, is inside information.[84] Again, the Code of Market Conduct provides information, on what an insider would look like.[85] In essence, the Code lays out a set of criteria where, if a person is in possession of inside information such as a senior manager in an organization that is the target of a takeover, then they will be classified as being an insider for the purpose of the market abuse provisions.

It is quite transparent that the definition of 'insider' primarily relates to a person in possession of 'inside information', and therefore it is arguable that the definition of 'inside information' is key to being able to bring a successful action for market abuse against that 'insider'. What amounts to inside information is contained in sections 118C(2) and (3) of the FSMA 2000 with guidance again provided in the Code of Market Conduct.[86] The provisions are split between qualifying or related investments which are *not* commodity derivatives[87] and which *are* commodity derivatives.[88] For both elements, information is 'inside information' of a precise nature if it is not generally available;[89] relates, directly or indirectly to issuers of qualifying investments or qualifying investments themselves;[90] and, in the case of commodities, to one or more derivatives.[91] In relation to qualifying investments, the requirement is that the information would have a significant effect on the price of the qualifying or related investments.[92] In relation to commodities, it is 'inside information' if users of such markets would expect to receive such information in accordance with any accepted practices on those markets.[93] The different section dealing with commodities reflects the physical nature of commodities and, as such, markets for commodities may have access to information in different forms.[94] 'Precise' is defined in section 118C(5) of the FSMA as circumstances that exist or may reasonably be expected to come into existence or an event that has occurred or may reasonably be expected to occur,[95] and is specific enough to enable a conclusion to be drawn as to the possible effect of those circumstances or that event on the price of qualifying investments or related investments.[96] This is not a particularly well-defined section and could conceivably lead to some debate. The question remains as to how precise or how specific the 'inside information' needs to be. If too specific then the FSA will struggle to bring successful enforcement

---

84   Financial Services and Markets Act 2000, s 118B(e).
85   MAR 1.2.7. 1.2.8E and 1.2.9G.
86   MAR 1.2.10.
87   Financial Services and Markets Act 2000, s 118C(2).
88   Financial Services and Markets Act 2000, s 118C(3).
89   Financial Services and Markets Act 2000, s 118C(2)(a), 118C(3)(a).
90   Financial Services and Markets Act 2000, s 118C(2)(b).
91   Financial Services and Markets Act 2000, s 118C(3)(b).
92   Financial Services and Markets Act 2000, s 118C(2)(c).
93   Financial Services and Markets Act 2000, s 118C(3)(c).
94   A. Hudson, *The Law of Finance* (Sweet and Maxwell 2009) at p. 282.
95   Financial Services and Markets Act 2000, s 118(C)(5)(a).
96   Financial Services and Markets Act 2000, s 118(C)(5)(b).

actions. It is submitted that this is the correct approach in that the requirement for inside information should not be overly restricted by a requirement of too great a specificity. Many issues have an impact on the price of securities and such a broad approach is thus to be welcomed.[97]

In addition to the need to be precise, the information needs to be 'likely to have a significant effect on the price of those qualifying investments or related investments.'[98] In similar fashion to the older criminal provisions, this requirement leads to the conclusion that for the prohibition to apply the action on the part of the person accused of market abuse must be more than trivial, in that minor movements in the prices of qualifying investments will not amount to market abuse. Exactly what will amount is a matter for the FSA to determine, and a trawl through the Authority's enforcement actions list will give some idea as to what 'significant' will mean in practice.[99] Thus, the FSA will consider what the reasonable investor would be likely to do. For example, the more significant the price movement gained from the 'inside information' the more likely that the FSA will see it as 'significant' within the meaning of the provision.[100]

A further key issue is whether or not the information has been made public. Information is only 'inside information' if it 'is not generally available',[101] and once it is regarded as generally available it ceases to be information for the purposes of market abuse. Section 118C(8) and the Code of Market Conduct provides the section, assistance and examples to determine whether or not information is to be regarded as generally available.[102] These include information disclosed in the proper manner to a prescribed market,[103] publicly available documents,[104] papers only available on payment of a fee,[105] and documents obtained by analysing or developing other information which is generally available.[106] It is not relevant if the information is only available outside of the UK,[107] nor is it relevant if the analysis is only possible by a person with considerable financial 'resources, expertise or competence.'[108] The example given in the Code of Market Conduct

---

97   For a look at Finnish case law on the issue of what is precise see J. Hayrynen, 'The Precise Definition of Inside Information?' (2008) *Journal of International Banking Law and Regulation*, 23(2), 64–70.

98   Financial Services and Markets Act 2000, s 118C(6).

99   See Financial Services Authority (n/d), 'Enforcement Notices, Financial Services Authority' <http://www.fsa.gov.uk/pages/About/What/financial_crime/market_abuse/library/notices/index.shtml> accessed 1 July 2010.

100   Hudson above, n 94 at 284.

101   Financial Services and Markets Act 2000, s 118C(2)(a), 118C(3)(a) and 118C(4)(b).

102   MAR1.2.12E.

103   MAR1.2.12E, Para (1).

104   MAR1.2.12E, Para (2).

105   MAR1.2.12E, Para (3).

106   MAR1.2.12E, Para (5).

107   MAR1.2.13E, Para (1).

108   MAR1.2.13E, Para (2).

is of a passenger on a train who sees a burning factory during his journey. If he calls his broker and tells him to sell shares in that company, this will not amount to market abuse as the information will be deemed to have been generally available.[109] Information is, however, available in many forms today and so it can be a difficult question as to whether information is no longer to be regarded as 'inside information' or whether it is generally available, with this being a matter of evidence. What does come through, however, is that the professional and talented market analyst and broker are protected against accusations of market misconduct, providing of course that the source of their information is not regarded as 'inside information'. The professional and thorough analysis of the broker will not fall foul of the regime, even if the information is paid for and if the information is not generally available to the market as a whole, unless of course they have done the same research. One of the new and innovative features required by the MAD was the introduction of more proactive measures to prevent market abuse. In this the MAD requires a system of suspicious transaction reporting,[110] and while not a new phenomenon by any means to the financial sector in respect of money laundering it was a new requirement for suspected market abuse.[111]

The new market abuse regime has been described as 'novel',[112] 'controversial'[113] and the 'new witchcraft'.[114] These comments arguably stem from the civil enforcement mechanisms contained within the provisions. The new regime is designed to complement the criminal provisions of the Criminal Justice Act 1993, by running parallel and in addition to these, rather than replacing and substituting them.[115] The original UK regime came into force in 2001 but was soon subject to a major revision by virtue of the MAD, which, as discussed above, aimed to set a minimum standard across EU markets.[116] The Directive was the first of the provisions to be brought through using the Lamfalussy process designed to speed up the implementation of provisions forming part of the EU's 'Financial Services Action Plan', and was designed to bring a level of uniformity to the communities approach to tackling market misuse, which had reported that the

---

109   MAR1.2.14G.

110   Article 6.9 MAD.

111   Detailed suspicious transaction reporting requirements as contained in the Supervision Handbook SUP at SUP 15.10.

112   Linklater above, n 44.

113   A. Alcock, 'Market Abuse' (2002) *Company Lawyer*, 23(5), 142–150 at 143.

114   Alcock above, n 31.

115   A. Sykes, 'Market Abuse: A Civil Revolution' (1999) *Journal of International Financial Markets*, 1(2), 59–67.

116   2003/6/EC.

existing regulatory system was slow and rigid and unevenly implemented.[117] The UK MAR incorporating the Directive has thus been active since 1 July 2005.[118]

The Extent of Market Abuse

The extent of market abuse, like the other types of financial crime addressed throughout this book, is extremely difficult to determine. Efforts to accurately determine its extent are flawed with methodological difficulties. However, several attempts have been made to measure the extent of market abuse in the UK. For example, in 2006 the FSA published its 'measure for the scale of market abuse.'[119] Here, the FSA were unable to illustrate the exact level of market abuse, but did 'suggest that some informed trading may have taken place prior to 28.9% of the takeover announcements and 21.7% of the FTSE350 trading announcements which were identified as being most likely to contain information of use to an insider trader.'[120] The informed trading, according to the FSA, could amount to instances of market abuse. In 2007, the FSA published an update on its 2006 report.[121] The 2007 Report indicated that there was a 'significant decrease in the level of possible informed trading ahead of FTSE 350 companies' trading announcements, with only 2% of significant announcements being preceded by informed price movements compared to 11.1% in the period 2002/03 and 19.6% in 1998–2000.'[122] Furthermore, in its 2010 Annual Report the FSA stated that the abnormal pre-announcement price movements dataset declined to the lowest figure since 2003.[123] However, the FSA admitted that although 'this fall has taken place against the backdrop of increasing focus on market abuse, due to the nature of the statistic, the reason behind this decline cannot be determined with certainty'.[124]

---

117   J. Hansen, 'MAD in a Hurry: The Swift and Promising Adoption of the EU Market Abuse Directive' (2007) *European Business Law Review*, 15(2), 183–221.

118   Amendments made to FSMA 2000 by the Financial Services and Markets Act 2000 (Market Abuse) Regulations 2005, SI 2005/381.

119   FSA (2006) 'FSA Publishes Measure of Scale of Market Abuse', 17 March 2006 <http://www.fsa.gov.uk/pages/Library/Communication/PR/2006/020.shtml> accessed 10 November 2011.

120   Financial Services Authority, *Measuring Market Cleanliness FSA Occasional Paper Series 23* (Financial Services Authority 2006) at p. 24.

121   Financial Services Authority, *Updated Measurement of Market Cleanliness FSA Occasional Paper Series 25* (Financial Services Authority 2007).

122   Financial Services Authority (2007) 'FSA Publishes Updated Measure of UK Market Cleanliness', 7 March 2007 <http://www.fsa.gov.uk/library/communication/pr/2007/031.shtmlm> accessed 9 December 2011. See also A. Hayes 'Market Abuse' (2010) *Compliance Officer Bulletin* 75(Apr), 1–31.

123   Financial Services Authority, *Annual Report 2010/2011* (Financial Services Authority: London 2011) at p. 62.

124   Ibid.

Nonetheless, Hector Sants, the former chief executive of the FSA stated that the levels of market abuse were still at an 'unacceptably high level'.[125] He added:

> There's no evidence that the UK marketplace is worse than other major financial centres but I don't think that should be our benchmark. Our benchmark should seek to have a market that participants really believe to be clean and fair and, as a general test, I think that if you were to ask the market participants, they would share my view that there is too much market abuse.[126]

Financial Institutions and Regulatory Bodies

The civil market abuse regime is primarily enforced by the FSA as a result of its statutory objective to reduce financial crime under the FSMA 2000. Under this Act, the FSA has been given an extensive array of enforcement powers to ensure that firms comply with the regime and impose sanctions for those firms that breach that regime. Therefore, it is arguable that the primary function of the MAR is to punish market abusers, and to that end Part VIII FSMA 2000 is actually entitled 'Penalties for Market Abuse'. While this was the position of the original intention of the Act, this has been emphasized by the Directive which requires member states' regulatory authorities to attempt to prevent market abuse occurring. This can be shown by the Code of Market Conduct and the many examples within the code of what amounts to market abuse and who commits it. By providing such examples, market participants should be able to ascertain when they are coming dangerously close to committing the prohibited activities contained in Part VIII of the FSMA 2000. Despite this help, the MAR still plays a vital role in bringing market abusers to account and to this aim the FSA has considerable power, as discussed below, to undertake investigations into alleged market abusers and issue financial penalties.

Reporting of Suspicious Transactions

The final part of UK policy towards market abuse is the reporting of suspicious transactions through the use of suspicious transactions reports. Comparisons can therefore be drawn with similar provisions outlined in chapters 2 and 4 for money laundering and fraud. The obligation to report suspected dealings of market abuse

---

125   BBC News (2010) 'UK Market Abuse Unacceptably High, Says FSA Boss' Sunday 14 March 2010 <http://news.bbc.co.uk/1/hi/8566904.stm> accessed 20 October 2011.

126   Andrew Cave (2010) 'Market Abuse is Unacceptably High', 13 March 2011 <http://www.telegraph.co.uk/finance/newsbysector/banksandfinance/7436104/Market-abuse-is-unacceptably-high-says-FSA-boss.html> accessed 14 December 2011.

exist as a result of the MAD, which was implemented into the UK on 1 July 2005. In determining whether or not to report the transaction, the firm or individual must have reasonable grounds of suspicion which is the same test as utilized by the Proceeds of Crime Act 2002. Furthermore, the FSA has its own rules for the reporting of suspicious transactions which provide that:

> a firm which arranges or executes a transaction with or for a client in a qualifying investment admitted to trading on a prescribed market and which has reasonable grounds to suspect that the transaction might constitute market abuse must notify the FSA without delay.[127]

If a firm or individual does not file a suspicious transaction report, the FSA has the power to impose a financial penalty, as seen below.

Sentencing and Recovery

A person found guilty of the criminal offence of misleading statements and practices is liable to a term of imprisonment not exceeding seven years, an unlimited fine, or both.[128] For misleading the Authority, the maximum penalty is a fine,[129] while for misleading the OFT, the maximum penalty is increased to a term of custody not exceeding two years and/or a financial penalty.[130] Even though market abuse is defined as a criminal offence under the FSMA 2000, the majority of market abusers are dealt with using financial penalties under the civil MAR rather than through a criminal route. These enforcement powers are contained in Part XI of the FSMA 2000, which allows the FSA to appoint professionals to undertake general investigations under section 167 or investigations in particular cases under section 168. The types of cases relevant to section 168 include insider dealing[131] and market abuse.[132] To bring a disciplinary action the FSA must be satisfied that a person has engaged in market abuse,[133] or has encouraged another person to undertake behaviour which, if he had engaged in such action, would amount to market abuse.[134] The outcome of such investigations is sent to the Regulatory Decisions Committee, an administrative decisionmaker, to decide whether or not to bring disciplinary actions against an individual.

---

127 Financial Services Authority, *FSA Handbook – SUP (Supervision)* (Financial Services Authority 2008) at SUP 15.10.2.
   128 Financial Services and Markets Act 2000, s 397(8).
   129 Financial Services and Markets Act 2000, s 398(3).
   130 Competition Act 1998, s 44(3).
   131 Financial Services and Markets Act 2000, s 168(2)(a).
   132 Financial Services and Markets Act 2000, s 168(2)(d).
   133 Financial Services and Markets Act 2000, s 123(1)(a).
   134 Financial Services and Markets Act 2000, s 123(1)(b).

Before a fine can be imposed, the FSA must prepare and issue a statement of its intention to fine, known as a statement of fining policy. Once this has been issued, the public are invited to make representations.[135] Such statements will be taken into account when setting the level of the fine. When the level has been decided upon, the FSA must then issue a warning notice which will state the amount involved. Likewise, if the proposal is to publish a censure, a warning notice setting out the terms of the censure must be issued.[136] It is at this point that the named individual or company will be able to argue that any of the defences apply. If, having taken any representations into account, a financial penalty is still deemed appropriate, the FSA will issue a decision notice which will contain the final decision regarding the level of fine.[137] An important check and balance here is that if the FSA decides to take action against a person, that person may refer the matter to the Financial Services and Markets Tribunal, an independent Tribunal set up to hear appeals against FSA decisions and, if necessary, can appeal this decision to the Court of Appeal, as long as this appeal is on a point of law.

Where market abuse has been proved, the FSA has a number of options, dependent on the severity of the abuse. For instance, through the FSMA 2000, the FSA is authorised to impose 'a penalty of such amount as it considers appropriate.'[138] In determining what this amount should be, the Authority must have regard to:

a. whether the behaviour in respect of which the penalty is to be imposed had an adverse effect on the market in question and, if it did, how serious that effect was;
b. the extent to which that behaviour was deliberate or reckless; and
c. whether the person on whom the penalty is to be imposed is an individual.[139]

In addition to these guidelines, since 6 March 2010, the FSA also has a financial penalties policy which provides a framework for calculating the size of fines. Under this framework, fines are linked to the income of companies and are based on:

- up to 20 per cent of a firm's revenue from the product or business area linked to the breach over the relevant period;
- up to 40 per cent of an individual's salary and benefits (including bonuses) from their job relating to the breach in non-market abuse cases; and
- a minimum starting point of £100,000 for individuals in serious market abuse cases.

---

135   Financial Services and Markets Act 2000, s 125.
136   Financial Services and Markets Act 2000, s 126(3).
137   Financial Services and Markets Act 2000, s 127.
138   Financial Services and Markets Act 2000, s 123(1).
139   Financial Services and Markets Act 2000, s 124(2).

The above framework has led to quite sizeable penalties being imposed, many of which have been imposed in relation to instances whereby individuals or companies have failed to submit accurate and/or timely suspicious transaction reports to the FSA. For example in 2010, the FSA fined the London branch of Societe Generale (SocGen) £1,575,000; the London branch of Commerzbank AG £595,000; Credit Suisse £1.75 million; Getco Europe Limited £1.4 million; and Instinet Europe Limited £1.05 million for such offences. Similarly, in 2009 Barclays Capital Securities Limited and Barclays Bank plc were fined £2.45 million.[140] For deliberately and systematically engaging in manipulative trading, Swift Trade Inc were fined £8 million in 2011[141] and in the same year individuals Michiel Weiger Visser and Oluwole Modupe Fagbulu were fined £2 million and £100,000 respectively for market abuse and deception offences.[142] Interestingly, the FSA is also able to obtain High Court injunctions restraining individuals from committing future instances of market abuse. These are reserved for those individuals who have previously been involved in market abuse activity, with breach of the injunction resulting in the possibility of a custodial sentence. The first of these injunctions was issued against Samuel Kahn in May 2011, who was also fined £1,094,000 – the second largest fine given to an individual in FSA history.[143]

Furthermore, the FSA has the power to publicly censure market participants by publishing a statement that a person has engaged in market abuse;[144] presumably to damage his/her reputation and standing. In some cases this 'naming and shaming' will be sufficient punishment and deterrence. Additionally, it can either apply to the courts for restitution or it can order restitution itself.[145] As part of the measures to ensure greater transparency and to head off civil liberties concerns the FSA is required to publish a 'Statement of Policy'[146] outlining how it intends to implement its penalties regime, detailing when and how it will impose these and the amount

---

140   Financial Services Authority (2011) Transaction Reporting Cases <http://www.fsa.gov.uk/pages/About/What/financial_crime/market_abuse/library/index.shtml> accessed 18 October 2011.

141   Financial Services Authority (2011) 'FSA Decides to Fine Firm £8m for Market Abuse' <http://www.fsa.gov.uk/pages/Library/Communication/PR/2011/075.shtml> accessed 18 October 2011.

142   Financial Services Authority (2011) 'Tribunal Upholds FSA Decision to Ban and Fine Hedge Fund CEO and CFO £2.1m for Deceiving Investors and Market Abuse' <http://www.fsa.gov.uk/pages/Library/Communication/PR/2011/071.shtml> accessed 18 October 2011.

143   J. Russell (2011) 'FSA Fine of £1m and High Court Injunction For Market Abuse', *The Telegraph*, 25 May 2011 <http://www.telegraph.co.uk/finance/financial-crime/8533980/FSA-fine-of-1m-and-High-Court-injunction-for-market-abuse.html> accessed 20 October 2011.

144   Financial Services and Markets Act 2000, s 123(3).

145   Financial Services and Markets Act 2000, s 3840.

146   Financial Services and Markets Act 2000, s 124.

of any penalty imposed along with other relevant factors.[147] As with the insider dealing provisions, any imposition of a penalty does not render any transaction void or unenforceable.[148]

One of the most controversial and initially confusing elements of the MAR has surrounded the nature of the offence. As already noted the intention of Part VIII of the FSMA 2000 was to introduce a civil enforcement regime parallel to the criminal provision contained in the Criminal Justice Act 1993. The confusion is not helped by the terms used to describe the regime, such as 'offence' and 'prosecute',[149] words normally associated with criminal sanctions. The introduction of the civil enforcement mechanisms forced the FSA to consult,[150] beyond its original intention, due to the volume of comments on their original consultation.[151] The key issue here is whether or not the so-called civil sanctions are compatible with the European Convention on Human Rights as incorporated into English law by the Human Rights Act 1998, a relevant question when a decision of the FSA has been referred to the Financial Services and Markets Tribunal.[152] Section 123 of the FSMA 2000 merely states that the FSA has to be 'satisfied' that market abuse or encouraging such activity has occurred, which does not create a particularly high standard. This argument relates to whether the civil penalties in the regime can accurately be described as civil or whether, in reality, they are more akin to criminal sanctions. The controversy has centred on the two key issues of the reduced burden of proof required to prove market abuse as opposed to the criminal standard required by the criminal provisions of the Criminal Justice Act 1993, and whether or not the allegation of market abuse is a criminal charge, which should then be subject to the usual due process protections.[153]

Future Recommendations

As discussed in Chapter 5, the criminalization of insider dealing in the UK is principally seen as a failure, largely because of the high burden of proof required in such difficult evidentiary cases. There has therefore been an attempt to address

---

147   See DEPP 6 Decision Procedure and Penalties Manual FSA Handbook.

148   Financial Services and Markets Act 2000, s 131.

149   Filby above, n 29.

150   Financial Service Authority (1999), 'Feedback Statement on Responses to Consultation Paper 10: Market Abuse' <http://www.fsa.gov.uk/pubs/cp/cp10_response.pdf> accessed 5 July 2010.

151   Financial Services Authority (1998) 'Consultation Paper 10 Market Abuse Part 1: Consultation on a Draft Code of Market Conduct' <http://www.fsa.gov.uk/pubs/cp/cp10.pdf> accessed 5 July 2010.

152   C. Conceicao, 'The FSA's Approach to Taking Action Against Market Abuse' (2007) *Company Lawyer*, 29(2), 43–45.

153   Additionally there have been concerns that the market abuse regime lacks certainty required by Article 7 ECHR.

this in the form of a civil regime, enacted as part of FSMA 2000, which covers not just insider dealing but all forms of market abuse. Whether or not this regime has been more successful is difficult to judge, even though some considerable time has elapsed since its initial enactment. This is partly due to the requirements of the MAD which altered UK policy within only four years of it coming into force. It is certainly evident, however, that the level of fines issued for market abuse remain high and this coupled with a more aggressive approach taken by the FSA, particularly in respect of criminal prosecutions for insider dealing, should allow it to claim success in its mission to combat insider dealing and market manipulation. Despite this, challenges will undoubtedly still remain. The perception of the victimless crime and the ongoing difficulties in proving the offence will remain problematic, especially if the Financial Services and Markets Tribunal apply a criminal standard of proof to the more important cases, an issue which could bring the MAR to a halt. As Rider notes, the compromises seen in respect of civil liberties issues have resulted in civil offences becoming as difficult to prove as the criminal ones they were designed to remedy and replace.[154]

Further Reading

Alcock, A. 'Market Abuse – The New Witchcraft' (2001) *New Law Journal*, 151, 1398.

Alcock, A. 'Market Abuse' (2002) *Company Lawyer*, 23(5), 142–150.

Alcock, A. 'Five Years of Market Abuse' (2007) *Company Lawyer*, 28(6), 163–171.

Alexander, R. 'Corporate Crimes: Are the Gloves Coming Off?' (2009) *Company Lawyer*, 30(11), 321–322.

Barnes, P. 'Insider Dealing and Market Abuse: The UK's Record on Enforcement' (2011) *International Journal of Law Crime and Justice*, 39(3), 174–189.

Burger, R. 'A Principled Front in the War Against Market Abuse' (2007) *Journal of Financial Regulation and Compliance*, 15(3), 331–336.

Burger, R. and G. Davies 'What's New in Market Abuse – Part 2' (2005) *New Law Journal*, 155, 964.

Conceicao, C. 'The FSA's Approach to Taking Action Against Market Abuse' (2007) *Company Lawyer*, 29(2), 43–45.

Editorial, 'Insiders Beware!' (1993) *Company Lawyer*, 14(11), 202.

Filby, M. 'Part VIII Financial Services and Markets Act: Filling Insider Dealing's Regulatory Gaps' (2004) *Company Lawyer*, 23(12), 363–370.

Haines, J. 'FSA Determined to Improve the Cleanliness of Markets: Custodial Sentences Continue to be a Real Threat' (2008) *Company Lawyer*, 29(12), 370.

Hansen, J. 'MAD in a Hurry: The Swift and Promising Adoption of the EU Market Abuse Directive' (2007) *European Business Law Review*, 15(2), 183–221.

154   B. Rider, 'An Abominable Fraud?' (2010) *Company Lawyer*, 31(7), 197–198.

Hayes, A. 'Market Abuse' (2010) *Compliance Office Bulletin*, 75(Apr), 1–31.

Haynes, A. 'Market Abuse: An Analysis of its Nature and Regulation' (2007) *Company Lawyer*, 28(11), 323–335.

Haynes, A. 'Market Abuse, Northern Rock and Bank Rescues' (2009) *Journal of Banking Regulation*, 10(4), 321–334.

Hayrynen, J. 'The Precise Definition of Inside Information?' (2008) *Journal of International Banking Law and Regulation*, 23(2), 64–70.

Linklater, L. 'The Market Abuse Regime: Setting Standards in the Twenty-First Century' (2001) *Company Lawyer*, 22(9), 267–272.

Rider, B. 'Where Angels Fear!' (2008) *Company Lawyer*, 29(9), 257–258.

Sheikh, S. 'FSMA Market Abuse Regime: A Review of the Sunset Clauses' (2008) *International Company and Commercial Law Review*, 19(7), 237–236.

Swan, E. 'Market Abuse: A New Duty of Fairness' (2004) *Company Lawyer*, 25(3), 67–68.

Sykes, A. 'Market Abuse: A Civil Revolution' (1999) *Journal of International Financial Markets*, 1(2), 59–67.

Chapter 7
Bribery and Corruption

Introduction

Bribery and corruption have received a considerable amount of attention since the introduction and implementation of the Bribery Act 2010 and the extension of the remit of the Serious Fraud Office (SFO). Bribery has been referred to as an illegal gratuity, extortion, conflict of interest, kickback, corporate espionage and a commission or fee. According to the Organisation for Economic Co-operation and Development (OECD), bribery is defined as 'the offering, promising or giving [of] something in order to influence a public official in the execution of his/her official duties.'[1] Perhaps one of the simplest definitions, however, is offered by the SFO who argues that bribery is the 'giving or receiving [of] something of value to influence a transaction.'[2] A bribe can include,

> ... money, other pecuniary advantages, such as [a] scholarship for a child's college education, or non-pecuniary benefits, such as favourable publicity. In the international context, bribery involves a business firm from country A offering financial or non-financial inducements to officials of country B to obtain a commercial benefit.[3]

It has been argued that bribery can be divided into two categories – direct and indirect.[4] The more common of these two types is indirect, and this is usually conducted via an agent or a go-between. This type of conduct traditionally arises where the respective parties agree to meet in order to try and gain, for example, a competitive advantage. The agent is normally paid a commission from the additional revenue generated by the resultant work or trade.[5] Beale and Esposito offer the following useful example of what constitutes a direct bribe,

---

1   OECD Observer, *The Fight against Bribery and Corruption* (OECD 2000) as cited in R. Sanyal and S. Samanta, 'Trends in International Bribe-giving: Do Anti-bribery Laws Matter?' (2011) *Journal of International Trade Law & Policy*, 10(2), 151–164, 152.

2   Serious Fraud Office, 'Bribery and Corruption' <http://www.sfo.gov.uk/bribery--corruption/bribery--corruption.aspx> accessed 23 November 2011.

3   R. Sanyal and S. Samanta, 'Trends in International Bribe-Giving: Do Anti-Bribery Laws Matter?' (2011) *Journal of International Trade Law & Policy*, 10(2), 151–164, 153.

4   K. Beale and P. Esposito, 'Emergent International Attitudes Towards Bribery, Corruption and Money Laundering' (2009) *Arbitration*, 75(3), 360–373, 362.

5   K. Beale and P. Esposito, 'Emergent International Attitudes Towards Bribery, Corruption and Money Laundering' (2009) *Arbitration*, 75(3), 360–373, 362.

A company commences an arbitration against the government of a country and the government's defence is that it has recently learned that the company paid bribes to government employees or officials in connection with the project; that is an allegation of direct bribery.[6]

Denning, citing Latymer, stated that bribery was 'a princely kind of thieving',[7] yet despite these simple definitions, it is still a very difficult term to define.[8] This point is illustrated by the different statutory definitions of bribery offered by the Public Bodies Corrupt Practices Act 1889, the Prevention of Corruption Act 1906 and the Prevention of Corruption Act 1916. The uncertainty over its definition was clarified by the Bribery Act 2010. To aid with this clarity, the chapter begins by outlining the relevant offences created by the Bribery Act and then goes on to look at the United Kingdom's (UK) bribery policy, which is administered by the Ministry of Justice and enforced by the SFO in conjunction with the Financial Services Authority (FSA). The policy, which has been adopted, is very similar to that outlined in the previous chapters of this book and can be divided into three parts: criminalization, regulatory agencies and the use of suspicious transaction reports. The primary focus of this chapter will therefore be to analyse these initiatives including also an attempt at quantifying the extent of the problem. The final part of the chapter reviews the available criminal and civil sentencing options and practices.

What is the Offence of Bribery?

Prior to the Bribery Act 2010, the criminal offence of bribery was housed in the provisions of the Public Bodies Corrupt Practices Act 1889, the Prevention of Corruption Act 1906 and the Prevention of Corruption Act 1916.[9] These laws were described as an 'untidy and unsatisfactory jumble',[10] which needed replacing with a 'concise modern mini-code, which should ensure rather more

---

6   K. Beale and P. Esposito, 'Emergent International Attitudes Towards Bribery, Corruption and Money Laundering' (2009) Arbitration, 75(3), 360–373, 362. For other examples of conduct that amounts to a bribe see J. Horder, 'Bribery as a Form of Criminal Wrongdoing' (2011) *Law Quarterly Review*, 127(Jan), 37–54, 37–38.

7   A. Denning, 'Independence and Impartiality of the Judges' (1954) *South African Law Journal*, 71, 345.

8   The Law Commission, *Reforming Bribery* (The Stationery Office 2008).

9   OECD, 'Steps Taken to Implement and Enforce the OECD Convention on Combating Bribery of Foreign Public Officials in International Business Transactions: UNITED KINGDOM' (28 May 2010) <http://www.oecd.org/dataoecd/17/30/48362318. pdf> accessed 27 March 2012.

10   Editorial, 'The Bribery Act 2010' (2010) *Criminal Law Review*, 6, 439–440, 439.

effective compliance with the United Kingdom's international obligations to curb bribery and corruption.'[11] Furthermore, these statutory provisions have been described as being 'inconsistent, anachronistic and inadequate'[12] in terms of complying with international anti-corruption obligations.

The impetus for the reform of the law of bribery was undoubtedly sparked by the recommendation of the Committee on Standards in Public Life, that the government should clarify the law on bribery.[13] Resultantly, the Law Commission published its proposals in 1998, although it wasn't until the Bribery Act 2010 that its recommendations were finally implemented.[14] Other relevant statutory measures included the Anti-terrorism, Crime and Security Act 2001 and the Criminal Justice and Immigration Act 2008 which both extended the scope of the UK's bribery and corruption laws, although, it was not until the implementation of the Bribery Act on 1 July 2011 that the four current bribery offences were actually introduced.

Offences of bribing another person

Section 1 of the Bribery Act 2010 states that a person is guilty of an offence if he/she offers, promises or gives a financial or other advantage to another person in one of two possible circumstances. These circumstances are set out in the Act as separate 'cases' as follows:

Case 1 is where –

a. P offers, promises or gives a financial or other advantage to another person, and
b. P intends the advantage:
    i. to induce a person to perform improperly a relevant function or activity, or
    ii. to reward a person for the improper performance of such a function or activity.[15]

---

11 Editorial, 'The Bribery Act 2010' (2010) *Criminal Law Review*, 6, 439–440, 439.

12 D. Aaronberg and N. Higgins, 'Legislative Comment The Bribery Act 2010: All Bark and No Bite ...?' (2010) *Archbold Review*, 5, 6–9, 6.

13 Committee on Standards in Public Life, *First Report 'Standards in Public Life'* (Cm 2850–1, 1995) 43.

14 Law Commission, *Legislating the Criminal Code: Corruption No. 248* (Law Commission 1998).

15 Bribery Act 2010, s 1(2).

Case 2 is where –

a. P offers, promises or gives a financial or other advantage to another person, and
b. P knows or believes that the acceptance of the advantage would itself constitute the improper performance of a relevant function or activity.[16]

For the purposes of the Act, a function or activity is defined as either,

a. any function of a public nature,
b. any activity connected with a business,
c. any activity performed in the course of a person's employment, [or]
d. any activity performed by or on behalf of a body of persons (whether corporate or unincorporate).[17]

It must also meet one or more of three set conditions, i.e. that a person performing the function or activity is expected to perform it in 'good faith', 'impartially' or 'is in a position of trust by virtue of performing it.'[18] Furthermore, there is no requirement either that the activity or function is performed in the UK or even has any connection with the UK.[19]

A further definitional term, given by the Act is that of 'improper performance'. This is taken to relate to the situation whereby either the activity or function has been 'performed in breach of a relevant expectation', or the failure to carry out the said activity or function is in 'itself a breach of a relevant expectation.'[20] What is to be expected is decided by implementing what is known as the 'expectation test'. This is defined as 'a test of what a reasonable person in the United Kingdom would expect in relation to the performance of the type of function or activity concerned.'[21] This is therefore a question for jurors to decide.

A person is, therefore, guilty of an offence under section 1 if he/she pledges, promises or provides a monetary, pecuniary or other benefit to another person with the purpose that there should be an illicit or shady performance of a function or activity, or knowing that approval would amount to this unlawful conduct. Arguably, it is this offence which 'targets those who offer or pay bribes.'[22] It is also important to note that the improper performance is rewarded by the 'advantage'.[23]

---

16   Bribery Act 2010, s 1(3).
17   Bribery Act 2010, s 3(2).
18   Bribery Act 2010, s 3(3–5).
19   Bribery Act 2010, s 3(6).
20   Bribery Act 2010, s 4(1).
21   Bribery Act 2010, s 5.
22   D. Aaronberg and N. Higgins, 'Legislative Comment The Bribery Act 2010: All Bark and No Bite…?' (2010) *Archbold Review*, 5, 6–9, 6.
23   Bribery Act 2010, s 1.

The Act stipulates that it is irrelevant if the advantage was offered, assured or directly given between the participants or whether a third party was utilized. Furthermore, it is immaterial if the person receiving the offer is the same person due to perform the activity.[24] According to the City of London Police, a person commits an offence under section 1 of the Bribery Act 2010 if he/she 'offers, promises or gives a financial or other advantage to another person, intending to induce them to perform improperly a relevant function or activity or to reward a person for such improper performance.'[25] Similarly, Gentle notes that an offence is committed under section 1 where 'a person offers, promises or gives an advantage to another, intending that the advantage should induce him to perform improperly a function which he is expected to carry out impartially, in good faith or as a consequence of his being in a position of trust.'[26]

Offences relating to being bribed

Section 2 of the Bribery Act 2010 provides that a person 'R' commits an offence if the following cases apply,

> Case 3 is where R requests, agrees to receive or accepts a financial or other advantage intending that, in consequence, a relevant function or activity should be performed improperly (whether by R or another person).[27]
>
> Case 4 is where –
>
> a. R requests, agrees to receive or accepts a financial or other advantage, and
> b. the request, agreement or acceptance itself constitutes the improper performance by R of a relevant function or activity.[28]
>
> Case 5 is where R requests, agrees to receive or accepts a financial or other advantage as a reward for the improper performance (whether by R or another person) of a relevant function or activity.[29]

---

24   Bribery Act 2010, s 1(4)(5).

25   City of London Police 'Bribery Act 2010 summary' <http://www.cityoflondon. police.uk/CityPolice/Departments/ECD/anticorruptionunit/briberyact2010summary.htm> accessed 24 November 2011.

26   S. Gentle, 'The Bribery Act 2010: Part 2: The Corporate Offence' (2011) *Criminal Law Review*, 2, 101–110, 102.

27   Bribery Act 2010, s 2(2).

28   Bribery Act 2010, s 2(3).

29   Bribery Act 2010, s 2(4).

Case 6 is where, in anticipation of or in consequence of R requesting, agreeing to receive or accepting a financial or other advantage, a relevant function or activity is performed improperly –

a. by R, or
b. by another person at R's request or with R's assent or acquiescence.[30]

Therefore a person is guilty of an offence under this section if he/she wishes, consents to, or accepts an advantage with the specific purpose that he/she will perform a relative function or activity improperly either by himself or by another person, or as a reward for such a performance.[31] Arguably, this section of the Act 'targets those who accept or solicit bribes.'[32] The mere request, agreement or acceptance of a benefit constitutes improper performance and it does not matter whether the advantage is received directly or through a third party nor whether the benefit is to those same parties or another.[33] This applies to instances where the improper performance has either been done or is yet to be done by the person or someone acting under his instruction or acquiescence. It is also irrelevant whether the person performing the function or activity knows that it is improper. This is therefore the counter-part of the first offence. The City of London Police has noted that a person is guilty of an offence under this section of the Act where he/she,

> ... requests, agrees to receive or accepts a financial or other advantage intending that, in consequence, a relevant function or activity should be performed improperly by themselves or another. In the above it does not matter whether the advantage is direct or through a third party, nor whether the benefit is for that person or another.[34]

Similarly, Gentle notes that 'in broad terms, the criminal conduct consists of a person requesting, agreeing to receive or accepting an advantage or prospective advantage to perform improperly a relevant function.'[35]

---

30   Bribery Act 2010, s 2(5).

31   Bribery Act 2010 s 2.

32   D. Aaronberg and N. Higgins, 'Legislative Comment The Bribery Act 2010: All Bark and No Bite…?' (2010) *Archbold Review*, 5, 6–9, 7.

33   Bribery Act 2010, s 2(4–6)

34   City of London Police 'Bribery Act 2010 summary' <http://www.cityoflondon. police.uk/CityPolice/Departments/ECD/anticorruptionunit/briberyact2010summary.htm> accessed 24 November 2011.

35   S. Gentle, 'The Bribery Act 2010: Part 2: The Corporate Offence' (2011) *Criminal Law Review*, 2, 101–110, 102.

Bribing a foreign public official

By virtue of section 6 of the Bribery Act 2010, a person 'P' commits the offence of bribing a foreign public official 'F' if P's intention is to influence F in F's capacity as a foreign public official.'[36] P must also 'intend to obtain or retain (a) business, or (b) an advantage in the conduct of business.'[37] In relation to section 6, the Ministry of Justice has noted that this,

> creates a standalone offence of bribery of a foreign public official. The offence is committed where a person offers, promises or gives a financial or other advantage to a foreign public official with the intention of influencing the official in the performance of his or her official functions. The person offering, promising or giving the advantage must also intend to obtain or retain business or an advantage in the conduct of business by doing so. However, the offence is not committed where the official is permitted or required by the applicable written law to be influenced by the advantage.[38]

A person is, therefore, guilty of the offence if he/she aims to manipulate or induce the official in the performance of his role as a public official with the intention of obtaining or retaining business or a business advantage.[39] The City of London Police has taken the view that the offence has been committed,

> where a person in the act of intending to obtain or retain business, or an advantage in the conduct of business, bribes a foreign public official with the intent to influence them in their capacity ... This only applies if they directly, or through a third party, offer, promise or give any financial or other advantage to the foreign official or to another at the official's request or with their assent or acquiescence and the official is neither permitted nor required by the applicable local written law to be influenced in their capacity by the offer, promise or gift.[40]

Failure of commercial organizations to prevent bribery

In addition to individual liability, the Bribery Act 2010 also introduces a new form of corporate criminal liability. Therefore under section 7 of the Act, a commercial organization can also be found guilty of an offence if a person associated with the

---

36 Bribery Act 2010, s 6(1).
37 Bribery Act 2010, s 6(2).
38 Ministry of Justice, *The Bribery Act 2010 – Guidance* (Ministry of Justice 2011) 11.
39 Bribery Act 2010, s 6.
40 City of London Police 'Bribery Act 2010 summary' <http://www.cityoflondon.police.uk/CityPolice/Departments/ECD/anticorruptionunit/briberyact2010summary.htm> accessed 24 November 2011.

organization bribes another, intending to obtain or retain business or a business advantage for that organization.[41] In essence it creates an additional direct rather than alternative vicarious liability, when the commission of a section 1 or section 6 bribery offence has taken place on behalf of an organization. For there to be any liability, however, the organization in question must be stipulated as a 'relevant commercial organization'. This is defined as,

a. a body which is incorporated under the law of any part of the United Kingdom and which carries on a business (whether there or elsewhere),
b. any other body corporate (wherever incorporated) which carries on a business, or part of a business, in any part of the United Kingdom,
c. a partnership which is formed under the law of any part of the United Kingdom and which carries on a business (whether there or elsewhere), or
d. any other partnership (wherever formed) which carries on a business, or part of a business, in any part of the United Kingdom.[42]

For the purposes of this section, an 'associated person' is seen as an individual who 'performs services for or on behalf of' the organization,[43] with the person being, for example, the organization's agent, subsidiary or employee.[44] This has been stated to be a 'matter of substance rather than form',[45] with it being necessary for all surrounding circumstances to be taken into account, although a presumption will exist if the associated person is an employee of the organization. The scope of section 7 is intentionally broad, so as to encompass the whole range of individuals who may be committing bribery on behalf of a third party organization. To be held as an 'associated person', however, 'the perpetrator of the bribery must be performing services for the organization in question and must also intend to obtain or retain business or an advantage in the conduct of business for that organization.'[46]

Due to this introduction of corporate criminal liability, section 7 of the Bribery Act 2010 has been described as a significant move 'away from the current approach',[47] with the Ministry of Justice providing that under section 7,

---

41   Bribery Act 2010, s 7.
42   Bribery Act 2010, s 7(5).
43   Bribery Act 2010, s 8(1).
44   Bribery Act 2010, s 8(3).
45   Ministry of Justice, *Bribery Act 2010, Circular 2011/05* (Ministry of Justice 2011) para. 23.
46   Ministry of Justice, *Bribery Act 2010, Circular 2011/05* (Ministry of Justice 2011) para. 23.
47   T. Pope and T. Webb. 'Legislative Comment – the Bribery Act 2010' (2010) *Journal of International Banking Law and Regulation*, 25(10), 480–483, 482.

a commercial organization will be liable to prosecution if a person associated with it bribes another person intending to obtain or retain business or an advantage in the conduct of business for that organization.[48]

It is also worth noting that for the offence to be made out, there is no requirement to prove that the activity was committed in the UK or elsewhere. Indeed, there is no need to even show a close connection to the UK as is needed for the other bribery offences under the Act.[49]

Moreover, the existence of section 7 does not affect the common law principle which governs the liability of corporate bodies for criminal offences. Under this provision, prosecuting bodies must prove a mens rea or fault element in addition to the actus reus or conduct element. This common law principle, also known as the identification principle, should still be used instead of section 7 of the Bribery Act 2010, where it is possible to prove 'that a person who is properly regarded as representing the "directing mind" of the body in question possessed the necessary fault element required for the offence.'[50]

Defences

Applicable only to section 7 offences, it is a defence if the relevant commercial organization can prove that it had in place 'adequate procedures' designed to prevent persons associated with the commercial organization from bribing another person.[51] 'In accordance with established case law, the standard of proof which the commercial organization would need to discharge in order to prove the defence, in the event it was prosecuted, is the balance of probabilities.'[52] The expression adequate procedures has generated much debate. The Ministry of Justice, as required by the Act, has published guidance to commercial organizations to enable the Act to take effect from July 2011. This guidance sets out the six general principles of adequate procedures namely,

1. Proportionality;
2. Top-level commitment to anti-bribery measures;
3. Risk assessment;
4. Due diligence regarding business partners;

---

48   Ministry of Justice, *The Bribery Act 2010 – Guidance* (Ministry of Justice 2011) 15.

49   Ministry of Justice, *Bribery Act 2010, Circular 2011/05* (Ministry of Justice 2011) para. 22.

50   Ministry of Justice, *Bribery Act 2010, Circular 2011/05* (Ministry of Justice 2011) para. 18.

51   Bribery Act 2010, s 7.

52   Ministry of Justice, *The Bribery Act 2010 – Guidance* (Ministry of Justice 2011) 15.

5. Communication; and,
6. Monitoring and review.[53]

The SFO is keen to underline that section 7 does not provide an offence of strict liability, because of the availability of the defence of adequate procedures. Thus, if there are adequate procedures, then no offence has been committed. This is a complete defence and not just mitigation.[54]

In addition to the section 7 defence, the Bribery Act 2010 also details a general defence which is available to the bribery offences contained in sections 1 and 2 of the Act. It is also applicable to attempting, aiding, abetting, counselling, procuring, conspiring to commit or inciting the commission of these offences.[55] The defence is contained within section 13 of the Act which states that,

> It is a defence for a person charged with a relevant bribery offence to prove that the person's conduct was necessary for –
>
> a. the proper exercise of any function of an intelligence service, or
> b. the proper exercise of any function of the armed forces when engaged on active service.[56]

The aim of the defence is to enable the intelligence services or the armed forces to undertake legitimate functions which may 'require the use of a financial or other advantage to accomplish the relevant function.'[57] It has therefore been introduced to allow for operational necessities. To rely on the defence, the defendant needs to prove, on the balance of probabilities, that his/her conduct was necessary. As explained by Lord Bach, the Parliamentary Under-Secretary of State for the Ministry of Justice,

> the police and other law enforcement agencies have an important role to play in protecting and defending the public from the threat caused by serious crime. Our objective is to ensure that these law enforcement agencies are not hindered in tackling serious crime.[58]

---

53   Ministry of Justice, *The Bribery Act 2010 – Guidance* (Ministry of Justice 2011) 15.

54   Serious Fraud Office, 'Richard Alderman, Speech The Bribery Act 2010 – The SFO's Approach and International Compliance' (9 February 2011) <http://www.sfo.gov.uk/about-us/our-views/director's-speeches/speeches-2011/the-bribery-act-2010---the-sfo's-approach-and-international-compliance.aspx> accessed 13 November 2011.

55   Bribery Act 2010, s 13(6).

56   Bribery Act 2010, s 13(1).

57   The Government's Explanatory Notes to s 3 Bribery Act 2010.

58   Hansard, HL Vol 716, col.GC89, 13 January 2010.

The Extent of Bribery

The threat posed by bribery cannot be underestimated and is graphically illustrated by the following quote from Pope and Webb.

> Such practices damage businesses through market distortion, prevention of fair competition, and by undermining confidence and business ethics. However, it is the human tragedy of corrupt business cultures that highlights the need for action in particular: where bribes and embezzlement of public funds are commonplace, citizens of that state suffer the most. Money meant to be used to improve schools, hospitals, roads, water supply and the like is instead transferred to a limited group of corrupt individuals.[59]

While this threat has far ranging consequences, as with all forms of financial crime, any attempt to measure the full extent of bribery and corruption is fraught with methodological difficulties, with it being virtually impossible to determine the exact extent. It has been estimated by some commentators, nevertheless, that approximately $1 trillion is paid in bribes on a worldwide basis each year.[60] This is also backed up by the World Bank.[61] Sanyal and Samanta take the view that,

> the enormous growth in international commerce over the past 60 years has been accompanied by an increase in bribery. The World Bank estimates that more than USD1 trillion in bribes are paid each year out of a world economy of USD30 trillion – 3 per cent of the world's economy. And, the impact is particularly severe on foreign investment. In fact, the World Bank estimates that corruption serves, essentially, as a 20 per cent tax.[62]

There are two organizations, in particular, which study global bribery and corruption: the World Bank and Transparency International. The World Bank believes that 'corruption is a product of bad governance and the weaknesses inherent in public sector institutions'.[63] Similarly, Transparency International defines corruption as the 'abuse of entrusted power for private gain. It hurts everyone whose life, livelihood or happiness depends on the integrity of people

---

59   T. Pope and T. Webb. 'Legislative Comment – the Bribery Act 2010' (2010) *Journal of International Banking Law and Regulation*, 25(10), 480–483, 480.

60   T. Pope and T. Webb. 'Legislative Comment – the Bribery Act 2010' (2010) *Journal of International Banking Law and Regulation*, 25(10), 480–483, 480.

61   C. William, 'Trillion Dollar Bribery' (2011) *New Law Journal*, 161(7447), 25–26, 25.

62   R. Sanyal and S. Samanta, 'Trends in International Bribe-giving: Do Anti-bribery Laws Matter?' (2011) *Journal of International Trade Law & Policy*, 10(2), 151–164, 151.

63   I. Carr, 'Fighting Corruption Through the United Nations Convention on Corruption 2003: A Global Solution to a Global Problem?' (2005) *International Trade Law and Regulation*, 11(1), 24–29, 28.

in a position of authority'.[64] In this context, the Bribery Act 2010, by overhauling the UK's patchwork of archaic corruption laws,[65] is regarded in the industry as 'the single most important development' in combating white collar crime.[66] Other commentators, including Aaronberg and Higgins, state that the Act 'provides the United Kingdom with some of the most draconian and far-reaching anti-corruption legislation in the world',[67] with Salens commenting that it has the potential to 'propel the UK to the forefront' in the international fight against bribery and corruption.[68] On a scale of 1–10, where 10 is very clean, Transparency International in 2010 gave the UK a rating of 7.6, placing it in 20th position out of 178. While this may appear satisfactory, the UK was still behind Denmark, New Zealand, Ireland, Barbados and Qatar – with the leading nation being Singapore with a 9.3 rating. This would therefore indicate that there is still some work to do. The USA, in 23rd place, had a rating of 7.1 whereas the bottom place was reserved for Somalia with a 1.1 rating. When a score of zero amounts to a labelling of a country as being 'highly corrupt', this is not an enviable position for Somalia to be in.[69]

Policy Background

The UK's policy towards bribery, like the other types of financial crime discussed in this book, has been influenced by a series of international legislative measures introduced by the United Nations (UN), the European Union (EU) and the OECD. One of the first international measures, introduced in 1994, was when the OECD accepted a recommendation that required member states to 'take effective measures to deter, prevent and combat the bribery of foreign public officials in connection

---

64 Transparency International, The Global Coalition Against Corruption, 'Corruption Perceptions Index 2010' <http://www.transparency.org/policy_research/surveys_indices/cpi/2010> accessed 28 June 2011.

65 J. Benstead, 'Biting the Bullet' (2010) _New Law Journal_, 160(7434), 1291–1292, 1291.

66 Salens 'Anti-bribery and Corruption: The UK Propels Itself to the Forefront of Global Enforcement' <http://www.salans.com/~/media/Assets/Salans/Publications/Salans%20Client%20Alert%20UK%20Bribery%20Act%20Implementation%20Date.ashx> accessed 24 July 2010.

67 D. Aaronberg and N. Higgins, 'Legislative Comment The Bribery Act 2010: All Bark and No Bite...?' (2010) _Archbold Review_, 5, 6–9, 6.

68 Salens 'Anti-bribery and Corruption: The UK Propels Itself to the Forefront of Global Enforcement' <http://www.salans.com/~/media/Assets/Salans/Publications/Salans%20Client%20Alert%20UK%20Bribery%20Act%20Implementation%20Date.ashx> accessed 24 July 2010.

69 Transparency International, The Global Coalition Against Corruption, 'Corruption Perceptions Index 2010' <http://www.transparency.org/policy_research/surveys_indices/cpi/2010> accessed 28 June 2011.

with international business transactions.'[70] This requirement was strengthened by the OECD Convention on Combating Bribery of Foreign Public Officials in International Business Transactions.[71] In response to this, the EU introduced its first bribery related provisions in 1995 in its Convention of the European Union on the Fight against Corruption involving officials of the European Communities or officials of member states.[72] In 1997, it approved a Convention on the Fight against Corruption involving Officials of the European Communities or Officials of Member States.[73] Furthermore, in 2003, the UN introduced its Convention against Corruption, which is administered by the UN Office on Drugs and Crime.[74]

The OECD Convention, which the UK signed in 1997[75] has 37 other countries as signatories,[76] and 'establishes legally binding standards to criminalize bribery of foreign public officials in international business transactions.'[77] It is the only international anti-corruption instrument focused on the supply side of the bribery transaction, that is, the person making the bribe rather than the recipient.[78] The OECD argues that its convention is working and reports that 'more than 135 individuals and companies have been convicted of foreign bribery.' This occurred in the first 10 years of the convention's existence, with fines during this period of

---

70   S. Sheikh, 'The Bribery Act 2010: Commercial Organisations Beware!' (2011) *International Company and Commercial Law Review*, 22(1), 1–16, 3.

71   See G. Sacerdoti, 'The 1997 OECD Convention on Combating Bribery of Foreign Public Officials in International Business Transactions' (1999) *International Business Law Journal*, 1, 3–18.

72   S. Sheikh, 'The Bribery Act 2010: Commercial Organisations Beware!' (2011) *International Company and Commercial Law Review*, 22(1), 1–16, 3.

73   Convention on the Fight Against Corruption Involving Officials of the European Communities or Officials of Member States, done at Brussels, 26 May 1997, 37 I.L.M. 12; OJ 1997 C 195.

74   For a more detailed and critical commentary on the provision of the 2003 Convention see P. Webb, 'The United Nations Convention Against Corruption: Global Achievement or Missed Opportunity?' (2005) *Journal of International Economic Law*, 8(1), 191–229 and M. Kubiciel, 'Core Criminal Law Provisions in the United Nations Convention Against Corruption' (2009) *International Criminal Law Review*, 9(1), 139–155.

75   OECD Convention on Combating Bribery of Foreign Public Officials in International Business Transactions 1997 <http://www.oecd.org/dataoecd/4/18/38028044.pdf> accessed 13 December 2011.

76   OECD Convention on Combating Bribery of Foreign Public Officials in International Business Transactions 1997 <http://www.oecd.org/dataoecd/4/18/38028044.pdf> accessed 13 December 2011.

77   OECD Convention on Combating Bribery of Foreign Public Officials in International Business Transactions 1997 <http://www.oecd.org/dataoecd/4/18/38028044.pdf> accessed 13 December 2011.

78   OECD Convention on Combating Bribery of Foreign Public Officials in International Business Transactions 1997 <http://www.oecd.org/dataoecd/4/18/38028044.pdf> accessed 13 December 2011.

time amounting to €1.24 billion.[79] Interestingly, there is no collective enforcement governance; with enforcement action carried out by individual countries. The OECD does not therefore act as global policemen. The UK's initial response to these conventions was the passing of the Anti-Terrorism, Crime and Security Act 2001. This was only ever meant to be a transient and temporary instrument until more comprehensive corruption legislation could be introduced.[80] This has obviously now taken place through the Bribery Act 2010.

The UK's reform of its bribery laws began with the publication of a Law Commission Report in 1998.[81] The Law Commission recommended that 'the common law offence of bribery and the statutory offences of corruption should be replaced by a modern statute.'[82] The then Labour government responded by publishing a Corruption Bill, which after being subjected to pre-legislative scrutiny by the Joint Committee,[83] was rejected, resulting in a revised version which was published in 2005.[84] This was followed by another consultation exercise by the Law Commission in 2007,[85] which subsequently led to the publication of its 2008 Report.[86] In response to this Report, and to emphasize the impetus to address the threat posed by bribery, the then Justice Secretary, Jack Straw stated,

> bribery is a cancer which destroys the integrity, accountability and honesty that underpins ethical standards both in public life and in the business community. The fight against bribery is not an optional extra or a luxury to be dispensed with in testing economic times. Our current law is old, complex and fragmented … A new law will provide our investigators and prosecutors with the tools they need to deal with bribery much more effectively.[87]

---

79 OECD, *OECD Working Group on Bribery 'Annual report 2008'* (OECD 2008) 2.

80 M. Raphael, *Blackstone's Guide to the Bribery Act 2010* (OUP 2010) 116.

81 Law Commission, *Legislating the Criminal Code: Corruption No. 248* (Law Commission 1998). For a more detailed discussion of this report see G. Sullivan, 'Proscribing Corruption – Some Comments on the Law Commission's Report' (1998) *Criminal Law Review*, August, 547–555.

82 S. Sheikh, 'The Bribery Act 2010: Commercial Organisations Beware!' (2011) *International Company and Commercial Law Review*, 22(1), 1–16, 4.

83 For an excellent discussion of the scrutiny of the Corruption Bill see A. Kennon, 'Pre-Legislative Scrutiny of Draft Bills' (2004*) Public Law*, Aut, 477–494.

84 Home Office, *Reform of the Prevention of Corruption Acts and SFO Powers in Cases of Bribery Against Foreign Officials* (Home Office 2005).

85 The Law Commission, *Reforming Bribery: A Consultation* (Law Commission 2007). For a more detailed discussion see P. Alldridge, 'Reforming Bribery: Law Commission Consultation Paper 185: (1) Bribery Reform and the Law – Again' (2008) *Criminal Law Review*, 9, 671–686.

86 Law Commission, *Reforming Bribery: A Consultation* (Law Commission 2007).

87 Ministry of Justice, 'Government Welcomes New Bribery Law Recommendations' (20 November 2008) <http://www.wired-gov.net/wg/wg-news-1.nsf/0/329BD09E4E75E8 138025750700478C2E?OpenDocument> accessed 25 November 2011.

The Report was followed by the publication of a White Paper in 2009 that finally resulted in the enactment of the Bribery Act 2010.[88] Prior to its introduction, Kenneth Clarke, the Secretary of State for Justice, stated that the Act would,

> reinforce its [the UK's] reputation as a leader in the global fight against corruption –... The Act will ensure that the UK is at the forefront of the battle against bribery allowing the country to clamp down on corruption without being burdensome to business.[89]

The provisions of the Bribery Act 2010 have received a mixture of responses from commentators. For example, some writers have suggested that the provisions 'go too far and fear [that] the new "gold standard" legislation poses a threat to UK competitiveness.'[90] Other concerns have been raised in relation to the increased prosecutorial powers under the Act and the compliance costs which firms in the UK are expected to meet.[91] Conversely, it has also been described as a 'major piece of legislation, of immense practical importance to the conduct of business, whether in the public or private sphere.'[92] Alexander further argues that the Act is desperately needed because 'corruption is not merely a regrettable evil; it kills';[93] identifying examples including that of children dying from unsafe medication which has been approved by corrupt health officials. In many respects it is still too early to determine who is correct; although it should go without saying that the Bribery Act 2010 is significantly better than the UK's previous patchwork quilt.

Financial Institutions and Regulatory Bodies

As mentioned above, there are two main regulatory bodies that enforce the provisions of the Bribery Act 2010, namely the SFO and the FSA. In addition to these agencies, the City of London Police has also begun to investigate allegations of

---

88   The Ministry of Justice, *Bribery: Draft Legislation* (The Stationery Office 2009). For an excellent commentary on the draft law see C. Well, 'Bribery: Corporate Liability under the Draft Bill' (2009) *Criminal Law Review*, 7, 479–487.

89   Ministry of Justice, press release 'UK Clamps Down on Corruption with New Bribery Act' <http://www.justice.gov.uk/news/press-release-300311a.htm> accessed 29 November 2011.

90   T. Pope and T. Webb. 'Legislative Comment – the Bribery Act 2010' (2010) *Journal of International Banking Law and Regulation*, 25(10), 480–483, 480.

91   T. Pope and T. Webb. 'Legislative Comment – the Bribery Act 2010' (2010) *Journal of International Banking Law and Regulation*, 25(10), 480–483, 480.

92   Editorial, 'The Bribery Act 2010' (2010) *Criminal Law Review*, 6, 439–440, 439.

93   R. Alexander, 'The Bribery Act 2010: Time to Stand Firm' (2011) *Journal of Financial Crime*, 18(2), Editorial.

bribery and corruption.[94] As part of its efforts to reduce this type of financial crime, the SFO has placed 'huge emphasis on raising awareness, education, persuasion, and ultimately prevention.'[95] Moreover, as outlined in earlier sections of this book, the FSA has a statutory obligation to reduce financial crime under the Financial Services and Markets Act 2000.[96] Clearly, bribery falls within the definition of financial crime under this statutory objective, with bribery also being relevant to its secondary statutory objective of maintaining market confidence. Bribery affects the latter statutory aim because 'bribery and corruption distort natural competition and could affect the UK's reputation, making it a less attractive place for firms to conduct insurance or other business.'[97] The FSA, therefore, pinpointed the threat posed by bribery in its 2008 Financial Risk Outlook stating that,

> International efforts to combat corruption combined with the continuing development of the UK's legal framework on corruption may increase the level of interest in the financial services sector's efforts to combat corruption and bribery. There is a risk that firms could come under pressure to pay bribes, especially if they are operating in jurisdictions where paying bribes is widely expected. In addition, financial services firms may launder the proceeds of corruption or be used to transmit bribes.[98]

It is important to note here, however, that the FSA does not actually enforce the provisions of the Bribery Act 2010, with its role only applying where 'authorised firms fail adequately to address corruption and bribery risk, including where these risks arise in relation to third parties acting on behalf of the firm.' The FSA has nevertheless argued that it does 'not need to obtain evidence of corrupt conduct to take regulatory action against a firm.'[99] Therefore, firms who are regulated by the FSA are bound to comply with its anti-bribery provisions as set out in its Hand Book and in particular its 11 Principles for Business. These include:

1. Integrity
2. Skill care and diligence

---

94   T. Duthie and D. Lawler, 'Legislative Comment The United Kingdom Bribery Bill' (2010) *Construction Law Journal*, 26(2), 146–152, 147.

95   C. Monteity, 'The Bribery Act 2010: Part 3: Enforcement' (2011) *Criminal Law Review*, 2, 111–121, 114.

96   Financial Service and Markets Act 2000, s 6(3).

97   Financial Services Authority, *Anti-Bribery and Corruption in Commercial Insurance Broking Reducing the Risk of Illicit Payments or Inducements to Third Parties* (Financial Services Authority 2010) 6.

98   Financial Services Authority, *Financial Risk Outlook 2008* (Financial Services Authority 2008) 35.

99   Financial Services Authority, 'One-Minute Guide – Anti-Bribery and Corruption in Commercial Insurance Broking' <http://www.fsa.gov.uk/smallfirms/resources/one_minute_guides/insurance_intermed/anti_bribery.shtml> accessed 24 November 2011.

3. Management and control
4. Financial prudence
5. Market conduct
6. Customer's interest
7. Communications with clients
8. Conflict of interest
9. Customers: relationships of trust
10. Client assets
11. Relationships with regulators

Of particular relevance to bribery and corruption are Principles 1, 2 and 3. Principle 1 provides that a firm is obliged to 'conduct business with integrity'. This is especially relevant as 'broker firms and their employees may themselves be engaged in corrupt practices.' Principle 2 states that a firm must 'conduct its business with due skill, care and diligence', while Principle 3 sets out an obligation that 'a firm must take reasonable care to organize and control its affairs responsibly and effectively, with adequate risk management systems.' In addition to adhering to the FSA's Principles of Business, a firm's senior management team is also 'responsible for making an appropriate assessment of financial crime risks, including those relating to bribery and corruption.'[100] Furthermore, Rule SYSC[101] 3.2.6R states that firms are required to 'establish and maintain effective systems and controls ... for countering the risk that the firm might be used to further financial crime.'[102] This means that firms have the responsibility to assess the risks of becoming involved in, or facilitating, bribery and corruption and are obliged to take all reasonable steps in preventing such risks from crystallising. Authorised firms, therefore have an additional, regulatory, obligation. This makes them responsible for putting in place and maintaining relevant policies and processes which can be utilized in preventing corruption and bribery and thus allows them to conduct their businesses with integrity.[103] Gentle notes that,

> ... the FSA has shown itself ready to take action against authorised firms for breaches of principle 3 (of the Principles for Business) when firms fail to comply with systems and controls designed to prevent criminal activity such as bribery. [For example, t] he FSA fined Aon Limited (Aon Ltd) £5.25 million for failing

---

100   Financial Services Authority, *Anti-Bribery and Corruption in Commercial Insurance Broking. Reducing the Risk of Illicit Payments or Inducements to Third Parties* (Financial Services Authority 2010) 10.

101   Senior Management Arrangements, Systems and Controls.

102   Financial Services Authority, *The Full Handbook* – SYSC Senior Management Arrangements, Systems and Controls (Financial Services Authority 2011) at Rule SYSC 3.2.6R.

103   Financial Services Authority, 'One-Minute Guide - Anti-Bribery and Corruption in Commercial Insurance Broking' <http://www.fsa.gov.uk/smallfirms/resources/one_minute_guides/insurance_intermed/anti_bribery.shtml> accessed 24 November 2011.

to take reasonable care to establish and maintain effective systems and controls to counter the risks of bribery and corruption associated with making payments to overseas firms and individuals.[104]

If a firm breaches any of these 11 Principles, the FSA has an extensive array of enforcement powers that it can use. These will be discussed in the sentencing and recovery section below.

Financial Intelligence

In addition to the creation of criminal offences designed to capture individuals intimately involved in bribery and corruption, it is also the intention of the Bribery Act 2010 to extend the responsibility for bribery to those who are involved on a peripheral basis. Therefore, it additionally includes those who could be described as the controlling minds and all those organizations involved or on whose behalf bribery took place or was even contemplated. This can include individuals and organizations that are many steps away from the organization itself. Any peripheral involvement can be subject to a financial penalty in addition to any action taken against individuals intimately involved. The wide scope of the Act, therefore, significantly increases the responsibility of commercial organizations to manage such risk issues. The ambit of the law thus covers any commercial organization with a business presence in the UK. This brings into consideration any part of that organization, even if the controlling body was overseas and the alleged bribery was also offshore.[105] Consequently, this should encourage businesses to review their existing anti-bribery policies and procedures and ensure that their associates are similarly compliant.

Internationally, the OECD Guidelines for Multinational Enterprises[106] and the OECD Business Approaches to Combating Corrupt Practices[107] provide guidance, as do USA Federal Sentencing Guidelines.[108] In the UK, the SFO has been designated as the national reporting point for allegations of bribery of foreign public officials by British nationals or companies incorporated in the UK, even if the matter occurred overseas. This should be helpful because a key element

---

104   S. Gentle, 'The Bribery Act 2010: Part 2: The Corporate Offence' (2011) *Criminal Law Review*, 2, 101–110, 110.

105   Ministry of Justice, 'Bribery Act Implementation' (20 July 2010) <http://www.justice.gov.uk/news/newsrelease200710a.htm> accessed 15 December 2011.

106   OECD, 'Guidelines for Multinational Enterprises' <http://www.oecd.org/document/28/0,3343,en_2649_34889_2397532_1_1_1_1,00.html> accessed 24 July 2010.

107   OECD, 'Business Approaches to Combating Bribery' <http://www.oecd.org/dataoecd/45/32/1922830.pdf> accessed 24 July 2010.

108   US Federal Sentencing Guidelines 'Chapter Eight – Part B – Remedying Harm From Criminal Conduct, and Effective Compliance and Ethics Program' <http://www.ussc.gov/2007guid/8b2_1.html> accessed 24 July 2010.

in combating bribery and corruption is the requirement to report such instances to the authorities. However, in the UK the obligation to report is not that well established. This is largely because there is no actual statutory obligation to report bribery, corruption or fraud, unlike that which exists for money laundering where reporting is required by the Proceeds of Crime Act 2002.[109] This omission is demonstrated in the fraud arena, where 'not having a centralized body to co-ordinate fraud intelligence across the public and private sectors has made it easier for criminals to operate undetected and [remain] free to re-offend.'[110] The National Fraud Intelligence Bureau thus seems to rely on 'best endeavours' and 'encouragement' to report[111] although such crimes *should,* nevertheless, still be reported to the police.[112]

By contrast, the other significant actor in the UK, namely the FSA, which is responsible for regulating financial services, does have the ability to *impose* reporting obligations.[113] Regulated firms are obliged to inform the FSA, 'promptly, of anything relating to the firm of which the FSA would reasonably expect prompt notice' (SYSC 6.3 Financial Crime).[114] The outcome is that the SFO, which is tasked with taking the lead in bribery matters and which is designated as the reporting centre, lacks statutory backing to compel reporting, whereas the FSA, in the sector it regulates, can instil bribery reporting obligations. The relationship between the SFO and the FSA therefore lies at the heart of the UK's efforts to control economic crime and this inconsistency in designation and power needs to be addressed to enable the situation whereby the agency that is responsible for dealing with cases of bribery, corruption and fraud, also has the power to make the reporting of it a statutory obligation.

In an attempt to try and control such crime, the SFO has published its 'Approach to Dealing with Overseas Corruption'.[115] This provides guidance and industry specific codes of practice including, for example, advice that 'a negotiated settlement rather than a criminal prosecution' would give protection against a

---

109   Proceeds of Crime Act 2002, ss 327–340.

110   NFA, 'National Fraud Intelligence Bureau' <http://www.homeoffice.gov.uk/agencies-public-bodies/nfa/about-us/who-we-work-with/nfib/> accessed 17 September 2012.

111   NFA, 'National Fraud Intelligence Bureau' <http://www.homeoffice.gov.uk/agencies-public-bodies/nfa/about-us/who-we-work-with/nfib/> accessed 17 September 2012.

112   Home Office, 'Counting Rules For Recorded Crime' <http://rds.homeoffice.gov.uk/rds/pdfs10/countgeneral10.pdf> accessed 29 April 2010.

113   Financial Services Authority, 'What We Do: Who We Regulate' 'We regulate most financial services markets, exchanges and firms. We set the standards that they must meet and can take action against firms if they fail to meet the required standards' <http://www.fsa.gov.uk/pages/About/What/Who/index.shtml> accessed 27 September 2011.

114   FSA, 'Principles for Business' <http://www.fsa.gov.uk/Pages/Library/Communication/PR/1999/099.shtml> accessed 29 April 2010.

115   SFO, 'Approach of the Serious Fraud Office to Dealing with Overseas Corruption' <http://www.sfo.gov.uk/media/107247/approach%20of%20the%20serious%20fraud%20office%20v3.pdf> accessed 24 July 2010.

mandatory European Union procurement.[116] Corporate hospitality is also covered, with the government recognizing that the provision of corporate hospitality is a part of business life. In the past, the government has not been prescriptive in establishing sufficient protective parameters in this regard, preferring rather to leave the issue to prosecutorial discretion and common sense.[117] The ultimate consequence of this, however, is fundamental uncertainty which is likely to remain until test cases are brought to trial. For example, while lavish corporate hospitality, such as taking clients to, say, a Rugby World Cup match in New Zealand, or the Rio de Janeiro Olympic Games, would clearly be open to scrutiny for proportionality, the Justice Secretary has nevertheless stated that the government does not want 'to stop firms getting to know their clients by taking them to events like Wimbledon or the Grand Prix.'[118] The guidance, therefore, while it recognises that corporate hospitality and promotional expenditure is an everyday part of business life, does not provide detail on when that boundary is crossed, even though the government additionally states that 'it is, however, clear that hospitality and promotional or similar business expenditure *can* be employed as bribes' (emphasis added).[119] This means that commercial organizations are obliged to put in place clear procedures and give directions to their employees to ensure that, at best, their motives are not misinterpreted.

Sentencing and Recovery

A person found guilty of any of the offences contained in sections 1, 2 and 6 of the Bribery Act 2010 is liable to a maximum custodial sentence of 10 years' imprisonment and/or an unlimited fine. For the offence found in section 7, the maximum penalty is an unlimited fine.[120] Although the SFO is arguably the lead agency in prosecuting cases of bribery and corruption, proceedings under the Act require the personal consent of not just the Director of the SFO but also, either the Director of Public Prosecutions or the Director of Revenue and Customs Prosecutions.[121]

---

116   EU Public Services Procurement Directive 2004/18/EC Art. 45.

117   Wragge & Co, 'Bribery Act to Come into Force April 2011 – Time to Take Action' (23 July 2010) <http://www.wragge.com/analysis_6175.asp> accessed 24 July 2010.

118   Ministry of Justice. 'The Bribery Act: Guidance' (March 2011) <http://www. justice.gov.uk/downloads/guidance/making-reviewing-law/bribery-act-2010-guidance. pdf> accessed 5 May 2011.

119   Ministry of Justice. 'The Bribery Act: Guidance' (March 2011) <http://www. justice.gov.uk/downloads/guidance/making-reviewing-law/bribery-act-2010-guidance. pdf> accessed 5 May 2011.

120   Bribery Act 2010, s 11(3).

121   Bribery Act 2010, s 10.

Historically, however, and particularly with reference to the situation prior to the Bribery Act 2010, there have been few criminal cases taken to trial;[122] with this situation continuing even after the *de Grazia* review in 2008.[123] The few examples which do exist include one case from September 2009, where a British construction company, Mabey and Johnson, were held liable for bribing foreign officials in order to win business contracts. The company pleaded guilty to overseas corruption charges, for paying €1 million in bribes through middlemen with reference to £60–£70 million contracts, and to the breaching of UN Iraq sanctions relating to Saddam Hussein's 'Oil for Food Programme'. The case concluded with a plea bargain, which led to a financial penalty of £3.5 million, in addition to compensation payable to the countries of Ghana, Jamaica and Iraq and legal costs totalling £3.1 million. Interestingly, this was the first conviction in the UK of a company for such offences with the SFO deciding to prosecute the company rather than the actual individuals involved.[124]

It is obviously too early to say whether there will be more criminal prosecutions for bribery and corruption, following the introduction of the Bribery Act 2010. However, the Crown Prosecution Service (CPS) has stated that not only is bribery a serious offence, but that 'there is an inherent public interest in bribery being prosecuted.'[125] In determining whether or not to prosecute, the CPS will take into account both aggravating and mitigating factors. These might include the amount of money involved; whether there has been a breach of a position of trust; whether it involved a vulnerable or elderly victim; the period over which the offence was carried out; whether any voluntary repayments had been made and whether there were any personal factors such as disability, illness or family difficulties.[126] Despite the existence of CPS legal guidance, there are no sentencing guidelines for bribery, with the only available aid coming in the form of two Court of Appeal cases; both of which were decided prior to 2010. The first *R v Anderson (Malcolm John)*,[127] involved the appeal of a sentence of 12 months' imprisonment for accepting a bribe in return for contracts which were beneficial to the appellant's business. On the basis that the appellant was of previous good character and that the financial gain was relatively small, a sentence of six months was held to be more appropriate.

---

122   D. Aaronberg and N. Higgins, 'Legislative Comment The Bribery Act 2010: All Bark and No Bite…?' (2010) *Archbold Review*, 5, 6–9, 6.

123   J. de Grazia, *Review of the Serious Fraud Office – Final Report* (Serious Fraud Office 2008).

124   Case Comment 'First UK Company Convicted for Overseas Corruption' (2010) *Company Lawyer*, 31(1), 16.

125   The Crown Prosecution Service 'Bribery Act 2010: Joint Prosecution Guidance of the Director of the Serious Fraud Office and the Director of Public Prosecutions' <http://www.cps.gov.uk/legal/a_to_c/bribery_act_2010/> accessed 29 November 2011.

126   The Crown Prosecution Service, *'Bribery', Legal Guidance* (Crown Prosecution Service 2008).

127   [2003] 2 Cr. App. R. (S) 28.

The second is that of *R v Francis Hurell*.[128] The sentence in question was again for 12 months, but this time was for attempting to bribe a police officer, through the offering of £2,000 so that the officer would not carry out a breath test. Even though the Court held that any attempt to bribe a police officer in the execution of his duty was serious, it nevertheless substituted the sentence for one of three months. What is therefore needed is more up-to-date guidance on what is appropriate for the four offences under the new Act.

One recent criminal conviction for bribery and corruption can however be seen in the case of Mark Jessop, who in April 2011 was sentenced to a two year custodial sentence and ordered to pay £150,000 in compensation and £25,000 in prosecution costs. The orders were in relation to ten counts of engaging in activities which made funds available to the Iraqi government in contravention of UN Iraq sanctions, again in relation to the Oil for Food Programme.[129] Recent criminal prosecutions include Dennis Kerrison, Paul Jennings and David Turner, all former executives of Innospec Ltd, who in October 2011 were charged with corruption in relation to making and conspiring to make corrupt payments to public officials in Indonesia and Iraq in order to secure contracts for the business.[130] In January 2012 Turner pleaded guilty to three counts of conspiracy to corrupt, with sentencing still to take place.[131] Also in October 2011, Victor Dahdaleh was also charged with bribery offences for making payments of bribes to officials of an aluminium smelting company in Bahrain, again in order to secure contracts for a business.[132]

In addition, and perhaps instead of, criminal liability, the FSA also has the power to impose civil fines under section 206(1) of the Financial Services and Markets Act 2000.[133] The use of this was seen, for example, in July 2011, when the FSA fined Willis Limited £6.895 million for weaknesses in its anti-bribery and

---

128   [2004] 2 Cr. App. R. (S.) 23.

129   Serious Fraud Office, 'Medical Goods to Iraq Supplier Jailed for Paying Kick-Backs' (Press release 13 April 2011) <http://www.sfo.gov.uk/press-room/latest-press-releases/press-releases-2011/medical-goods-to-iraq-supplier-jailed-for-paying-kick-backs.aspx> accessed 29 November 2011.

130   Serious Fraud Office, 'Innospec Ltd: Two More Executives Charged with Corruption' (Press Release 27 October 2011) <http://www.sfo.gov.uk/press-room/latest-press-releases/press-releases-2011/innospec-ltd-two-more-executives-charged-with-corruption.aspx> accessed 29 November 2011.

131   Serious Fraud Office, 'Innospec Ltd: Former Director Pleads Guilty to Corruption' (17 January 2012) <http://www.sfo.gov.uk/press-room/latest-press-releases/press-releases-2012/innospec-ltd-former-director-pleads-guilty-to-corruption.aspx> accessed 27 March 2012.

132   Serious Fraud Office, 'Victor Dahdaleh Charged with Bribery' (Press Release 24 October 2011) <http://www.sfo.gov.uk/press-room/latest-press-releases/press-releases-2011/victor-dahdaleh-charged-with-bribery.aspx> accessed 29 November 2011.

133   J. Horder, 'Bribery as a Form of Criminal Wrongdoing' (2011) *Law Quarterly Review*, 127(Jan), 37–54, 43.

corruption systems and controls.[134] As a result of an extensive investigation, the FSA determined that Willis Limited had failed to:

1. guarantee that it established and recorded an adequate commercial rationale to support its payments to overseas third parties;
2. ensure that adequate due diligence was carried out on overseas third parties to evaluate the risk involved in doing business with them; and
3. adequately review its relationships on a regular basis to confirm whether it was still necessary and appropriate for Willis Limited to continue with the relationship.[135]

In this particular instance the FSA concluded that Willis Limited had,

> … failed to take the appropriate steps to ensure that payments it was making to overseas third parties were not being used for corrupt purposes. This is particularly disappointing as we have repeatedly communicated with the industry on this issue and have previously taken enforcement action for failings in this area. The involvement of UK financial institutions in corrupt or potentially corrupt practices overseas undermines the integrity of the UK financial services sector. The action we have taken against Willis Limited shows that we believe that it is vital for firms not only to put in place appropriate anti-bribery and corruption systems and controls, but also to ensure that those systems and controls are adequately implemented and monitored.[136]

Additionally, as mentioned above, the FSA, in 2011, fined Aon Limited £5.25 million for 'failing to take reasonable care to establish and maintain effective systems and controls to counter the risks of bribery and corruption associated with making payments to overseas firms and individuals.' Here, the FSA determined that Aon Ltd had 'failed to properly assess the risks involved in its dealings with overseas firms and individuals who helped it win business and failed to implement effective controls to mitigate those risks.'[137]

---

134 Financial Services Authority, 'FSA Fines Willis Limited 6.895m for Anti-Bribery and Corruption Systems and Controls Failings' (21 July 2011) <http://www.fsa.gov.uk/pages/Library/Communication/PR/2011/066.shtml> accessed 24 November 2011.

135 Financial Services Authority, 'FSA Fines Willis Limited 6.895m for Anti-Bribery and Corruption Systems and Controls Failings' (21 July 2011) <http://www.fsa.gov.uk/pages/Library/Communication/PR/2011/066.shtml> accessed 24 November 2011.

136 Financial Services Authority, 'FSA Fines Willis Limited 6.895m for Anti-Bribery and Corruption Systems and Controls Failings' (21 July 2011) <http://www.fsa.gov.uk/pages/Library/Communication/PR/2011/066.shtml> accessed 24 November 2011.

137 Financial Services Authority, 'FSA Fines Willis Limited 6.895m for Anti-Bribery and Corruption Systems and Controls Failings' (21 July 2011) <http://www.fsa.gov.uk/pages/Library/Communication/PR/2011/066.shtml> accessed 24 November 2011.

The Civil Recovery Order

As well as criminal and civil financial penalties, the court can also make a Civil Recovery Order (CRO) under the Proceeds of Crime Act 2002. The order is applicable when, on the balance of probabilities, it can be established that the individual or company in question is in possession of property which was obtained through unlawful conduct. The order allows for the recovery of such property and interestingly, does not require a criminal conviction for it to be made. Examples of when this has been used include Balfour Beatty who was ordered to pay £2.25 million for 'payment irregularities' by an African subsidiary on an Egyptian construction contract and AMEC plc, whose order was for almost £5 million due to the making of irregular payments in connection with a bridge building contract in South Korea.[138] More recently, in February 2011, the SFO recovered £7 million from the engineering group M.W. Kellogg who pleaded guilty to the payment of bribes amounting to more than £100 million to Nigerian Government officials by its parent company. Commenting on the case, the Director of the SFO stated,

> … in cases such as this a prosecution is not appropriate. Our goal is to prevent bribery and corruption or remove any of the benefits generated by such activities. This case demonstrates the range of tools we are prepared to use.[139]

The Serious Crime Prevention Order

Furthermore, the court has the option of making a Serious Crime Prevention Order (SCPO) under Part 1 of the Serious Crime Act 2007, which came into force on the 6 April 2008. A SCPO is a civil order which is intended to restrict, discipline and prevent future involvement in serious crime and which can be made either by the High Court or by application to the Crown Court. For an order to be made, the court must be satisfied, on the balance of probabilities, that the person has been involved in serious crime, and, it has reasonable grounds for believing that the making of the order would protect the public from further such crime.[140] This can be easily established if the person in question has been convicted of such an offence. For the purposes of the order, serious crime is defined in Part 1 of Schedule 1 of the Act, and includes money laundering, fraud, corruption and bribery. The order can contain a number of requirements, prohibitions, restrictions and other terms which are considered by the court to be appropriate in protecting the public from future

---

138   T. Duthie and D. Lawler, 'Legislative Comment The United Kingdom Bribery Bill' (2010) *Construction Law Journal*, 26(2), 146–152, 146.

139   J. Russell, 'SFO Settles Nigeria Bribery Case for £7m' (*The Telegraph* 2011), <http://www.telegraph.co.uk/finance/newsbysector/industry/8329298/SFO-settles-Nigeria-bribery-case-for-7m.html> accessed 29 November 2011.

140   Serious Crime Act 2007, s 1(1).

offending.[141] Examples of such requirements are detailed in section 5(3) of the Act including for example, restrictions on working arrangements, travel both abroad and within the UK, the means of communication and association with named individuals and access to certain premises. An order can also require a person to answer questions, provide information and/or provide documents at a time or place specified in the order.[142] When such requirements are made, the court must ensure that their prohibitive effect is proportionate to the purpose of protecting the public against future serious crime. Interestingly, however, a SCPO cannot require a person to,

- provide oral answers to questions or requirements to provide information (Section 11);
- answer questions, or provide information or documents which are covered by legal professional privilege (Section 12);
- produce excluded material as defined by section 11 of the Police and Criminal Evidence Act (Section 13(1)(a));
- disclose any information or produce any document held by him in confidence as part of a banking business unless there is consent from the person to whom confidence is owed,
- the order specifically required disclosure of information or documents of this kind, or it required disclosure of specified information or documents of this kind (Section 13 (2)–(4)); or,
- provide information or documents or answer questions if it would involve a disclosure prohibited by another enactment (Section 14).[143]

A SCPO can last for a maximum of five years, although the commencement of this can be delayed to coincide with release from custody. The court can also set different start and end dates for specific requirements, prohibitions or restrictions.[144] In addition to orders being made against named individuals, a SCPO can also be issued against a body corporate, a partnership or an unincorporated association.[145]

In a speech given on 26 February 2009, the Director of the SFO, Richard Alderman stated how SCPOs,

> … enable prosecutors to obtain court orders regulating the future conduct of those who have been engaged in serious crime. SCPOs can be obtained before or after a conviction. The conditions that can attach to such orders are almost

---

141   Serious Crime Act 2007, s 1(3).

142   Serious Crime Act 2007, s 5(5).

143   Crown Prosecution Service, 'Serious Crime Prevention Orders' <http://www.cps. gov.uk/legal/s_to_u/serious_crime_prevention_orders_%28scpo%29_guidance/> accessed 29 November 2011.

144   Serious Crime Act 2007, s 16.

145   Serious Crimes Act 2007, ss 30–32.

limitless. A company might, for example, be asked to submit its trading accounts for scrutiny every six months. I am very interested in these orders. An SCPO obtained from the High Court quickly without prosecution is a very important weapon for us.[146]

Perhaps controversially, on the basis that an SCPO is a civil order, breach of it without reasonable excuse amounts to a criminal offence. On summary conviction this can make the individual liable for up to 12 months' imprisonment, which can be extended on conviction on indictment by up to five years.[147]

Further Recommendations

The Bribery Act 2010 represents a significant development in the UK's financial crime legislative agenda. It provides the SFO with a welcome extension of its remit in a time of uncertainty following the impending creation of the National Crime Agency. The provisions of the Bribery Act seek to extend and modify the existing related provisions and to bring them in line with its international obligations. Nonetheless, concerns remain about some of the Acts provisions. One particular concern, is the overlapping regulatory remit of the SFO and FSA. Whether or not this problem remains is uncertain, and a great deal with depend on the enactment of the Financial Services Bill and the statutory objective of the FSA to reduce financial crime. It is hoped that the SFO will adopt a rigorous stance toward enforcing the criminal provisions of the Bribery Act 2010.

Further Reading

Aaronberg, D. and N. Higgins, 'Legislative Comment The Bribery Act 2010: All Bark and No Bite...?' (2010) *Archbold Review*, 5, 6–9.

Alldridge, P. 'Reforming Bribery: Law Commission Consultation Paper 185: (1) Bribery Reform and the Law – Again' (2008) *Criminal Law Review*, 9, 671–686.

Beale, K. and P. Esposito, 'Emergent International Attitudes Towards Bribery, Corruption and Money Laundering' (2009) *Arbitration*, 75(3), 360–373.

Editorial, 'The Bribery Act 2010' (2010) *Criminal Law Review*, 6, 439–440.

Gentle, S. 'Legislative Comment – The Bribery Act 2010: Part 2: The Corporate Offence' (2011) *Criminal Law Review*, 2, 101–110.

Law Commission, *Reforming Bribery, Law Commission No. 313* (Law Commission 2007).

---

146   Cameron McKenna, 'The Serious Fraud Office' <http://www.law-now.com/law-now/2009/anticorruptionthesfo?cmckreg=true> accessed 29 November 2011.

147   Serious Crime Act 2007, s 25.

Ministry of Justice, *The Bribery Act 2010 – Guidance* (Ministry of Justice 2011).

Pope, T. and T. Webb, 'Legislative Comment – The Bribery Act 2010' (2010) *Journal of International Banking Law and Regulation*, 25(10), 480–483.

Raphael, M. *Blackstone's Guide to the Bribery Act 2010* (Oxford University Press 2010).

Sanyal, R. and S. Samanta, 'Trends in International Bribe-giving: Do Anti-bribery Laws Matter?' (2011) *Journal of International Trade Law & Policy*, 10(2), 151–164.

Sheikh, S. 'The Bribery Act 2010: Commercial Organisations Beware!' (2011) *International Company and Commercial Law Review*, 22(1), 1–16.

Well, C. 'Bribery: Corporate Liability Under the Draft Bill 2009'. *Criminal Law Review*, 7, 479–487.

Chapter 8
Conclusions and Recommendations

Introduction

The purpose of this book is to provide a detailed overview of the law relating to financial crime in the United Kingdom (UK). To aid in this endeavour, each chapter has followed the same structure,

1. The criminal offences and defences;
2. The extent of each financial crime;
3. The policy background;
4. Financial institutions and regulatory bodies;
5. Financial intelligence;
6. Sentencing and recovery, and
7. Future recommendations

Throughout each chapter we have tried to demonstrate the threat posed by financial crime towards the UK and explain how its negative implications cannot be underestimated or ignored. For example, in the case of money laundering, this has been used by a large proportion of organized criminals to disguise their proceeds of crime and subsequently to fund and facilitate their so-called champagne lifestyles. This unlawful laundering process has also been used by drug cartels in order to hide the proceeds of the sale of illegal narcotics. It has thus been argued that money laundering, in the UK, poses a significant threat to the integrity of the City of London and to its financial services sector. This is especially the case given the contribution that the City of London makes towards the UK's gross domestic product. In relation to money laundering, it is also important to note the danger posed by electronic or virtual money laundering, with research suggesting that this is becoming an even more popular and effective mechanism for organized criminals to launder their dirty proceeds of crime into clean untainted profits.

Terrorist financing is another threat to the UK, but here there is also a threat against national security and to the safety of the UK population. This was clearly illustrated by the terrorist attacks of the Irish Republican Army (IRA) in Warrington and more recently by the al-Qaeda inspired attacks in London in July 2005. We have shown how the detection and prevention of terrorist financing is extremely difficult, especially given the vast array of sources of financing that are currently available. This is made even more problematic when combined with the relatively small amounts of money which is required to carry out such attacks as mentioned above. Moreover, the risks of, and devastation which can be caused by, fraud have also been highlighted by a significant reported increase in such activity. Recent examples of fraudulent activities include those of Bernard Madoff and his massive Ponzi scheme and instances of mortgage fraud and identity theft. Our awareness of such activities has been supplemented by the implementation of an unprecedented array of counter fraud measures which have been recently implemented by the government. These include, for example, the introduction of the Fraud Act 2006, the publication of the Fraud Review, the creation of Action Fraud, the setting up of the National Fraud Reporting Centre and the publication of a national fraud strategy by the National Fraud Authority (NFA).

Furthermore, this book has also shown how insider dealing poses a specific threat to the City of London, as famously illustrated in the United States of America (USA) by Michael Douglas who played the character Gordon Gekko in the 1987 20th Century Fox film, *Wall Street*. The true extent of insider dealing is difficult to ascertain, but nevertheless has been highlighted by the increased number of recent enforcement actions of the Financial Services Authority (FSA). Many of these cases arose due to the Credit Crunch and have resulted in the first successful insider dealing prosecutions brought by the FSA and the imposition of a record number of financial penalties for individuals and firms. Despite such advancements, however, there are still a number of weaknesses in the UK's approach to the regulation of insider dealing and coupled with the introduction of the Market Abuse Directive, this has resulted in the implementation of the Market Abuse Regime by the FSA. This operates in conjunction with the insider dealing provisions of the Criminal Justice Act 1993 and has resulted in a series of enforcement measures being used against firms who breach the FSA regime. Finally we looked at bribery and corruption and it is in this area that there has been the most recent legislation; the Bribery Act 2010. This has brought the UK's legislation in line with its international obligations and it is very much hoped will play a significant role towards tackling the problems posed by bribery and corruption, by extending the regulatory remit of the Serious Fraud Office (SFO).

Money Laundering

The first type of financial crime that is considered in this book is money laundering. Due to the damaging effects of the illegal activity, it is unsurprising that the UK has adopted a very tough stance towards this crime. For example, the UK is largely compliant with its international obligations imposed by several United Nations (UN) Conventions and the '40 Recommendations' of the Financial Action Task Force (FATF). In furtherance of this, the UK has criminalized money laundering by virtue of part 7 of the Proceeds of Crime Act 2002, which is additionally supported by the Money Laundering Regulations of 2007. Both of these measures play a central part in the UK's anti-money laundering (AML) policy, which is administered by HM Treasury. The provisions of the Proceeds of Crime Act 2002 that criminalize money laundering are generally regarded as effective and if breached, carry a maximum sentence of 14 years' imprisonment. These provisions are furthermore supported by the statutory objective of the FSA, which is to reduce financial crime under the Financial Services and Markets Act (FSMA) 2000.[1] In order to achieve this statutory objective the FSA has an extensive array of enforcement, prosecutorial and investigative powers, although despite such authority has been very reluctant to use its prosecutorial powers. This was a point which was clearly illustrated by the decision in *R v Rollins*,[2] where the Supreme Court confirmed that the FSA *did* have the ability to prosecute allegations of money laundering under the Proceeds of Crime Act 2002; and were perhaps suggesting that such powers should be used on a more regular basis.

In addition to its prosecutorial role, the FSA requires authorised firms to have in place an AML system so that they can detect any alleged instances of money laundering. The system, as it currently stands, requires authorised firms, such as banks and building societies, to act as financial policemen and to report any suspicious activity to the FSA via a suspicious transaction report. While this may appear to be sound in theory, in practice it has proven to be extremely controversial. For example, authorised firms have complained about an increase in compliance costs since the introduction of these reporting obligations, to the extent that the requirements have created a fear factor amongst the regulated sector. This has consequently resulted in the adoption of a defensive reporting strategy by firms towards their AML obligations which has subsequently led to a significant increase in the number of reports submitted to the FSA. To complicate matters even further, the Proceeds of Crime Act 2002 also requires the reporting of suspicious transaction reports to the UK's Financial Intelligence Unit (FIU) which is situated within the Serious Organised Crime Agency (SOCA). This repetition of gathering financial intelligence via suspicious transaction reports is unnecessary and causes confusion and uncertainty amongst the regulated sector. It is, however, important to note that the future role of SOCA as the UK's FIU is uncertain due to the probable creation of the National Crime Agency (NCA). Consultation papers released by the Home Office have called for the creation of an NCA, which will delegate its financial crime role to one of its four Commands, which in the case of financial crime will be the Economic Crime Command. However, with the introduction of the NCA there is no mention in the consultation papers with regards to the inclusion or delegation of SOCA's role as the UK's FIU. The future situation is therefore presently unclear.

One of the most important facilities used by the FSA against firms who breach its AML rules and regulations is the imposition of financial penalties. These have arguably become one of the most popular and consistently used powers of the FSA in recent times. For instance, the FSA has imposed a series of high profile and media friendly fines on a number of financial institutions and individuals, even though there was *no* actual evidence of money laundering, a practice which could

---

1   Financial Services and Markets Act 2000, s 6.
2   [2010] UKSC 39, 1.

not take place within the criminal justice system. Furthermore, law enforcement agencies have also used the confiscation powers provided by the Proceeds of Crime Act 2002 through the implementation of confiscation[3] and restraint orders.[4] A confiscation order can be made against any convicted offender who is thought to have a criminal lifestyle with the main purpose behind the order being to recover the proceeds of crime. Moreover, the purpose of a restraint order is to prevent the disposal of criminal assets, prior to criminal proceedings, so that if a confiscation order is made at a later date there are sufficient assets left to cover the amount which has been ordered to be seized. For this purpose a restraint order can be made even before a defendant has been charged with a criminal offence, provided that this is the expected course of action. The existence of such orders is especially important when HM Treasury currently estimates that serious crime involves approximately £5 billion of assets which are in a seizable form.[5]

Despite the existence of such mechanisms it is nevertheless extremely difficult to determine if the introduction of such a wide range of AML legislative and reporting devices have had their desired effect. This is further complicated by the fact that there is no reliable estimation of the exact level of money which is laundered in the UK on an annual basis. As outlined in Chapter 2 of this book, estimates can vary between £19 billion and £48 billion; but if we do not know the size of the problem it is therefore impossible for us to accurately assess whether in all reality we are actually dealing with it. This therefore makes the task of assessing the efficacy of the financial institutions involved in regulating and preventing money laundering even more problematic.

Terrorist Financing

In addition to AML rules and regulations, the UK has also been proactive in establishing a fairly impressive counter-terrorist financing (CTF) policy which predates the international legislative measures introduced by the UN. Such measures were introduced following the terrorist attacks in the USA in September 2001 and the instigation of the financial war on terror by the then USA President George Bush. In an attempt to stop the financing of terrorism, the UK's CTF policy has three measures,

1. Safeguards to prevent terrorists using common methods to raise funds, or using the financial system to move money;
2. Financial intelligence and financial investigation tools; and

---

3   Proceeds of Crime Act 2002, ss 6–13.
4   Proceeds of Crime Act 2002, s 41.
5   HM Treasury, *The Financial Challenge of Terrorism and Crime* (HM Treasury 2007).

3. Asset freezing, which can be used to disrupt the activity of terrorists and their supporters.

The policy is jointly managed by HM Treasury and the Office of Security and Counter Terrorism, situated within the Home Office, with both institutions playing an important role in ensuring compliance with the '9 Special Recommendations' of the FATF. In addition to this, HM Treasury also liaises with overseas governments and international entities to create and enforce international CTF standards. As part of our assessment, we have established that the UK is largely compliant with the international obligations imposed by the UN Security Council Resolutions 1267 and 1373, in addition to the '9 Special Recommendations' of the FATF.

The UK criminalized the financing of terrorism by virtue of the Prevention of Terrorism Act 1989 which was later significantly extended by the provisions of the Terrorism Act 2000. However, it is important to note that since the introduction of the Terrorism Act 2000, only a handful of people have been convicted of funding terrorism which has resulted in the effectiveness of these provisions being questioned. Nevertheless, there are a number of important players that form an integral part of the UK's CTF policy. For example, the financial services sector plays an important role by undertaking its customer due diligence obligations and thereby providing financial intelligence to SOCA via its suspicious transaction reporting system. In addition to the roles outlined above, HM Treasury also works closely with the Charities Commission to prevent the charitable sector being abused by terrorists, a role which it again jointly shares with the Office of Security and Counter Terrorism. Furthermore, HM Revenue and Customs has created a fit and proper test for money services businesses and a registration system so that such institutions are not misused for the purposes of terrorist financing.

Aside from safeguards and financial intelligence and reporting, perhaps one of the most controversial CTF measures in the UK is the ability of HM Treasury to freeze the assets of suspected or known terrorists. This is managed by HM Treasury's Asset Freezing Scheme which is responsible for,

- Domestic legislation on financial sanctions;
- The implementation and administration of domestic financial sanctions;
- Domestic designations under the Terrorist Asset-Freezing etc. Act 2010;
- Providing advice to Treasury Ministers, on the basis of operational advice, on domestic designation decisions;
- The implementation and administration of international financial sanctions in the UK, including those relating to terrorism;
- Working with the Foreign and Commonwealth Office on the design of individual financial sanctions regimes and listing decisions at the UN and European Union (EU);

- Working with international partners to develop the international frameworks for financial sanctions; and,
- Licensing exemptions to financial sanctions where permitted.[6]

The Asset Freezing Scheme was introduced by the Anti-terrorism, Crime and Security Act 2001, which broadly implemented the provisions of UN Security Council Resolution 1373, under which signatory states are required to freeze the assets of individuals. Resultantly, HM Treasury has targeted the financial assets of known al-Qaeda terrorists and in total has frozen approximately £120 million of suspected terrorist assets. This figure, however, may be somewhat misleading as approximately £80 million of this amount had previously been frozen under the Terrorism Act 2000 and therefore was not the result of the implementation of the Anti-terrorism, Crime and Security Act 2001.

The appropriateness of the freezing of terrorist assets under the Anti-terrorism, Crime and Security Act 2001 and the Terrorism (United Nations Measures) Order 2006 has been questioned by several commentators.[7] Its legality was also considered by the Supreme Court in the UK in *Ahmed & Others v HM Treasury*,[8] which determined that the Terrorism (United Nations Measures) Order was beyond the remit of the authority provided by the United Nations Act 1946 and therefore must be abolished. The government responded to the decision of the Supreme Court in an expedient manner and thus introduced and implemented the Terrorist Asset-Freezing (Temporary Provisions) Act 2010. This was subsequently amended by the Terrorist Asset-Freezing etc Act 2010, part 1 of which implemented UN Security Council Resolution 1373.

Fraud

The next financial crime considered in this book is that of fraud. The prevention of fraud in the UK has gained significant momentum since the publication of the Fraud Review and the implementation of the Fraud Act in 2006. Until the introduction of such measures, however, it can be argued that the prevention of fraud had been largely neglected, notwithstanding the creation of the SFO and the introduction of the Criminal Justice Act in 1987. This level of inattention combined with the deregulation of banking legislation resulted in the UK gaining an unwanted reputation for being a safe haven for fraudsters and other types of financial criminals. This position, however, thankfully changed with the election of the Labour government in 1997 and the eventual publication of a set of proposals by the Law Commission which ultimately resulted in the implementation of the

---

6   HM Treasury, 'Financial sanctions' <http://www.hm-treasury.gov.uk/fin_sanctions_index.htm> accessed 17 February 2012.

7   S.I. 2006/2657.

8   [2010] UKSC 2.

Fraud Act 2006. The criminalization of fraud in 2006 replaced the ad hoc legislative framework contained in the Theft Acts of 1968 to 1996 and the eight common law offences of conspiracy to defraud. This was particularly welcoming considering that the deception offences which prosecutors had to rely on prior to the Fraud Act 2006 were notoriously difficult to enforce and were incredibly technical in terms of understanding. As the Home Office stated at the time, it 'is not always clear which offence should be charged, and defendants have successfully argued that the consequences of their particular deceptive behaviour did not fit the definition of the offence with which they have been charged.'[9] The Fraud Act 2006 therefore took away such confusion and made the enforcement of the law much simpler.

In terms of preventing fraud, there are two principal regulatory agencies in the UK that have been given the task of limiting the threat posed by fraud, namely the SFO and the FSA. The SFO is the principal law enforcement agency for fraud, and is arguably the most recognizable out of the two. It was created in 1987 and was given an extensive collection of enforcement and investigative powers under the Criminal Justice Act 1987. Its effectiveness, however, has been arguably limited, mainly due to a large number of high profile and costly prosecutions which have failed in terms of securing a conviction. Examples include Ernest Saunders (one of the Guinness Four), Barlow Clowes, Robert Maxwell, and Blue Arrow. Such failure has resulted in the probability of a successful prosecution in this area being compared to an England victory in a cricket test match! Nevertheless, and as outlined above, the FSA does have a statutory objective to reduce all aspects of financial crime, which also extends to the prevention of fraud.

The development of the FSA's fraud policy can arguably be said to have been overshadowed by its AML policy, and so it wasn't until the impact of the recent Credit Crunch on the financial services sector that the FSA began to fully utilize its enforcement powers to prevent fraud. The FSA has therefore adopted a largely preventative stance towards combating fraud and thus requires the regulated sector to have in place anti-fraud measures and a fraud reporting system as prescribed by its Handbook. If a company fails to implement such measures, the FSA is able to impose a series of financial penalties which can be applied to both authorised firms and individuals. In addition to the regulatory agencies, the NFA also has an important role in devising and measuring the impact of the UK's fraud strategy. The NFA has consequently achieved several notable victories since its creation; for example, it has increased the knowledge and understanding of the impact of fraud through the publication of its Annual Fraud Indicator and has established a strong working relationship with key stakeholders in determining the success of the UK's anti-fraud strategy. Importantly, the NFA has also established Action Fraud,[10] which not only provides invaluable support for victims of fraud but also

---

9   A. Doig, *Fraud* (Willan Publishing 2006, 22–35). For a more detailed illustration of this problem see generally *R v Preddy* [1996] AC 815, 831.

10   See <http://www.actionfraud.police.uk/thedevilsinyourdetails>.

a hotline where instances of fraud can be reported by individuals, charities, small businesses and large corporations.

Notwithstanding such advancements, we nevertheless argue that these measures are still insufficient. It is therefore recommended that lessons could be learnt from the AML reporting system whereby firms are compelled to report suspicious activity to their money laundering reporting officers who then report such instances to SOCA. Such a system has proven to be extremely effective in the USA where all allegations of financial crime from money laundering, terrorist financing, insider trading and fraud are all reported to the Financial Crimes Enforcement Network. The National Fraud Intelligence Bureau, which is managed by the City of London Police force, does deal with reports of fraud from members of the public and does gather financial intelligence that can be distributed to police forces across the UK, but we believe that more than this can be done in the fight against fraud.

It is also important to note, once more, how the scope and future role of each of these agencies, mentioned above, is uncertain due to the impending creation of the NCA. As a result of the 2010 general election and the creation of the Coalition government there are plans for controversial reforms to the UK's financial crime and banking regulation policies. The Coalition government initially stated that it would create an Economic Crime Agency, which would be a single financial crime agency that would see the merging of the SFO, the FSA financial crime team and SOCA. In June 2011, however, the Home Office announced that it had abandoned this idea and had rather decided to create the NCA. As previously stated the NCA will contain four commands 1) The Organised Crime Command; 2) The Border Policing Command; 3) The Economic Crime Command; and 4) The Child Exploitation and Online Protection Centre; of which the third – the Economic Crime Command – will deal with financial crime.

As detailed in Chapter 4 of this book, fraud has developed at such an unprecedented level that it is becoming increasingly difficult for regulatory and prosecutorial agencies to combat. In particular the increasing usage of Internet banking and online shopping has created vast opportunities which many fraudsters are exploiting. Even though certain offences may be covered, from a financial point of view, through insurance companies or financial institutions, there is ultimately always a primary victim of fraud.[11] The Fraud Advisory Panel has introduced indicators to help employers recognize fraud in a bid to prevent it,[12] but in reality fraud is increasingly becoming more subtle and thus difficult, for even the experts, to spot. With fraudsters pushing boundaries and consequently continuing to punish and test the private and public markets, it is difficult to see how fraud in all reality can be slowed down to such an extent that it could ever be completely eradicated.

---

11   J. Burrows and M. Levi, 'Measuring the Impact of Fraud in the UK: A Conceptual and Empirical Journey' (2008) British Journal of Criminology, 48(3), 304.

12   Fraud Advisory Panel, 'An Introduction to Fraud Indicators' <http://www.fraudadvisorypanel.org/new/pdf_show.php?id=170> accessed on 17 November 2011.

It is also difficult to know whether the NCA will really have as much of an impact on fraud prevention as the government believes it will, or whether the SFO and other fraud regulatory bodies will in actuality retain their enforcement powers and render the NCA effectively useless. Perhaps because of this confusion over which of the current regulatory bodies are in control, some firms are currently offering fraud prevention services in an attempt to help institutions and companies combat fraud. Such services even go as far as to state that the use of their service will equate to a 40 per cent reduction in lost revenue.[13] The difficulty experienced by us all, however, is that fraudsters are moving forward at a significant pace yet the process of introducing new legislation is painfully slow. It could be argued therefore that because legislation takes time to be implemented and even with the NCA in place, new frauds may come into existence and thus become even more difficult to combat. The reporting regimes in place that focus on 'whistle-blowers' are arguably out-dated and un-incentivized, making it even more difficult to provide arguments for their complete success. The NCA may therefore require even more powers to tackle fraud in certain areas should new fraud develop in certain ways, particularly in relation to cross-border fraud or frauds that did not initially originate within the UK. One thing is for certain though, the NCA will need to be both dynamic and forceful to successfully adapt to constant variations in national and global markets. A fraud investigation can be damaging to a company or individual's reputation and a successful conviction would be detrimental; but getting it wrong and following the pattern of successive failed prosecutions would be even more devastating.

Insider Dealing

The slow approach towards the prevention of fraud has not thankfully been mirrored with regards to the regulation and prevention of insider dealing. The UK's stance towards insider dealing has been heavily influenced by the introduced of the Council of Europe's Insider Dealing Directive in 1989, which was implemented into the UK by virtue of the Criminal Justice Act 1993. Prior to its introduction, the UK's legislative approach against such illegal dealing was contained in the Companies Act 1980 and the Company Securities (Insider Dealing) Act 1985, which were also supported by the Financial Services Act of 1986. The insider dealing provisions were initially enforced by the then Department of Trade and Industry (DTI) and the Securities and Investment Board (SIB) who were given an extensive assortment of enforcement mechanisms, mandated for in the Financial Services Act 1986.

---

13 PKF Accountants and Business advisers, 'The Financial Cost of Fraud – What Data From Around the World Shows' <http://www.pkf.co.uk/web/pkf.nsf/0/F459DDCCE 5269C818025792D002A830E/$FILE/The%20Financial%20Cost%20of%20Fraud_WEB. pdf> accessed 9 November 2011.

The enforcement of such provisions, by both the DTI and the SIB can arguably, however, be said to have been largely ineffective. This is perhaps due to a number of reasons. The first is the fact that the scope of the insider dealing provisions of the Financial Services Act 1986 only applied to authorised persons, thus limiting their scope. Furthermore, it had been notoriously difficult to secure a criminal conviction for insider dealing. Such factors led to the well documented reform of the SIB into the FSA which subsequently resulted in the perceived introduction of a much tougher insider dealing regime. The new regime is thus contained in the provisions of the FSMA 2000 and the FSA Handbook, under which the FSA was given broad enforcement powers. As a result of such reforms, the FSA has since secured an impressive number of criminal convictions through adopting an aggressive stance towards enforcing the insider dealing provisions.[14] Examples include Christopher McQuoid and James William Melbourne,[15] Matthew and Neel Uberoi,[16] Malcolm Calvert,[17] Anjam Ahmad,[18] Neil Rollins,[19] Christian and Angie Littlewood,[20] Helmy Omar Sa'aid[21] and Rupinder Sidhu.[22] Moreover, the FSA

14   Financial Services Authority, 'Management Consultant Found Guilty of Insider Dealing and Sentenced to Two Years' (15 December 2011) <http://www.fsa.gov.uk/library/communication/pr/2011/114.shtml> accessed 16 February 2012.

15   Financial Services Authority, 'Solicitor and Father-in-Law Found Guilty in FSA Insider Dealing Case' (27 March 2009) <http://www.fsa.gov.uk/library/communication/pr/2009/042.shtml> accessed 16 February 2012.

16   Financial Services Authority, 'Former Corporate Broker Intern and Father Found Guilty of Insider Dealing' (4 November 2009) <http://www.fsa.gov.uk/pages/Library/Communication/PR/2009/149.shtml> accessed 16 February 2012.

17   Financial Services Authority, 'Former Cazenove Broker Sentenced to 21 Months in Prison for Insider Dealing (11 March 2011) <http://www.fsa.gov.uk/pages/Library/Communication/PR/2010/043.shtml> accessed 16 February 2012.

18   Financial Services Authority, 'Hedge Fund Trader Sentenced for Insider Dealing' (22 June 2010) <http://www.fsa.gov.uk/pages/Library/Communication/PR/2010/104.shtml> accessed 16 February 2012.

19   Financial Services Authority, 'Insider Dealing: Financial Services Authority Prosecutes Mr Neil Rollins' (7 January 2009) <http://www.fsa.gov.uk/pages/Library/Communication/PR/2009/002.shtml> accessed 16 February 2012.

20   Financial Services Authority, 'Investment Banker, His Wife and Family Friend Plead Guilty to Insider Dealing' (10 January 2011) <http://www.fsa.gov.uk/pages/Library/Communication/PR/2011/002.shtml> accessed 16 February 2012.

21   Financial Services Authority, 'Investment Banker, His Wife and Family Friend Plead Guilty to Insider Dealing' (10 January 2011) <http://www.fsa.gov.uk/pages/Library/Communication/PR/2011/002.shtml> accessed 16 February 2012.

22   Financial Services Authority, 'Management Consultant Found Guilty of Insider Dealing and Sentenced to Two Years' (15 December 2011) <http://www.fsa.gov.uk/library/communication/pr/2011/114.shtml> accessed 16 February 2012.

has been active in prosecuting a large number of alleged breaches of the insider dealing provisions of the Criminal Justice Act 1993.[23]

It is likely, however, that one of the reasons that the FSA has increased its enforcement activities is due to the announcement by the Coalition government in 2010 that it would be reforming the UK's approach towards the regulation of the financial services sector in light of the ineffective approach adopted by the FSA towards Northern Rock. Subsequently, the publication of the Financial Services Bill in 2012 proposes to replace the FSA with the Financial Conduct Authority. The FSA has, to date, adopted what is best described as a preventative approach towards insider dealing, which requires regulated firms to have appropriate and effective systems and controls to prevent insider dealing, which also extends to money laundering, fraud and bribery. Moreover, there is also an obligation to report any alleged instances of insider dealing to the FSA as a result of their 2005 Market Abuse Directive. A failure to report any suspicious activity will result in a breach of the FSA Handbook and could result in prosecution and/or a financial penalty.

Market Abuse

The market abuse regime is often used in conjunction with the insider dealing provisions of the Criminal Justice Act 1993. The FSA manages and enforces the UK's market abuse regime via the FSMA 2000 and its Handbook. The FSA has enforced this role by imposing several high profile financial penalties, which has proven to be extremely controversial. Yet, it is highly likely that the FSA, and its replacement the Financial Conduct Authority, will continue to use the civil sanctions as opposed to pursuing criminal prosecutions under the Criminal Justice Act 1993. Since introducing the market abuse regime, the FSA has imposed over 60 financial penalties on firms and individuals who have breached its provisions. It appears that the market abuse provisions under FSMA 2000 and the Handbook compliment the criminal provisions of the Criminal Justice Act 1993 and this approach has also been adopted by several other jurisdictions, including for example, the USA. Interestingly, a large proportion of the financial penalties imposed by the FSA have been issued since the start of the 'Credit Crunch' in 2007. This is a matter that is beyond the scope of this book, but represents an intriguing link between breaches of the market abuse regime and the global financial crisis.

---

23   Financial Services Authority, 'Management Consultant Found Guilty of Insider Dealing and Sentenced to Two Years' (15 December 2011) <http://www.fsa.gov.uk/library/communication/pr/2011/114.shtml> accessed 16 February 2012.

Bribery and Corruption

The final financial crime considered in this book is that of bribery and corruption. The prevention of bribery has recently gained significant impetus in the UK with the introduction of the Bribery Act 2010 which replaced the patchwork framework of the Public Bodies Corrupt Practices Act 1889, the Prevention of Corruption Act 1906 and the Prevention of Corruption Act 1916. With the introduction of the Act, the jurisdiction of the SFO has been extended to incorporate the criminal offences created by the Bribery Act 2010 and in the short time that has passed since the Act's implementation the SFO has already used its new enforcement powers. For example, in 2011 several ex-directors of Maybey and Johnson, were convicted of bribing foreign public officials to secure contracts in Iraq in contravention of the UN Oil for Food Programme.[24] Furthermore, in February 2011 the SFO recovered over £7 million from M.W. Kellogg which was generated by contracts that had been obtained through bribery and corruption committed by the company's parent company.[25] Finally, Mark Jessop was sentenced to six months' imprisonment for making illegal payments to Saddam Hussein's government.[26]

The Act contains, what some may regard as, a number of controversial provisions that have caused unease amongst commercial entities. For example, Richard Alderman, the Director of the SFO, has argued that facilitation payments are bribes and that they 'have a corrosive effect. ... Corruption [he states] becomes systematic and endemic in the society [in which facilitation payments are paid] and produces a culture in which others look for much larger bribes as well. ... I am looking for companies to adopt a zero tolerance approach to these payments.'[27] Furthermore, in relation to the provisions of the Bribery Act 2010 that apply to corporate hospitality, Chris Walker, Head of Policy at the SFO has stated,

---

24   See Serious Fraud Office, 'Mabey & Johnson Directors Made Illegal Payments to Sadam Hussein's Iraq to Gain Contract' (10 February 2011) <http://www.sfo.gov.uk/press-room/latest-press-releases/press-releases-2011/mabey--johnson-directors-made-illegal-payments-to-sadam-hussein's-iraq-to-gain-contract.aspx> accessed 16 February 2012.

25   Serious Fraud Office, 'MW Kellogg Ltd to Pay £7million in SFO High Court Action' (16 February 2011) <http://www.sfo.gov.uk/press-room/latest-press-releases/press-releases-2011/mw-kellogg-ltd-to-pay-7-million-in-sfo-high-court-action.aspx> accessed 16 February 2012.

26   Serious Fraud Office, 'Medical Goods to Iraq Supplier Jailed for Paying Kick-Backs' (13 April 2011) <http://www.sfo.gov.uk/press-room/latest-press-releases/press-releases-2011/medical-goods-to-iraq-supplier-jailed-for-paying-kick-backs.aspx> accessed February 2012.

27   Serious Fraud Office, 'Breakfast Seminar Hosted by Kingsley Napley & Carmichael Fisher' speech by Richard Alderman, Director, Serious Fraud Office (21 June 2011) <http://www.sfo.gov.uk/about-us/our-views/director's-speeches/speeches-2011/break fast-seminar-hosted-by-kingsley-napley--carmichael-fisher.aspx> accessed 16 February 2012.

Sensible and proportionate promotional entertainment expenditure is not an offence under the Act. However, when hospitality is done *so that people will be induced to act in a certain way* – when the expenditure is beyond what is sensible and proportionate, the relevant provisions of the Act will be triggered. [emphasis added][28]

Interestingly, the Bribery Act also requires companies to have in place adequate procedures to prevent people associated with them from being bribed. Indeed, the Bribery Act 2010 provides that a commercial organization[29] which fails to prevent an associated person from committing bribery on their behalf, has also committed an offence.[30] However, it is a defence for the commercial organization to have in place 'adequate procedures to prevent persons associated with the commercial entity from undertaking such conduct.'[31] This defence is similar to the obligations contained in the FSA Handbook which provides that firms are required to 'establish and maintain effective systems and controls ... for countering the risk that the firm might be used to further financial crime.'[32] The creation and implementation of an effective system and control has traditionally been used to combat money laundering and fraud, but the FSA has further extended this to include bribery and corruption. This can only be a good thing. The FSA has stated 'that firms therefore have a responsibility to assess the risks of becoming involved in, or facilitating, bribery and corruption and to take reasonable steps to prevent those risks crystallising.'[33]

Despite such advancements, we still argue that the extension of the jurisdiction of the FSA towards imposing an obligation on authorised firms in relation to bribery is yet another unnecessary duplication of roles with the SFO. Furthermore, the Bribery Act 2010 does not impose a duty on commercial organizations to report any suspicious activity that might amount to bribery. Therefore, the government has adopted a similar stance towards reporting instances of bribery to that of fraud. This is in sharp contrast with the approaches used to prevent money laundering and terrorist financing and is therefore in opposition to the approach which we would seek to encourage.

---

28   Serious Fraud Office, 'Best Practices in Fighting Bribery and Corruption: The Bribery Act 2010 Enforcing the Bribery Act, Chris Walker, Head of Policy, Serious Fraud Office' (15 February 2011) <http://www.sfo.gov.uk/about-us/our-views/other-speeches/speeches-2011/icc-conference-hosted-by-herbert-smith.aspx>, accessed 16 February 2012.

29   As defined by the Bribery Act 2010, s 7(5).

30   Bribery Act 2010, s 7(1).

31   Bribery Act 2010, s 7(2).

32   SYSC 3.2.6R.

33   Financial Services Authority, *Anti-Bribery and Corruption in Commercial Insurance Broking: Reducing the Risk of Illicit Payments or Inducements to Third Parties* (Financial Services Authority 2010) 10.

Final Thoughts

The UK has implemented at times a robust financial crime policy that often exceeds the minimum standards set by the UN, the EU and the FATF. What has become clear from reviewing the plethora of legislative provisions, regulations, law enforcement agencies and different enforcement mechanisms involved in regulating and preventing financial crime is that there are a number of important findings and recommendations that could improve the UK's current stance towards such illegal activity. For example, there is a sense of uncertainty as to the future direction of SOCA's role as the UK's FIU and consultation papers published by the Home Office have referred to an Economic Crime Command, positioned in the NCA that will lead and implement the future financial crime strategy. Yet, there is no reference to, or indication of what becomes of this integral AML and CTF role. It is therefore surprising that given the early rhetoric from the Coalition government to create a single financial crime agency that institutions such as the SFO will continue to enforce the provisions of the Fraud Act 2006 and the Bribery Act 2010. While we would welcome an all encompassing agency, we would like to see more certainty in what the future holds and more proactive reporting requirements so that fraud and bribery prevention are brought to the forefront of agendas and dealt with as rigorously as is seen with the policies for money laundering and terrorist financing.

Bibliography

Aaronberg, D. and Higgins, N. 'Legislative Comment, The Bribery Act 2010: All Bark and No Bite …?' (2010) *Archbold Review*, 5, 6–9.

Abarca, M. 'The Need for Substantive Regulation on Investor Protection and Corporate Governance in Europe: Does Europe Need a Sarbanes-Oxley?' (2004) *Journal of International Banking Law and Regulation*, 19(11), 419–431.

Alexander, K. 'The International Anti-money Laundering Regime: The Role of the Financial Action Task Force' (2001) *Journal of Money Laundering Control*, 4(3), 231–248.

Alexander, R. 'Corruption as a Financial Crime' (2009) *Company Lawyer*, 30(4), 98.

Alexander, R. 'Money Laundering and Terrorist Financing: Time for a Combined Offence' (2009) *Company Lawyer*, 30(7), 200–204, 202.

Alkaabi, A., Mohay, G., Mccullagh, A. and Chantler, N. 'Comparative Analysis of the Extent of Money Laundering in Australia, UAE, UK and the USA' (20 January 2010) Finance and Corporate Governance Conference 2010 Paper <http://ssrn.com/abstract=1539843> accessed 6 July 2011.

Alldridge, P. *Money Laundering Law* (Hart 2003).

Alldridge, P. 'Reforming Bribery: Law Commission Consultation Paper 185: (1) Bribery Reform and the Law – Again' (2008) *Criminal Law Review*, 9, 671–86.

Anderson, T., Lane, H. and Fox, M. 'Consequences and Responses to the Madoff Fraud' (2009) *Journal of International Banking and Regulation*, 24(11), 548–555.

Arora, A. 'The Statutory System of the Bank Supervision and the Failure of BCCI' (2006) *Journal of Business Law*, August, 487–510.

Attorney General's Office, *Extending the Powers of the Crown Court to Prevent Fraud and Compensate Victims: A Consultation* (Attorney General's Office 2008).

Attorney General's Office, *Fraud Review – Final Report* (Attorney General's Office 2006).

Australian Government and Australian Institute of Criminology, *Charges and Offences of Money Laundering Transnational Crime Brief No. 4* (Australian Institute of Criminology 2008).

Bagge, J. 'The Future For Enforcement Under the New Financial Services Authority' (1998) *Company Lawyer*, 19(7), 194–197.

Bale, R. and Volpe, T. 'Ponzi schemes and financial fraud regulation' (2011) *Brief*, Summer, 40, 8.

BBC News, 'Arrogant Muslim Preacher Jailed' (18 April 2008) <http://news.bbc.co.uk/1/hi/uk/7354397.stm> accessed 28 June 2011.

BBC News, 'Asil Nadir jailed for ten years for Polly Peck thefts' (23 August 2012) <http://www.bbc.co.uk/news/uk-19352531> accessed 26 September 2012.

BBC News, 'UK Maximum Sentence for Money Launder' (25 February 1999) <http://news.bbc.co.uk/1/hi/uk/285759.stm> accessed 6 June 2011.

Beale, K. and Esposito, P. 'Emergent International Attitudes Towards Bribery, Corruption and Money Laundering' (2009) *Arbitration*, 75(3), 360–373.

Bell, R. 'The Confiscation, Forfeiture and Disruption of Terrorist Finances' (2003) *Journal of Money Laundering Control*, 7(2), 105–125, 113.

Benstead, J. 'Biting the Bullet' (2010) *New Law Journal*, 160(7434), 1291–1292.

Bentley, D. and Fisher, R. 'Criminal Property Under PCOA 2002 – Time to Clean up the Law?' (2009) *Archbold News* 2, 7–9.

Binning, P. 'In Safe Hands? Striking the Balance Between Privacy and Security – Anti-terrorist Finance Measures' (2002) *European Human Rights Law Review*, 6, 737–749.

Booth, R., Farrell, S., Bastable, G. and Yeo, N. *Money Laundering Law and Regulation: A Practical Guide* (Oxford University Press 2011).

Bosworth-Davies, R. 'Investigating Financial Crime: The Continuing Evolution of the Public Fraud Investigation Role – A Personal Perspective' (2009) *Company Lawyer*, 30(7), 195–199.

Brown, G. and Evans, T. 'The Impact: The Breadth and Depth of the Anti-money Laundering Provisions Requiring Reporting of Suspicious Activities' (2008) *Journal of International Banking Law and Regulation*, 23(5), 274–277.

Building Societies Association, 'Financial Crime Prevention' <//www.bsa.org.uk/policy/policyissues/fcpandphysec/financialcrime.htm> accessed 1 July 2011.

Bunyan, N. and Edwards, R. 'Canoe Wife Trial: Darwin's Jailed for More Than Six Years' (*The Daily Telegraph* 23 July 2008) <http://www.telegraph.co.uk/news/2448044/Canoe-wife-trial-Darwins-jailed-for-more-than-six-years.html> accessed 10 June 2011.

Cabinet Office, *The UK and the Campaign Against International Terrorism – Progress Report* (Cabinet Office 2002).

Carr, I. 'Fighting Corruption Through the United Nations Convention on Corruption 2003: A Global Solution to a Global Problem?' (2005) *International Trade Law and Regulation*, 11(1), 24–29.

Charity Commission, 'Compliance Toolkit: Protecting Charities from Harm' (2009) Module 7, Page 1 <http://www.charity-commission.gov.uk/Library/tkch1mod7.pdf> accessed 17 June 2011.

Chase, A. 'Legal Mechanisms of the International Community and the United States Concerning the State Sponsorship of Terrorism' (2004) *Virginia Journal of International Law*, 45, 41.

City of London Police, 'Bribery Act 2010 summary' <http://www.cityoflondon.police.uk/CityPolice/Departments/ECD/anticorruptionunit/briberyact2010summary.htm> accessed 24 November 2011.

City of London Police, *Assessment: Financial Crime Against Vulnerable Adults* (Social Care Institute for Excellence November 2011).

Collins, J. and Kennedy, A. 'The Cheat, His Wife and Her Lawyer' (2003) *Taxation*, November 136.

Croall, H. 'Who is the White-Collar Criminal?' (1989) *British Journal of Criminology*, 29(2), 157.

Crown Prosecution Service, 'DPP Announces New Head of Fraud Prosecution Division' (2009) <http://www.cps.gov.uk/news/press_releases/136_09/> accessed 22 January 2010.

Crown Prosecution Service, 'Proceeds of Crime Act 2002 Part 7 – Money Laundering Offences' <http://www.cps.gov.uk/legal/p_to_r/proceeds_of_crime_money_laundering/> accessed 6 July 2011.

Crown Prosecution Service, 'The Fraud Act 2006' (2008) <http://www.cps.gov.uk/legal/d_to_g/fraud_act/> accessed 8 June 2011.

Deem, D. 'Notes From the Field: Observations in Working with the Forgotten Victims of Personal Financial Crimes' (2000) *Journal of Elder Abuse & Neglect*, 12(2), 33–48.

de Grazia, J. *Review of the Serious Fraud Office – Final Report* (Serious Fraud Office 2008).

Denning, A. 'Independence and Impartiality of the Judges' (1954) *South African Law Journal*, 71, 345.

Dennis, I. 'Fraud Act 2006' (2007) *Criminal Law Review*, January, 1–2.

Doig, A. *Fraud* (Willan Publishing 2006).

Donohue, L. 'Anti Terrorist Finance in the United Kingdom and the United States' (2005–2006), *Michigan Journal of International Law*, 27, 303.

Duthie, T. and Lawler, D. 'Legislative Comment: The United Kingdom Bribery Bill' (2010) *Construction Law Journal*, 26(2), 146–152.

Editorial, 'The Bribery Act 2010' (2010) *Criminal Law Review*, 6, 439–440.

European Commission, 'Financial Crime' <http://ec.europa.eu/internal_market/company/financial-crime/index_en.htm> accessed 21 March 2012.

Evans, M. 'Shortage of Money Led to 7/7 Security Failures'. *The Times* (London, 11 May 2006).

Federal Bureau of Investigation (n/d) 'Mortgage Fraud' <http://www.fbi.gov/hq/mortgage_fraud.htm> accessed 22 April 2010.

Federal Bureau of Investigation, 'Financial Crimes Report to the Public' <http://www.fbi.gov/stats-services/publications/financial-crimes-report-2010-2011/financial-crimes-report-2010-2011#Financial> accessed 21 March 2012.

Financial Action Task Force, *International Standards on Combating Money Laundering and the Financing of Terrorism & Proliferation* (Financial Action Task Force 2012).

Financial Action Task Force, 'FATF steps up the fight against money laundering and terrorist financing', 16 February 2012 <http://www.fatf-gafi.org/document/17/0,3746,en_32250379_32236920_49656209_1_1_1_1,00.html> accessed 14 March 2012.

Financial Action Task Force, *Report on Money Laundering and Terrorist Financing Typologies 2003–2004* (Financial Action Task Force 2004).

Financial Action Task Force, *Third Mutual Evaluation Report Anti-Money Laundering and Combating the Financing of Terrorism – United Kingdom* (Financial Action Task Force 2007).

Financial Services Authority, *Annual Report 2007/2008* (Financial Services Authority 2008, 23).

Financial Services Authority, *Anti-bribery and Corruption in Commercial Insurance Broking: Reducing the Risk of Illicit Payments or Inducements to Third Parties* (Financial Services Authority 2010).

Financial Services Authority, *Developing our Policy on Fraud and Dishonesty – Discussion Paper 26* (Financial Services Authority 2003).

Financial Services Authority, 'Fake Stockbroker Sentenced to 15 months' <http://www.fsa.gov.uk/pages/Library/Communication/PR/2008/011.shtml> accessed 28 March 2010.

Financial Services Authority, 'Fighting Financial Crime' <http://www.fsa.gov.uk/about/what/financial_crime> accessed 21 March 2012.

Financial Services Authority, *Financial Risk Outlook 2008* (Financial Services Authority 2008).

Financial Services Authority, 'Frequently Asked questions' (Financial Services Authority 2011) <http://www.fsa.gov.uk/pages/About/What/financial_crime/money_laundering/faqs/index.shtml> accessed 6 June 2011.

Financial Services Authority, 'FSA Fines Capita Financial Administrators Limited £300,000 in First Anti-fraud Controls Case', <http://www.fsa.gov.uk/pages/Library/Communication/PR/2006/019.shtml> accessed 16 March 2006.

Financial Services Authority, 'FSA Fines Nationwide £980,000 for Information Security Lapses' <http://www.fsa.gov.uk/pages/Library/Communication/PR/2007/021.shtml> accessed 14 February 2007.

Financial Services Authority, 'FSA Fines Norwich Union Life £1.26m' <http://www.fsa.gov.uk/pages/Library/Communication/PR/2007/130.shtml> accessed 4 November 2009.

Financial Services Authority, 'FSA Returns £270,000 to Victims of Share Fraud' <http://www.fsa.gov.uk/pages/Library/Communication/PR/2010/032.shtml> accessed 21 March 2010.

Financial Services Authority, 'One-minute Guide – Anti-bribery and Corruption in Commercial Insurance Broking' <http://www.fsa.gov.uk/smallfirms/resources/one_minute_guides/insurance_intermed/anti_bribery.shtml> accessed 24 November 2011.

Financial Services Authority, Press Release 'FSA Fines Alpari and its Former Money Laundering Reporting Officer, Sudipto Chattopadhyay For Anti-money Laundering Failings' (5 May 2010) <http://www.fsa.gov.uk/pages/Library/Communication/PR/2010/077.shtml> accessed 6 July 2011.

Financial Services Authority, 'Principles for Business' <http://www.fsa.gov.uk/Pages/Library/Communication/PR/1999/099.shtml> accessed 29 April 2010.

Financial Services Authority, 'The FSA's New Approach to Fraud – Fighting Fraud in Partnership', speech by Philip Robinson, 26 October 2004 <http://www.fsa.gov.uk/library/communication/speeches/2004/sp208.shtml> accessed 3 August 2011.

Financial Services Authority *The Full Handbook – SYSC Senior Management Arrangements, Systems and Controls* (Financial Services Authority 2011).

Financial Services Authority, 'What We Do: Who We Regulate' 'We Regulate Most Financial Services Markets, Exchanges and Firms. We Set the Standards That They Must Meet and Can Take Action Against Firms if They Fail to Meet the Required Standards' <http://www.fsa.gov.uk/pages/About/What/Who/index.shtml> accessed 27 September 2011.

Financial Services Commission, *Guidance Notes – Systems of Control to Prevent the Financial System From Being Used for Money Laundering or Terrorist Financing Activities* (Financial Services Commission 2011).

Fisher, J. 'Recent Development in the Fight Against Money Laundering' (2002) *Journal of International Banking Law*, 17(3), 67–72.

Fisher, J. and Sumpster, T. *Fighting Fraud and Financial Crime* (Policy Exchange 2010).

Forston, R. 'Money Laundering Offences Under POCA 2002' in W. Blair and R. Brent (eds) *Banks and Financial Crime – The International Law of Tainted Money* (Oxford University Press 2010).

Fraud Advisory Panel, *Roskill Revisited: Is There a Case for a Unified Fraud Prosecution Office?* (Fraud Advisory Panel 2010).

Gallagher, J., Lauchlan, J. and Steven, M. 'Polly Peck: The Breaking of an Entrepreneur?' (1996) *Journal of Small Business and Enterprise Development*, 3(1), 3–12.

Gentle, S. 'The Bribery Act 2010: Part 2: The Corporate Offence' (2011) *Criminal Law Review*, 2, 101–110.

Global Witness, *Broken Vows – Exposing the "Loupe" Holes in the Diamond Industry's Efforts to Prevent the Trade in Conflict Diamonds* (Global Witness Publishing Inc 2003).

Gottschalk, P. 'Categories of Financial Crime' (2010) *Journal of Financial Crime*, 17(4), 441–458.

Greer, S. 'Human Rights and the Struggle Against Terrorism in the United Kingdom' (2008) *European Human Rights Law Review*, 2, 163–172.

Gurung, J., Wijaya, M. and Rao, A. 'AMLCTF Compliance and SMEs in Australia: A Case Study of the Prepaid Card Industry' (2010) *Journal of Money Laundering Control*, 13(3), 184–201.

Haines, J. 'The National Fraud Strategy: New Rules to Crack Down on Fraud' (2009) *Company Lawyer*, 30(7), 213.

Hardouin, P. 'Banks Governance and Public–Private Partnership in Preventing and Confronting Organized Crime, Corruption and Terrorism Financing' (2009) *Journal of Financial Crime*, 16(3), 199–209.

Harrison, K. 'Sentencing Financial Crime in England and Wales' in N. Ryder (ed.) *Financial Crime in the 21st Century – Law and Policy* (Edward Elgar 2011).

Harvey, J. 'An Evaluation of Money Laundering Policies' (2005) *Journal of Money Laundering Control*, 8(4), 339–345.

Harvey, J. 'Compliance and Reporting Issues Arising for Financial Institutions From Money Laundering Regulations: A Preliminary Cost Benefit Study' (2004) *Journal of Money Laundering Control*, 7(4), 333–346.

HM Crown Prosecution Service Inspectorate, *Inspectorate Review of the Fraud Prosecution Service* (HM Crown Prosecution Service Inspectorate 2008).

HM Customs and Excise, *Oils Fraud Strategy: Summary of Consultation Responses Regulatory Impact Assessment* (HM Customs and Excise 2002).

HM Government, *The Coalition: Our Programme for Government* (HM Government 2010).

HM Revenue and Customs, *Renewal of the 'Tackling Alcohol Fraud' Strategy* (HM Revenue and Customs 2009).

HM Treasury, 'Appointment of the UK President of the Financial Action Task Force' <http://www.gov-news.org/gov/uk/news/appointment_uk_president_financial_action/36083.html> accessed 3 July 2011.

HM Treasury, 'Asset Freezing Unit' <http://www.hm-treasury.gov.uk/fin_sanctions_afu.htm> accessed 14 March 2012.

HM Treasury, *Combating the Financing of Terrorism. A Report on UK Action* (HM Treasury 2002).

HM Treasury, 'George Osborne, Chancellor of the Exchequer. Speech at The Lord Mayor's Dinner for Bankers and Merchants of the City of London, at Mansion House 16 June 2010' <www.hm-treasury.gov.uk/press_12_10.htm> accessed 26 June 2010.

HM Treasury, *The Financial Challenge to Crime and Terrorism* (HM Treasury, 2007).

HM Treasury, *Anti-Money Laundering Strategy* (HM Treasury 2004).

HM Treasury, 'The Landsbanki Freezing Order' (2011) <http://www.hm-treasury.gov.uk/fin_stability_landsbanki.htm> accessed 24 June 2011.

Home Office, 'Counting Rules For Recorded Crime' <http://rds.homeoffice.gov.uk/rds/pdfs10/countgeneral10.pdf> accessed 29 April 2010.

Home Office, 'Economic Crime Press Release, 17 January 2011' <//www.homeoffice.gov.uk/media-centre/news/economic-crime> accessed 22 January 2011.

Home Office, 'Fraud' <http://www.crimereduction.homeoffice.gov.uk/fraud/fraud17.htm> accessed 7 December 2009.

Home Office Home office circular 47/2004 priorities for the investigation of fraud cases (Home Office 2004).

Home Office, *Reform of the Prevention of Corruption Acts and SFO Powers in Cases of Bribery Against Foreign Officials* (Home Office 2005).

Home Office, *Report on the Operation in 2004 of the Terrorism Act 2000* (Home Office 2004).

Home Office, *The United Kingdom's Strategy for Countering Terrorism* (London, 2011).

Home Office, *The National Crime Agency – A Plan for the Creation of a National Crime-fighting Capability* (Home Office 2011).

Home Office, *Local to Global: Reducing the Risk from Organised Crime* (Home Office 2011).

Hopton, D. *Money Laundering: A Concise Guide for all Businesses* (Gower 2009).

Horder, J. 'Bribery as a Form of Criminal Wrongdoing' (2011) *Law Quarterly Review*, 127(Jan), 37–54.

House of Commons, *Report of the Official Account of the Bombings in London on 7 July 2005* (House of Commons 2005).

House of Lords, 'Money Laundering and the Financing of Terrorism: European Union Committee' (2009) <http://www.publications.parliament.uk/pa/ld200 809/ldselect/ldeucom/132/9031811.htm> accessed 24 June 2011.

Hudson, A. *The Law of Finance* (Sweet and Maxwell 2009) at 345.

Hurst, T. 'A Post-Enron Examination of Corporate Governance Problems in the Investment Company Industry' (2006) *Company Lawyer*, 27(2), 41–49.

International Monetary Fund, *Financial System Abuse, Financial Crime and Money Laundering – Background Paper* (International Monetary Fund, 12 February 2001).

Johnson, J. 'Is the Global Financial System AML/CTF Prepared?' (2008) *Journal of Financial Crime*, 15(1), 7–21, 8.

Joint Money Laundering Steering Group, 'Who are the Members of the JMLSG?' <http://www.jmlsg.org.uk/bba/jsp/polopoly.jsp?d=777&a=9907> accessed 18 June 2010.

Kennon, A. 'Pre-legislative Scrutiny of Draft Bills' (2004) *Public Law*, Autumn, 477–494.

Kiernan, P. 'The Regulatory Bodies Fraud: Its Enforcement in the Twenty-first Century' (2003) *Company Lawyer*, 24(10), 293–299.

Kiernan, P. and Scanlan, G. 'Fraud and the Law Commission: The Future of Dishonesty' (2003) *Journal of Financial Crime*, 10(3), 199–208.

KPMG, *Money Laundering: Review of the Reporting System* (KPMG 2003).

Kruse, A. 'Financial and Economic Sanctions – From a Perspective of International Law and Human Rights' (2005) *Journal of Financial Crime*, 12(3), 217–220, 218.

Kubiciel, M. 'Core Criminal Law Provisions in the United Nations Convention Against Corruption' (2009) *International Criminal Law Review*, 9(1), 139–155.

Labour Party, *Labour Party Manifesto – Britain Forward Not Back* (Labour Party: 2005).

Lee, R. *Terrorist Financing: The US and International Response Report for Congress* (Congressional Research Service 2002).

Leigh, D. and Evans, R. 'Cost of New Economic Crime Agency Could Prove Prohibitive' <http://www.guardian.co.uk/business/2010/jun/02/economic-cri me-agency-scheme-cost> accessed 12 July 2010.

Lennon, G. and Walker, C. 'Hot Money in a Cold Climate' (2009) *Public Law*, January, 37–42.

Leong, A. 'Chasing Dirty Money: Domestic and International Measures Against Money Laundering' (2007) *Journal of Money Laundering Control*, 10(2), 140–156, 45.

Leroux, M. 'Michael Bright Gets Maximum Seven Years From Independent Insurance Fraud' (*The Times* 25 October) <http://business.timesonline.co.uk/ tol/business/industry_sectors/banking_and_finance/article2733660.ece> accessed 10 June 2011.

Levi, M. 'Combating the Financing of Terrorism. A History and Assessment of the Control of Threat Finance' (2010) *British Journal of Criminology*, 50, 650–669.

Levi, M. 'The Roskill Fraud Commission Revisited: An Assessment' (2003) *Journal of Financial Crime*, 11(1), 38–44.

Levi, M. and Burrows, J. 'Measuring the Impact of Fraud in the UK: A Conceptual and Empirical Journey' (2008) *British Journal of Criminology*, 48(3), 293–318.

Levi, M., Burrows, J., Fleming, M. and Hopkins, M. *The Nature, Extent and Economic Impact of Fraud in the UK* (ACPO 2007).

Levitt, M. 'Stemming the Flow of Terrorist Financing: Practical and Conceptual Challenges' (2003) *The Fletcher Forum of World Affairs*, 27(1), 63.

Linn, C. 'How Terrorists Exploit Gaps in US Anti-money Laundering Laws to Secrete Plunder' (2005) *Journal of Money Laundering Control*, 8(3), 200–214.

Lowe, P. 'Counterfeiting: Links to Organised Crime and Terrorist Funding' (2006) *Journal of Financial Crime*, 13(2), 255.

Lunt, M. 'The Extraterritorial Effects of the Sarbanes-Oxley Act 2002' (2006) *Journal of Business Law*, May, 249–266.

Mahendra, B. 'Fighting Serious Fraud' (2002) *New Law Journal*, 152(7020), 289.

Masters, J. 'Fraud and Money Laundering: The Evolving Criminalization of Corporate Non-Compliance' (2008) *Journal of Money Laundering Control*, 11(2), 103.

Maylam, S. 'Prosecution for Money Laundering in the UK' (2002) *Journal of Financial Crime*, 10, 157–158, 158.

Metropolitan Police, 'Man Jailed for 30 Years for Terrorism Offences' (Metropolitan Police Press Release 2011) <http://content.met.police.uk/News/Man-jailed-for-30-years-for-terrorism-offences/1260268719101/1257246745756> accessed 28 June 2011.

Metropolitan Police, 'Operation Overamp. Hassan Mutegombwa' (Metropolitan Police Press Release, 2010) <http://www.powerbase.info/images/6/6c/Metro politan_Police_Service_Press_Release_on_Conviction_of_Hassan_Mute gombwa.pdf> accessed 28 June 2011.

Ministry of Justice, 'Bribery Act Implementation' (20 July 2010) <http://www.justice.gov.uk/news/newsrelease200710a.htm> accessed 15 December 2011.

Ministry of Justice, *Bribery: Draft Legislation* (The Stationery Office 2009).

Ministry of Justice, 'Government Welcomes New Bribery Law Recommendations' (20 November 2008).

Ministry of Justice, Press Release 'UK Clamps Down on Corruption With New Bribery Act' <http://www.justice.gov.uk/news/press-release-300311a.htm> accessed 29 November 2011.

Ministry of Justice, *The Bribery Act 2010 – Guidance* (Ministry of Justice 2011).

Ministry of Justice, 'The Bribery Act: Guidance' (March 2011) <http://www.justice.gov.uk/downloads/guidance/making-reviewing-law/bribery-act-2010-guidance.pdf> accessed 5 May 2011.

Mitsilegas, V. and Gilmore, B. 'The EU Legislative Framework Against Money Laundering and Terrorist Finance: A Critical Analysis in Light of Evolving Global Standards' (2007) *International and Comparative Law Quarterly*, 56(1), 119–140.

Monteity, C. 'The Bribery Act 2010: Part 3: Enforcement' (2011) *Criminal Law Review*, 2, 111–121, 114.

National Criminal Intelligence Service, *UK Threat Assessment* (National Criminal Intelligence Service 2003).

National Fraud Authority, *Annual Fraud Indicator* (National Fraud Authority 2012).

National Fraud Authority, *Annual Fraud Indicator* (National Fraud Authority 2011).

National Fraud Authority, *Annual Fraud Indicator* (National Fraud Authority 2010).

National Fraud Authority, 'National Fraud Intelligence Bureau' <http://www.lslo.gov.uk/nfa/WhoWeWorkWith/Pages/NFIB.aspx> accessed 22 April 2010.

National Fraud Strategic Authority, *The National Fraud Strategy – A New Approach to Combating Fraud* (National Fraud Strategic Authority 2009).

National Fraud Strategic Authority, 'UK Toughens up on Fraudsters With New Anti-fraud Authority' <http://www.attorneygeneral.gov.uk/NewsCentre/Pages/UKToughensUpOn%20FraudstersWithNewAnti-FraudAuthority.aspx> accessed 2 October 2008.

Nunziato, M. 'Aiding and abetting, a Madoff family affair: why secondary actors should be held accountable for securities fraud through the restoration of the private right of action for aiding and abetting liability under the federal security laws' (2010) *Albany Law Review*, 73, 603–643.

OECD, 'Business Approaches to Combating Bribery' <http://www.oecd.org/dataoecd/45/32/1922830.pdf> accessed 24 July 2010.

OECD, 'Guidelines for Multinational Enterprises' <http://www.oecd.org/document/28/0,3343,en_2649_34889_2397532_1_1_1_1,00.html> accessed 24 July 2010.

Office of Fair Trading, *Anti-Money Laundering Future Supervisory Approach Consultation* (Office of Fair Trading 2010).

Office of Fair Trading, *Memorandum of Understanding Between the Office of Fair Trading and the Director of the Serious Fraud Office* (Office of Fair Trading 2003).

Office of Fair Trading, 'OFT and Nigerian Financial Crime Squad Join Forces to Combat Spam Fraud' (2005) <http://www.oft.gov.uk/news-and-updates/press/2005/210-05> accessed 2 August 2010.

Office of Fair Trading, *Prevention of Fraud Policy* (Office of Fair Trading).

Office of Fair Trading, *Scamnesty 2010 Campaign Strategy* (Office of Fair Trading 2009).

Ormerod, D. 'The Fraud Act 2006 – Criminalising Lying?' (2007) *Criminal Law Review*, 193–219, 219.

Oxford Analytica Ltd, 'Country Report: Anti-money Laundering Rules in the United Kingdom' in M. Pieith and G. Aiolfi (eds) *A Comparative Guide to Anti-money Laundering: A Critical Analysis of Systems in Singapore, Switzerland, the UK and the USA* (Edward Elgar 2004).

Pope, T. and Webb, T. 'Legislative Comment – The Bribery Act 2010' (2010) *Journal of International Banking Law and Regulation*, 25(10), 480–483.

Proctor, A. 'Supporting a Risk-based Anti-money Laundering Approach Through Enforcement Action' (2004) *Journal of Financial Regulation and Compliance*, 13(1) 10–14.

Proctor, L. 'The Barings Collapse: A Regulatory Failure, or a Failure of Supervision?' (1997) *Brooklyn Journal of International Law*, 22, 735–767.

Raphael, M. *Blackstone's Guide to the Bribery Act 2010* (Oxford University Press 2010).

Rider, B. 'A Bold Step?' (2009) *Company Lawyer*, 30(1), 1–2.

Robb, G. *White-collar Crime in Modern England – Financial Fraud and Business Morality 1845–1929* (Cambridge University Press 1992).

Royal Institute of Chartered Surveyors, *Money Laundering Guidance* (Royal Institute of Chartered Surveyors 2010).

Ryder, N. 'A false sense of security? An analysis of legislative approaches to the prevention of terrorist finance in the United States of America and the United Kingdom' (2007) *Journal of Business Law*, November, 821–850.

Ryder, N. 'Danger Money' (2007) *New Law Journal*, 157, 7300; Supp (Charities Appeals Supplement), 6, 8.

Ryder, N. *Financial Crime in the 21st Century* (Edward Elgar 2011).

Sacerdoti, G. 'The 1997 OECD Convention on Combating Bribery of Foreign Public Officials in International Business Transactions' (1999) *International Business Law Journal*, 1, 3–18.

Salans 'Anti-bribery and Corruption: The UK Propels Itself to the Forefront of Global Enforcement' <http://www.salans.com/~/media/Assets/Salans/Publications/Salans%20Client%20Alert%20UK%20Bribery%20Act%20Implementation%20Date.ashx> accessed 24 July 2010.

Sanyal, R. and Samanta, S. 'Trends in International Bribe-giving: Do Anti-bribery Laws Matter?' (2011) *Journal of International Trade Law & Policy*, 10(2), 151–164.

Sarker, R. 'Anti-money Laundering Requirements: Too Much Pain for Too Little Gain' (2006) *Company Lawyer*, 27(8), 250–251.

Sarker, R. 'Fighting Fraud – A missed opportunity?' (2007) *Company Lawyer*, 28(8), 243–244, 243.

Sarker, R. 'Guinness – Pure Genius' (1994) *Company Lawyer*, 15(10), 310–312.

Sarker, R. 'Maxwell: Fraud Trial of the Century' (1996) *Company Lawyer*, 17(4), 116–117.

Scanlan, G. 'Offences Concerning Directors and Officers of a Company: Fraud and Corruption in the United Kingdom – The Present and the Future' (2008) *Journal of Financial Crime*, 15(1), 22–37, 25.

Scanlan, G. 'The Enterprise of Crime and Terror – The Implications for Good Business. Looking to the Future – Old and New Threats' (2006) *Journal of Financial Crime*, 13(2), 164–176.

Sentencing Guidelines Council, 'Guideline Judgments Case Compendium' <http://sentencingcouncil.judiciary.gov.uk/docs/web_case_compendium.pdf> accessed 6 June 2011.

Sentencing Guidelines Council, *Sentencing for Fraud – Statutory Offences Definitive Guideline* (Sentencing Guidelines Secretariat 2009).

Serious Fraud Office (n/d), 'Our performance' <http://www.sfo.gov.uk/our-work/our-performance.aspx> accessed 26 September 2012.

Serious Fraud Office, *Achievements 2009–2010* (Serious Fraud Office 2010).

Serious Fraud Office, 'Approach of the Serious Fraud Office to Dealing with Overseas Corruption' <http://www.sfo.gov.uk/media/107247/approach%20of%20the%20serious%20fraud%20office%20v3.pdf> accessed 24 July 2010.

Serious Fraud Office, 'Bribery and Corruption' <http://www.sfo.gov.uk/bribery--corruption/bribery--corruption.aspx> accessed 23 November 2011.

Serious Fraud Office, 'Richard Alderman, Speech. The Bribery Act 2010 – The SFO's Approach and International Compliance' (9 February 2011) <http://www.sfo.gov.uk/about-us/our-views/director's-speeches/speeches-2011/the-bribery-act-2010---the-sfo's-approach-and-international-compliance.aspx> accessed 13 November 2011.

Serious Fraud Office, *SFO Budget 2009–2010* (Serious Fraud Office 2010).

Serious Organised Crime Agency, *Review of the Suspicious Activity Reports Regime* (Serious Organised Crime Agency 2006).

Serious Organised Crime Agency, *The Suspicious Activity Reports Regime Annual Report 2008* (Serious Organised Crime Agency, 2008).

Serious Organised Crime Agency, *The Suspicious Activity Reports Regime Annual Report 2009* (Serious Organised Crime Agency 2010).

Serious Organised Crime Agency, *The Suspicious Activity Reports Regime Annual Report 2010* (Serious Organised Crime Agency 2010).

Sheikh, S. 'The Bribery Act 2010: Commercial Organisations Beware!' (2011) *International Company and Commercial Law Review*, 22(1), 1–16.

Sidak, J. 'The Failure of Good Intentions: The WorldCom Fraud and the Collapse of American Telecommunications After Deregulation' (2003) *Yale Journal on Regulation*, 20, 207–261.

Simpson, M. 'International Initiatives' in M. Simpson, N. Smith and A. Srivastava (eds) *International Guide to Money Laundering Law and Practice* (Bloomsbury Professional 2010).

Simser, J. 'Money Laundering and Asset Cloaking Techniques' (2008) *Journal of Money Laundering Control*, 11(1), 15–24.

Spalek, B. 'Exploring the impact of financial crime: A study looking into the effects of the Maxwell scandal upon the Maxwell pensioners' (1999) *International Review of Victimology*, 6, 213–20.

Spalek, B. *Knowledgeable Consumers? Corporate Fraud and its Devastating Impacts, Briefing 4* (Centre for Crime and Justice Studies 2007).

Spalek, R. 'Regulation, White-Collar Crime and the Bank of Credit and Commerce International' (2001) *Howard Journal of Criminal Justice*, 40 166–179.

Sproat, P. 'Counter-terrorist Finance in the UK: A Quantitative and Qualitative Commentary Based on Open-source Materials' (2010) *Journal of Money Laundering Control*, 315–335, 318.

Sullivan, G. 'Proscribing Corruption – Some Comments on The Law Commission's Report' (1998) *Criminal Law Review*, Aug, 547–555.

The Law Commission, *Legislating the Criminal Code: Corruption No. 248* (Law Commission 1998).

The Law Commission, *Legislating the Criminal Code: Fraud and Deception – Law Commission Consultation Paper No. 155* (Law Commission 1999).

The Law Commission, *Informal Discussion Paper: Fraud and Deception – Further Proposals From the Criminal Law Team* (Law Commission: 2000).

The Law Commission, *Reforming Bribery: A Consultation* (Law Commission 2007).

The Law Commission, *Reforming Bribery* (The Stationery Office 2008).

The Law Society, *Anti-money Laundering Practice Note* (The Law Society 2009).

The Law Society, 'Anti-money Laundering' <http://www.lawsociety.org.uk/productsandservices/antimoneylaundering.page> accessed 1 July 2011.

The Telegraph, 'Two al-Qa'eda Terrorists Jailed for 11 Years' (2003) <http://www.telegraph.co.uk/news/1426290/Two-al-Qaeda-terrorists-jailed-for-11-years.html> accessed 28 June 2011.

The White House, *Progress Report on the Global War on Terrorism* (The White House 2003).

Times Online, 'Canoe Fraudster Anne Darwin to Repay Nearly £600,000' (*The Times* 11 November 2009) <http://www.timesonline.co.uk/tol/news/uk/article6912213.ece> accessed 10 June 2010.

Times Online, 'Conservatives Confirm Plans for Single Economic Crime Agency' <http://timesonline.typepad.com/law/2010/04/conservatives-confirm-plans-for-single-economic-crime-agency.html> accessed 26 April 2010.

Townsend, M. 'Leak Reveals Official Story of London Bombings', *The Observer* (London, 9 April 2006).

Transparency International, The Global Coalition Against Corruption, 'Corruption Perceptions Index 2010' <http://www.transparency.org/policy_research/surveys_indices/cpi/2010> accessed 28 June 2011.

Tupman, W. 'Where Has All the Money Gone? The IRA as a Profit-making Concern' (1998) *Journal of Money Laundering Control*, 1(4), 303–311.

United Kingdom Public Spending, 'UK Gross Domestic Product' <http://www.ukpublicspending.co.uk/downchart_ukgs.php?title=UK%20Gross%20Domestic%20Product&year=1950_2010&chart=> accessed 6 June 2011.

United Nations Office on Drugs and Crime, 'Money-laundering and Globalization' <http://www.unodc.org/unodc/en/money-laundering/globalization.html> accessed 6 July 2011.

United States Federal Sentencing Guidelines, 'Chapter Eight – Part B – Remedying Harm from Criminal Conduct, and Effective Compliance and Ethics Program' <http://www.ussc.gov/2007guid/8b2_1.html> accessed 24 July 2010.

Vaithilingham, S. and Nair, M. 'Factors affecting money laundering: Lesson for developing countries' (2008) *Journal of Money Laundering Control*, 10(3), 352–366.

van Cleef, C., Silets, H. and Motz, P. 'Does the Punishment Fit the Crime?' (2004) *Journal of Financial Crime*, 12(1), 57.

Walker, J. 'Modelling Global Money Laundering Flows – Some Findings' <http://www.johnwalkercrimetrendsanalysis.com.au/ML%20method.htm> accessed 6 June 2011.

Webb, P. 'The United Nations Convention Against Corruption: Global Achievement or Missed Opportunity?' (2005) *Journal of International Economic Law*, 8(1), 191–229.

Well, C. 'Bribery: Corporate Liability Under the Draft Bill' (2009) *Criminal Law Review*, 7, 479–487.

Welling, S. 'Smurfs, Money Laundering, and the Federal Criminal Law: The Crime of Structuring Transactions' (1989) *Florida Law Review*, 41, 287–339.

White, A. 'Freezing Injunctions. A Procedural Overview and Practical Guide' (2005) <http://www.parkcourtchambers.co.uk/seminar-handouts/16.11.05%20Commercial-Chancery%20_S%20White_.pdf> accessed 24 June 2011.

William, T. 'Trillion Dollar Bribery' (2011) *New Law Journal*, 161(7447), 25–26, 25.

Wragge & Co., 'Bribery Act to Come into Force April 2011 – Time to Take Action' (23 July 2010) <http://www.wragge.com/analysis_6175.asp> accessed 24 July 2010.

Wright, R. 'Developing Effective Tools to Manage the Risk of Damage Caused by Economically Motivated Crime Fraud' (2007) *Journal of Financial Crime*, 14(1), 17–27, 18.

Wright, R. 'Fraud After Roskill: A View from the Serious Fraud Office' (2003) *Journal of Financial Crime*, 11(1), 10–16.

Yeandle, M., Mainelli, M., Berendt, A. and Healy, B. *Anti-money Laundering Requirements: Costs, Benefits and Perceptions* (Corporation of London 2005).

Index